CW00481179

# EXCHANGING VOICES

Other titles in the
# Systemic Thinking and Practice Series
*edited by* David Campbell and Ros Draper
*published and distributed by* Karnac

Credit Card orders, Tel: + 44 (0)20 8969 4454; Fax: + 44 (0)20 8969 5585
Email: shop@karnacbooks.com

# EXCHANGING VOICES

## A Collaborative Approach to Family Therapy

*Lynn Hoffman*

Foreword by
*Gianfranco Cecchin*

Systemic Thinking and Practice Series

Series Editors
*David Campbell & Ros Draper*

London
KARNAC BOOKS

First published in 1993 by
H. Karnac (Books) Ltd.
6 Pembroke Buildings
London NW10 6RE

Second revised impression, 1995

Reprinted 2003

© 1993 by Lynn Hoffman

All rights reserved. No part of this publication may be reproduced, stored in a
retrieval system, or transmitted, in any form or by any means, electronic, mechanic
photocopying, recording, or otherwise, without the prior written permission of the
publisher.

British Library Cataloguing in Publication Data
A C.I.P. for this book is available from the British Library

ISBN: 1 85575 052 X
www.karnacbooks.com

Edited, designed, and produced by Communication Crafts

Printed & bound by Antony Rowe Ltd, Eastbourne

# CONTENTS

# EDITORS' FOREWORD

It is difficult to overestimate Lynn Hoffman's contribution to the development of systemic ideas and skills in the field of mental health and, in particular, family therapy. With the publication of *Foundations of Family Therapy*, she established herself as the chronicler of the brief history of this field. And since then she has continued to publish papers which, like milestones, help practitioners along their journey through the emerging ideas in family therapy. People ask, "What is she thinking about now?", and she has become trusted as the person who will challenge the new developments by asking the simple, telling questions that seem obvious to all of us, once we have heard her ask them.

The papers in this book, so aptly titled *Exchanging Voices*, reflect Lynn's critical observation of, first, herself and then of other influential contemporary thinkers over the past 25 years. In the 1980s, many people were infuriated that Lynn's current papers appeared to ditch the ideas in her previous papers, but by the 1990s we have begun to appreciate the way ideas evolve and to look for the patterns over time in the ecology of ideas which this book represents. This capacity to reflect on and discard ideas that are less than useful, or have gone beyond their "sell-by" date, is an interesting enactment of the process of co-evolution in the field. Our aim in putting this book together was to ask Lynn to reflect on the way her thoughts developed from one paper to another, and thereby shed light on the process by which ideas come to prominence, influence practice, and eventually incorporate or give way to new ones.

The ideas, as always, are not just Lynn's, and they have, in addition to her unique perspicacity, her particular brand of generosity to and encouragement of other thinkers and practitioners in the field. Lynn is both a friend and mentor to us. We are delighted to publish this particular part of the map in our series.

*David Campbell*
*Ros Draper*
London
July 1993

# FOREWORD

*Gianfranco Cecchin*

Having followed the evolution of family therapy in the last twenty years, it is a moving experience for me to read Lynn Hoffman's account of her struggles, periods of confusion, and the intellectual challenges that have characterized this period of time. Lynn has been an extremely sensitive witness to the evolution of family therapy: aware of the limits of every discovery and of every truth most of us thought to be reliable enough to be enjoyed for a while. Lynn would be the first to feel uncomfortable with an idea and try to move on to a new perspective.

She appears like one who, faced and fascinated by her own or someone else's therapeutic ideology or practice, would spend enough time studying it completely enough to describe it with the appropriate words, and then move on to make an epistemological shift.

I think Lynn experienced and worked through all the significant periods of family therapy, from interventive and strategic to the present so-called postmodern orientation. All these moments are described in some of her books. One of these periods was her interest in the so-called Milan group, of which I was a member. Her visits to Milan were a great stimulus for us. Firstly, her presence made it appear as an important moment in the story of family therapy; then she began to offer appropriate words. I remember the moment when she said, "What makes you different from other therapists is that you always have a hypothesis". This idea was the basis for an article we wrote in 1980, "Hypothesizing–Circularity–Neutrality".

I believe Lynn was the one who invented the term "Milan School". Later she was instrumental, together with Peggy Penn, in organizing the ideas coming from that school in the book *Milan Systemic Family Therapy* of which they were co-authors.

Of course, after that, Lynn moved on to other experiences and other descriptions. I remember, during a conference somewhere in England, when she and Harry Goolishian struggled to find a way out of the idea that a system in some way creates a problem. "What about a problem creating a system?" They said: "No, that is still causal lineal." "What about a problem-determined system?" "In such a way you don't have to 'solve' any problem to 'dis-solve' the system determined by the problem. At the end there is no 'problem', there is no 'system', there is no 'therapy', there is something else which it is better not to define otherwise you become an 'expert'." Later on, she would begin to have a problem also with the word "problem".

The issue of power and control began to be her preoccupation. Then in 1985 Lynn began to address her energy to a formidable challenge: can anyone do effective therapy without becoming an instrument of social control, without participating and contributing, often unknowingly, to the construction or the maintenance of a dominant discourse of oppression?

The voices were coming from the feminist field, narrative epistemology and postmodern thinkers, constructivism, constructionism, and hermeneutics. The challenge is complicated by the fact that any attempt to fight oppression in families or society at large can become a source of oppression itself. Lynn is acutely aware of this problem, and it is part of the fascination of this book to observe how she uses her clinical and intellectual skills to avoid the trap of using oppression to fight oppression.

Under her continuous irreverence towards an excessive loyalty to any discovered truth there seems to remain a constant premise: the premise that therapy cannot make a compromise with systems of social power. This is one of the premises towards which she seems not to be willing to be irreverent. One question comes to mind. Why did people like Hoffman, Anderson, Goolishian, and many others became so sensitive to this problem in the last five to six years, to the point of suggesting extreme positions like that of "not knowing", "not having an hypothesis", "being a silent listener", "doing imperceptible therapy"?—basically, a non-interventive stance. What explanations are there? It is very hard anyway to achieve a non-interventionist stance. Sometimes one could feel like giving up altogether any form of action or any form of knowing. Are we beginning, Lynn first of all, to feel that a new wave of refined and not easily detectable oppressive political structure will overcome all forms of therapy without us even knowing about it?

If so, this book is an antidote to that danger.

*Milan, 1993*

# EXCHANGING VOICES

# INTRODUCTION

Now we are going to make a new-way path. So you take a
shovel, you take a ground-*haker*, you take a hairpin. If all you
got is a hairpin, you take a hairpin and you start digging. And
you dig in all directions: up and down, in and out, right and
left. Not in a straight line. Nothing natural or interesting goes in
a straight line. As a matter of fact, it is the quickest way to the
wrong place. And don't pretend you know where you are
going. Because if you know where you are going, that means
you've been there, and you are going to end up exactly where
you came from.

Rifke, in Naomi Newman's play *Snake Talk: Urgent Messages from the
Mother* (quoted in Anderson & Hopkins, *The Feminine Face of God*,
1991)

This narration and its accompanying essays make up an
account of a voyage that proceeds like the course of a river
in an ancient alluvial plain. The river continually snakes
about or divides into streams, some of which trickle into nowhere,
while others continue independently, joining each other at the tip of
an island or the beginning of a lake. Its end is nowhere in sight. It is

1

still wandering towards some as yet unknown edge of land, some delta, where, like the Amazon, it presumably meets the sea.

I used this analogy and the beginning quote because the evolution of my work might otherwise be judged against a more logical causal path. I didn't intend to be so circuitous. It caused me much confusion and humiliation to continually have to "take it back" when I disagreed with something I had written the year before. Print commits you. So if you are trying to be taken seriously as a researcher, you make a case and stick to it. But that doesn't always work when you are trying to apply your hard-won ideas to human events. Too often you come up against intractable elements that simply laugh in your face.

\* \* \*

But let me summarize the content of this collection of papers. Published between 1985 and 1993, they represent a move towards a far less instrumental style of family therapy than the one I was trained in. They also record a major shift in the larger zeitgeist, from a "modern" Western mindset to what is being called a "postmodern" point of view. To this view I add my own version of the gender revolution, which I associate with Carol Gilligan's naming of a "different voice". Throughout, I am concerned with the implications of this different voice for family therapy practice.

The essays also reflect, not as consciously, a shift in writing style which is often caused by the purchase of a computer. Learning to write by computer is like taking a medication that prevents blood clots. Since you can change your words and sentences with lightning speed, a final version never quite jells. Your work, as it were, liquefies. And so, year after year, I found myself turning out a slightly different, and hopefully better, version of what I was trying to say.

All the same, there has been a single-mindedness to my quest. I started out enthralled with a view that emphasized the context in which emotional problems occurred, not the mind in which they occurred. Early on, before I read anything else of Gregory Bateson's, I ran across his book with psychiatrist Juergen Ruesch: *Communication: The Social Matrix of Psychiatry* (Ruesch & Bateson, 1951). Bateson, like Picasso (and Freud, for that matter), had different periods. For one thing, he was bent on applying the principles of the newly discovered field of cybernetics to evolution and ecology. Others in the research group he directed in Palo Alto between 1950 and 1960 applied these principles to the family—particularly to a family that contained an "abnormal" child. Thus the idea of the family system was born.

But Bateson's original and persisting belief was that there was a link between forms of communication and forms of what we call mental illness. The double-bind theory came out of this belief. It was subsequently discounted as too simple, but the idea persisted that people learn how to feel and act in complex, ongoing webs of interaction. If the patterns of interaction changed—so the thinking went—people's behaviours, no matter how bizarre, would change too.

This assumption flew in the face of the developmental theories upon which so many schools of modern psychology were based. From the beginning, the real conflict between family therapy and most individual therapies was over the cause of problems. Psychodynamic theories ascribed problems to early influences that interfered with normal psychic development. People who took the communicational position cared nothing for the psyche and its past. They looked at what was going on in the person's immediate field of connections. Individual therapy and family therapy became two rival clans.

However, in one respect at least they were similar. Each made the therapist into a detective looking for pathology. One day I realized that this detective theory was an invention and not an immutable truth. I began to feel less and less comfortable turning a person or a family into an object of medical attention. But if I abandoned a belief in pathology, I would have to look at therapy in an entirely new way. I found myself agreeing with writer Thomas Moore (1992), who has suggested that caring, not curing, is the operative word.

Along with this change came a change in the role of the professional. What if we abandoned the expert/non-expert dichotomy? Was there an alternative? If we found it, what would we call it? I spent a long time puzzling about a name, but I think Harlene Anderson and the late Harry Goolishian have given it to me. They began describing their work as a "collaborative language-systems approach". One day not long ago, it became clear to me that "collaborative" was the name.

The change from a hierarchical to a collaborative style in psychotherapy is a radical step. It calls into question the top-down structuring of this quasi-medical field called mental health and flies in the face of centuries of traditional Western practice. There is no, repeat no, school of psychotherapy—psychodynamic, behavioural, family, or otherwise—that is not based on an assumption of expertise, a series of respected texts, and a code of correct practice. To challenge these elements is to challenge the whole citadel. A tall order, and one that will be hard to defend, but let me start. I will tell you about the evolution of my thinking as it happened, chronologically, and the embedded essays will further explicate my journey at each stage.

# CHAPTER ONE

# The case against power and control

How did I begin this journey? In 1981, as I was finishing *Foundations of Family Therapy*, I was trying to write an epilogue for that book and had the problem that my prophetic abilities weren't working. The reason was that the road ahead had a ninety-degree turn in it, which I at that time couldn't see. However, clues were appearing, as if to a cosmic puzzle. I was fascinated by Harry Goolishian's and Paul Dell's interest in applying the ideas of the Nobel Prize-winning physicist Ilya Prigogine to family systems (Prigogine & Stengers, 1984). Prigogine believed that time was a one-way street into the future and that change was not the exception but the rule. However, which change would happen depended on how far the system in question was driven from equilibrium and which pebble in the dam, so to speak, began to crumble first.

I liked that notion. I had come to feel that human events meandered messily like bad eighteenth-century novels instead of occurring neatly in nice repetitive turns. So instead of imposing upon them the feedback loops of cybernetic theory, I began to contemplate them as if they were like waterfalls and streams. I said to myself: "Don't think of repeating cycles, think of rivers in time."

Gradually I began to realize that change by design, which had been the rallying cry of the early family therapists, didn't fit the new analogies. As the course of therapy became more subservient to chance, the centrality of the therapist diminished. At around this time, Harry Goolishian began to send me videotapes of sessions in which his former strategic brilliance played no part at all. I didn't know what to make of these rather drifting, aimless interviews, but looking back I see that they were harbingers of his later work. I rather jokingly told him I thought that what he was doing was "imperceptible therapy", without any realization that there would come a day when I too would be doing "imperceptible therapy", and of my own accord.

Another clue was the discovery that the original Bateson group, like the Gods on Mount Olympus, had had their differences. In 1978, I had joined the staff of the Ackerman Institute for Family Therapy and shortly thereafter Bradford Keeney came on board. He and I developed the friendship that is so special to two outsiders. A year or two before Gregory Bateson's death in 1979, Keeney had spent two or three weeks with him, soaking up his famous seamless stories and incorporating them into a dialogue between himself and Bateson, which I read.

It was Keeney who told me how strongly Bateson had disapproved of Haley's emphasis on power and control. Given his distrust of what he called "human conscious purpose", it made sense that he would look askance at the control-oriented family therapy that had come out of his research project. His views on the subject, later elaborated in the posthumous book *Angels Fear* (1987), which was edited and contributed to by his daughter Catherine, reinforced my own.

Then I read Carol Gilligan's *In a Different Voice* (1984). I had not plunged into the feminist family therapy movement because it reminded me too much in its fervour of the Marxism of the community I grew up in. Nevertheless, I was convinced that the gender revolution in the United States constituted the most important large-scale movement of my lifetime. It was also important for my tiny corner of the field of mental health. For instance, the results of Gilligan's research on male and female value-systems suggested that where men tended to stick to abstract principles of justice and truth, women (American middle-class women, at least) would often bend the rules in favour of relationships. Findings like these had immense implications for family therapy as I had learned it.

I became particularly aware of the unconscious sexism of all styles of family therapy. Up to that time, most family therapists had accepted them without question. Even when colleagues of mine applied feminist principles to their practice, they focused upon particular injustices like mother-bashing but did not question very much the models they had been trained in. Mainly pioneered by men, these styles went from a benign paternalism to an extreme focus on hierarchy, secrecy, and control. Even feminist versions kept therapists in a power position in relation to the people the therapists saw. How else could they "empower" them?

I began to ask questions. Why were there no styles that represented the ideals of connectedness and collaboration that feminist psychologists were linking to female development? Where was the family counterpart to the relational perspective of Wellesley's Stone Center (Surrey, 1984)? To become another activist seemed too close to becoming another kind of expert, so for the moment I stayed quiet on the subject. I still continued to search for a less hierarchically organized family therapy that would enlarge the options for all.

In 1983, I decided to relocate from New York City to Western Massachusetts. I told people that I was looking for "religious freedom", meaning that I wanted a space in which I could explore a style for family therapy analogous to Gilligan's different voice, and I felt that I could not do that within any established institution that I knew. I had no clear vision of what sort of practice could possibly come out of this search; philosophically I was convinced, but pragmatically speaking I was still totally locked into a view of therapy where the therapist held the reins.

Shortly thereafter, at a conference called "Maps of the Mind, Maps of the World", organized by the Mental Research Institute in Palo Alto, California, I met an elfin genius from Vienna called Heinz von Foerster. His enthusiasm and accessibility belied his reputation as one of the giants on whose shoulders the first computers had been built. Despite the 80-odd years he bore so lightly, I fell in love with him at once and jumped at an invitation to visit him for lunch at his house in Pescadero. Another Renaissance man of similar charm and talent, Ernst von Glasersfeld, was staying with him, so I got to know them both.

It turned out that these two, together with Chilean cognitive biologists Humberto Maturana and Francisco Varela, were planning a conference which was to be held in New Hampshire in 1984. Their idea was to replicate the famous Josiah Macy Conferences, interdisciplinary events that took place annually for ten years after World War II. It was at these meetings that the four scientists had met each other, along with researchers like Gregory Bateson, Margaret Mead, John von Neumann, and Norbert Wiener.

It was natural for family therapists with my background to gravitate to this group that seemed to inherit the mantle of ideas Bateson stood for. I was invited to the conference in New Hampshire, at which I met accomplished men and women from many countries and diverse areas of research. By one of those accidents of fate, Paul Watzlawick, who was to be the presenter for the interest group on family systems, couldn't come, and I was asked to take his place. Nervous at speaking before such a distinguished audience, I quickly arranged for several other family therapists who were there to share the time with me.

Luckily, my own presentation went well and I made many of the points that are elaborated here in "Beyond Power and Control" (published in 1986) and later in "A Constructivist Position for Family Therapy" (published in 1988). First, I emphasized the connection between a less instrumental style of family therapy and Maturana and Varela's (1980) idea that living systems are self-creating and cannot be manipulated like machines. Second, I found von Foerster's (1981) ideas about observing systems useful in reminding family therapists to be aware of their own effect upon the phenomena they observe and their own agendas in interpreting them.

But the most important application to my field was the central tenet of what von Glasersfeld (1984) called "radical constructivism": the idea that our sensory images of the world, far from representing "things out there", are literally constructed by our nervous system, the way a computer computes music from digital bits. This non-objectivist doctrine, so abstract when couched in philosophical terms, became a weapon in my hands against the idea of diagnosis and other attempts to assign objective causes for emotional or mental distress. To me, these were harmful social constructs, crude inventions of the human mind to explain mysteries that we as yet had few answers for. Constructivism, as I understood it, offered a rationale for attacking these and other questionable tenets of our psychotherapeutic faith. The following two essays, which in many ways are two versions of the same article, represent my attempts to apply constructivist ideas to family therapy.

# Beyond power and control: towards a "second-order" family systems therapy

While in the first quarter of this century physicists and cosmologists were forced to revise the basic notions that govern the natural sciences, in the last quarter of this century biologists will force a revision of the basic notions that govern science itself.

Heinz von Foerster
"Notes on an Epistemology for Living Things" (1981, p. 258)

## THE "LOST ATLANTIS"

When I first encountered the remains of Gregory Bateson's research project in Palo Alto in 1963, I had the sense of stumbling on the ruins of an old and remarkable civilization. In the grip of this conviction, I talked to everybody who had been there. I attended the Thursday bag lunch meetings organized by Don Jackson. As part of

From *Family Systems Medicine*, 3 (1985), no. 4: 381–396. By permission of Family Process, Inc.

the editing job I had been hired by Jackson to do on *Conjoint Family Therapy* (Satir, 1964), I watched Virginia Satir interview families. I ended up begging Jay Haley to let me do a book with him. All the same, I felt that I was merely watching ripples in the wake of a departed genius. I had a keen sense of disappointment about this.

In the ensuing 20 years, I continued to have the impression that I was on some kind of archeological dig, but the time signs were confusing. Was this a Lost Atlantis or a New Jerusalem? Was I unearthing a forgotten empire or helping to build a Promised Land? There was a sense of an evolving outline, but of something already there, the way secret writing is already on the page. Bateson himself noted that people who apprenticed themselves to him were convinced that he knew something that he was deliberately keeping from them. I suspect that Bateson was not only a scientist but a clairvoyant in that he could sense on-coming events before most people had any inkling of what was going on. He had a terrific sense of smell.

By the 1970s, Bateson (1972) had become something of a crusader for the integrity of the biosphere. He began to talk more and more about the dangers of "linear" or non-holistic thinking and epistemological errors implicit in ideas of power or control. Although not active politically, he was not above a bit of epistemological consciousness-raising, as evidenced by the 1968 conference at Burg Wartenstein called "The Effects of Conscious Purpose on Human Adaptation" and immortalized in Catherine Bateson's *Our Own Metaphor* (1972).

Thinking back, it seems clear that the cold-war years set a pattern that was informed by a fascination with control. Early cybernetic research was connected with experiments with guided missiles and rockets. There was a sense of Faustian expansion, as the new technology was used to investigate the brain and to create brain-like prostheses for the brain. Over the ensuing decades, a division began to build in the field of cybernetics between engineers involved in research on robotics and artificial intelligence, often underwritten by the military, and a group of visionary researchers that included not only Bateson but colleagues like Heinz von Foerster, Humberto Maturana, Francisco Varela, and Ernst von Glasersfeld.

This latter group shared the belief that the exploitative use of technology—indeed, the entire Western attitude towards science—

was based on a false illusion of objectivity. Von Foerster (Howe & von Foerster, 1974) summarized the two positions by comparing a "first-order" cybernetics in which the observer remains outside that which is observed with a "second-order" cybernetics where the observer is included in the total arc. Varela (Maturana & Varela, 1980), writing in the same vein, contrasts an "allopoietic" or control model for living systems (the input–output model of the engineers) with an "autopoietic" or autonomy model (living systems respected in the dimension of their wholeness rather than as objects to manipulate).

What is interesting from the point of view of a family theorist is that a similar division erupted back in the late 1950s between Bateson and some of his colleagues who were developing the first family therapy models. The articles on families and family therapy that were coming out of Palo Alto were imbued with a vocabulary based on war and adversarial games: "power-tactics", "strategy", being "one-up" or "one-down" (Haley, 1963). This language reflected the dominant value system of Western science, which was an eminently masculine value system in Carol Gilligan's (1982) sense. I am often struck by the resemblance between accounts of therapeutic prowess described within this framework and the sexual performance known as "scoring".

Bateson apparently also had reservations about these models of therapy. His chief quarrel with his co-researchers was over what he called the "myth of power". A peculiarity of the debate is that even when these younger theoreticians agreed that efforts to control others only begat more such efforts in "games without end", and subscribed to Bateson's hunch that a small admixture of complimentary or one-down behaviours might halt such progressions, they advocated this position for strategic reasons. Haley argued in *The Power Tactics of Jesus Christ* (1969) that Jesus only turned the other cheek to disarm his opponents, and the hallmark of the MRI therapist of that time was the technique of going one-down to be one-up. Thus power was kept as a central core and the masculine value system remained intact. My own thinking was highly coloured by this point of view, as anyone reading *Foundations of Family Therapy* (Hoffman, 1981) can plainly see.

After a long period underground, this debate began to make its way back into the family therapy field. It was sparked off by the

March 1982 issue of *Family Process,* which contained three essays by psychologists Bradford Keeney (with Douglas Sprenkle), Lawrence Allman, and Paul Dell. Keeney and Allman used Batesonian arguments to question the use of a narrowly pragmatic framework for family therapy. Dell attacked the concept of homeostasis, long a building block of family systems theory. The placing together of these pieces probably made them seem more like a mega-trend than they were. For whatever reasons, the result was a flurry of scathing dismissals from outraged "pragmatic" therapists. Epistemology was renamed "epistobabble" and from then on there was hardly anyone in the field who did not think they knew what epistemology meant.

In my view, these provocative articles and the overkill reaction to them temporarily dampened the free play of ideas in the field. Especially unfortunate was the support given to anti-intellectuals made nervous by the use of terms like "epistemology". For despite the negative publicity, epistemology is a heart-of-the-matter word. It had a special meaning for the pioneers who put it on the map, among whom were Bateson and the other scientists I have listed.

In using cybernetic principles to investigate the nervous system, these scientists invalidated the field of psychology as we know it. If, as their studies suggest, our perceptions do not represent impressions of an out-there reality but construct this reality in a totally turnabout fashion, psychology would have to find another name: lensology, or the science of lenses, perhaps. Because epistemology already meant the study of how we know our knowing, it was a likely candidate for the job. For family therapists, the ideas around epistemology put into question how almost everybody knew their knowing, and began to point the way to an intellectual revolution that was much more profound than early cybernetic thinking had led any of us to expect.

In the following pages, I outline what I believe are the consequences of this "new epistemology", or what is being alternatively called "second-order" cybernetics, for the family field. From the researchers mentioned above, I take a number of concepts that carry major implications for systems therapy: the idea of the observing system from von Foerster (1981); the complex that includes autopoiesis, informational closure, and conversational domains from Maturana and Varela (1980; Varela, 1979); and the idea of "fit" from the constructivist position of von Glasersfeld (1984). Related to all these concepts is Bateson's (1972, 1979) focus on circular organization which he equated, in some sense, with mental process. I try to show that the net effect of the new thinking is to point the way to an overall framework for systemic change that is as much as possible non-hierarchical, non-instrumental, and non-pejorative. But first I will have to send a herald on ahead, saying: "Enter the Observing System, Centre Stage."

## MAPS AND TERRITORIES

Let me start with a quote from a current joke: "I have a sea-shell collection. I keep it scattered on beaches all over the world." A sea-shell on a beach is part of an ecosystem. Add the collector, who is speaking, and you have the missing element—the idea in the mind of a person about beaches and shells and their relationship to each other and to that person. This is what I mean by saying: "Enter the Observing System, Centre Stage."

Heinz von Foerster (1983), whose book *Observing Systems* sets this stage, opened an address at a conference I attended with the remark, "Gregory Bateson says, 'The map is not the territory.' I disagree with Gregory Bateson." (Pause, for effect.) "I say, the 'Map *is* the Territory!'" At the same conference, von Foerster described an encounter with a blind graduate student who was asking his advice with regard to a paper he was working on. In talking about it, the student kept pointing to a spot on the wall behind von Foerster's head. Von Foerster asked, "Why do you point to the wall when you refer to your paper?" The student said, "Because my office is next-door and my paper is on the desk against that wall." So von Foerster observed to the audience that, in this instance, the man who was blind could "see", where he, von Foerster, was blind.

Von Foerster's thesis, derived from research on neural nets, is that learning is not a mapping of outside objects into some location in the brain but is a way that the organism computes a stable reality. Von Foerster's studies showed that neural nets do not encode little pictures of scenes or objects but merely register edges or sharp transitions, not only at sensorial surfaces but at any level within the brain. This research, of course, offers prestigious backing to Bateson's (1972) definition of information as news of a difference, since it implies that all the splendid visuals of our minds are formed from these totally contentless little blocks.

One could say, then, that the brain builds up invariances which are then seen as solid objects and ascribed to an objectively experienced world-out-there. One way to think about this process, as I see it, is to compare it to a person doing a rubbing of a gravestone. As the crayon goes back and forth across the paper, darker and lighter patches appear until a coherent picture takes shape. But this type of metaphor breaks down if you then extend it to mean that there are really gravestones out there to rub. The best we can do is to find someone else who perceives gravestones and will confirm our perception. This is why von Foerster defines reality as a "consistent frame of reference for at least two observers". Our ideas about the world are shared ideas, consensually arrived at and mediated through givens like culture and language.

Maturana, agreeing with von Foerster, takes the position that "anything said is said by an observer" (Maturana & Varela, 1980, p. 8). For him, the term "objectivity" is always in quotes. Maturana arrived at this view through research on the physiology of vision. A series of experiments with colour vision in the frog prompted him to challenge the accepted notion that there was a correlation between the perceived object and what the retinal cells received. Not finding the expected correspondence, his co-researchers had decided that the experiment with the frog was a failure. But Maturana posed the question to himself: Suppose there is really no correspondence? Suppose the retinal cells are activating the brain cells in a closed internal loop? Suppose this signalling goes on entirely within the nervous system, with no input from outside but a kind of general triggering? What then?

What then, indeed! The conventional way of thinking about perception and the operation of the nervous system would have to be completely thrown away. No longer could you describe an act of perception in terms of a little print being processed by the brain. Moreover, there would be no way to be sure that what we think we see is actually there.

With this idea in mind, Maturana devised an experiment with a newt: He rotated the newt's eye 180 degrees, then set a moving insect in front of it. The newt jumped completely around and attempted to pick up the insect as if it were behind it. Repetitions of the experiment made it clear that the newt would starve before it would discover where the insect really was. This seemed like a compelling proof of the self-enclosed nature of the nervous system that Maturana had postulated.

These and similar experiments led Maturana and his colleague, Francisco Varela, to ask: "*What is the organization of the living?*" (1980, p. xii). Their answer: Living systems are like homeostats where the organization of the entity is itself the critical variable that has to remain constant. The components may change many times over, as happens when body cells die and renew themselves, but the identity of the unit—which is the same thing as its organization—remains the same. Maturana and Varela wished to give a name to this process. They thought of using the term "circular organization" straight out, but changed their minds in favour of "autopoiesis," a term Maturana invented out of two Greek roots: *auto* (self) and *poiesis* (creation, production) (p. xvii).

Autopoiesis describes a biological unit not as a material entity exchanging matter and energy with its environment (which it also is) but as an information system that is operationally closed and folds recursively back upon itself. To illustrate what he means, Maturana uses the analogy of the pilot who makes a blind landing:

> What occurs in a living system is analogous to what occurs in an instrument flight where the pilot does not have visual access to the outside world and must function only as a controller of the values shown in his flight instruments. . . . When the pilot steps out of the plane he is bewildered by the congratulations of his friends on account of the perfect flight and landing that he performed in absolute darkness. He is perplexed because to his knowledge all that he did at any moment was to maintain the readings of his instruments within certain specified limits, a task which is in no way represented by the description that his friends (observers) make of his conduct. [p. 51]

Maturana would say that living organisms are always making blind landings, even though we are exchanging information with the outside world all the time. Then how does he describe how we, as informationally closed Helen Kellers, ever manage to communicate at all? Interestingly. He speaks of *structural coupling,* a process that seems to me to resemble a blindfold jump-rope game. It is as if (informationally speaking) we never "touch". All we can do is generate trajectories, invisible to us, that are mutually constraining and whose connections show up on our instrument panel. A baby and a mother shape each other in such a way that one day the mother puts the baby on the pot and the baby performs. This continues to happen. The mother says, "I toilet-trained my baby". The baby says (perhaps), "I toilet-trained my mother". The pair are, in this example, structurally coupled. One system has got together with another in what Maturana calls consensual validation of consensual validation.

Thus, all communication is necessarily indirect. In the movie *Close Encounters of the Third Kind* you have a good example of this. The earth people and the space people are trying to solve the problem of communicating when neither group knows whether the others are intelligent beings or how to arrive at a common language for determining that. The space people, who presumably have a highly developed sense of harmonics, emit a series of musical notes and wait. The earth people emit the same series back. The space ship explodes in a burst of jubilant noise, and the earth people jump up and down. Communication has not been established, but communication *about* communication has.

A corollary of this position is that you can have no "instructive interaction" in the sense of placing little packets of information into the heads of other people, or receiving such packets in turn. You cannot buy a round-trip ticket to the outside world, the way you can go to a foreign country, buy something, and bring it back. You can only buy a ticket to a loop inside your head. This is why Maturana, when he lectures about his theories, always puts an eye in profile on the upper corner of his blackboard. He is reminding us that objectivity is literally in the eye of the beholder.

Here one might ask: How do we link up this isolationist view, in which the biological unit is cordoned off, with Bateson's description of mental process as organism-plus-environment? In other words, how do we get "autopoiesis" and "mental process" to jibe? Varela (1979) is in a good position to help us with this issue, since he worked closely with both men: Maturana in Chile and Bateson at Southampton, Long Island. He has been somewhat more concerned than Maturana to find a way to generalize the concept of autopoiesis (which, strictly speaking, only describes biological organisms) to systems representing larger orders of inclusion. To do this, he offers the term "autonomous system" (p. 53). An autonomous system is any composite unity formed of elements that may or may not themselves be autopoietic. Varela includes in this category not only social groups like the family, managerial systems, nations, and clubs, but also organs like the brain and ecological aggregates like beehives.

In describing the processes of interaction that define these aggregates, Varela begins to get close to the definition of mental process which Bateson offers: "Mind is generated whenever the appropriate circuit structure of causal loops appears" (1972, p. 482). However, Varela chooses an interestingly different term: "conversational domain". [This concept reflects research by scientists like Gordon Pask on Conversation Theory and Linde and Goguen on Discourse Analysis (Varela, 1979, p. 269).] In explaining this term, he states that there is mind in every unity engaged in conversation-like actions, however spatially distributed or short-lived. He is moving towards defining higher-order unities not only as groups of material bodies but as groups or ecologies of ideas, enabling one to include items like the plays of Shakespeare, Chartres cathedral, and psychotherapy.

Basically, Varela brings in a controversial notion: that at a level above our own individual minds there is mind-like activity and that higher-order unities at this level, though not directly accessible to consciousness, are instances of autonomous systems. In this way he uses the idea of conversational domains to deny the possibility of solipsism and to bring us out of isolation:

> Thus we do not have, by necessity, a world of shared regularities that we can alter at whim. In fact, the act of understanding is basically *beyond our will* because the autonomy of the social and biological systems we are in goes *beyond* our skull, because our evolution makes us part of a social aggregate and a natural aggregate which have an autonomy compatible with but *not reducible to* our autonomy as biological individuals. This is precisely why I have insisted so much on talking about an observer-community rather than an observer; the knower is not the biological individual. Thus the *epistemology of participation* sees man in continuity with the natural world. [1979, p. 276]

## THE PROBLEM CREATES THE SYSTEM

How do these new ideas affect family systems work? For one thing, the treatment unit looks vastly different than it did before. The old idea of treating a psychiatric symptom was based on the medical notion of curing a part of the body. The illness is "in" some spatially defined, out-there unit. We can no longer say that it is "in" the family, nor is it "in" the unit. It is "in" the heads or nervous systems of everyone who has a part in specifying it. The old epistemology implies that *the system creates the problem*. The new epistemology implies that *the problem creates the system*. The problem is whatever the original distress consisted of plus whatever the distress on its merry way through the world has managed to stick to itself. You have to think of some kind of infernal tar baby or gingerbread man. The problem is the meaning system created by the distress and the treatment unit is everyone who is contributing to that meaning system. This includes the treating professional as soon as the client walks in the door.

This position has been supported recently by Harlene Anderson and Harry Goolishian (Anderson, Goolishian, Pulliam, & Winderman, 1986) in their discussion of the problem-oriented system. Goolishian (personal communication 1985) also makes a case against the prevailing emphasis on dividing therapy into individual, couple, or family treatment. His reason is that as long as we use a framework based on social units, we fall into a linear mind-trap. If it is an organization, it can be dysfunctional. If it is dysfunctional, it contains pathology. If it contains pathology, we can go ahead and cure it. This brings us inevitably back to the old epistemology and the dichotomy between the person who fixes and the person who is being fixed.

What we are basically challenging here is the representation of the family as a cybernetic system. This impression was fostered by the writings of general systems theorists like James Miller (1978), who posited an amoeba-like model for living systems that applied at any level on the Great Chain of Inclusiveness: cell, organ, organism, group, organization, society. This view, which first made its appearance in the family field in Don Jackson's "The Question of Family Homeostasis" (1957), is a good example of "first-order" cybernetics since it tended to set up the family as an allopoietic machine, in Varela's sense, which can be programmed or controlled from outside.

This homeostatic model of the family has been heavily criticized in recent years (Bogdan, 1984; Dell, 1982) on both philosophical and pragmatic grounds. For me, trying to move to an appreciation of "second-order" cybernetics, the idea of the family as a system was the greatest possible stumbling block. Not only did it put a cut between the observer and the observed, but it was an extremely pejorative formulation, as many a family that has been blamed for the condition of a troubled child has found out to its sorrow (more of that later).

One way out of this difficulty is to think of therapy in terms of a conversational domain. In that case, we would no longer be focusing on the client as the unit of attention, but would see the entire group, family plus other professionals, as a small, evolving meaning system. I think that Jeffrey Bogdan's "Family Organization as an Ecology of Ideas" (1984) is a very useful contribution here and moves us towards the concept of a conversation. However, I don't believe he goes far enough. I would prefer the formulation that the *problem is* an ecology of ideas and dismiss the thought that what comes in the clinician's door is ever a family organization per se.

This change in the idea of the treatment unit is only the beginning of a chain of changes. Next to go is the treatment structure as traditionally defined. In explaining what I mean, I will have to expand my discussion to include Bateson's concept of cybernetic circularities and the translation of this idea into clinical terms by the Milan Associates.

## LILIES OF THE FIELD

By the time Varela and Bateson met in Southampton in the 1970s, Bateson was proposing a position with regard to living systems that had ethical and spiritual overtones. Although initially interested in the workings of circular causal systems like the famous thermostat in a narrow, "first-order" sense, Bateson (1972) had moved to a consideration of what he called the unit of evolution: DNA-in-cell, cell-in-body, body-in-environment. All such sequences, as we have seen, Bateson subsumed under the rubric of "mind," which he felt was immanent not only inside the body but in the networks of connecting channels outside the body, reaching out to the entire planetary ecology.

Bateson warned against the human propensity for controlling social and environmental outcomes and in so doing ignoring the loop structure of this larger unity. He saw most of our worst errors coming from this tendency. For him, the concept of what he called "cybernetic circularities" included an awareness of this tendency, as well as an appreciation of the non-linear, equal participation of all elements in this bootstrap description of the processes of life.

There are also ethical considerations in Varela's distinction between an allopoietic or "control" model for living systems and an autopoietic or "autonomy" model. The first model lends itself to concerns of purpose, power, and control. You can program it; you can instruct it; you can change it. The second reflects the Biblical saying: "Consider the lilies of the field; they sew not, neither do they spin." The process of the entity is formally identical with its product, which is the maintenance of its identity. You can't control it from the outside or program it (no instructive interaction, remember?), but you can, as these scientists say, perturb it and see how it compensates. Or, as I say, give it a bump and watch it jump.

Bateson (1972) makes a different, if related, distinction between models for living systems: systems seen as distributions of energy (bioenergetics) and systems seen as distributions of information (entropy-reduction systems). In the former case, one is concerned with the flow-through aspect of energy across a spatial boundary. In the latter, one is concerned with ecologies of ideas that have no material borders. I think that we are dealing with a gestalt switch in the sense that if one thinks "this is a particle" one cannot think "but it is a wave" at the same time.

It may be that Varela's distinction between allopoietic and autopoietic systems is an artifact of the same gestalt switch. The danger arises when one gets inappropriately stuck in one or the other view. I think one value of the concept of autopoiesis lies in its function as a corrective to believing solely in a "particle world" that one can remain apart from and above. Stafford Beer, in his preface to *Autopoeisis and Cognition* (Maturana & Varela, 1980), takes the matter even further:

It seems to me that the architects of change are making the same mistake all over the world. It is that they perceive that system at their own level of recursion to be autopoietic, which is because they identify themselves with that system and know themselves to be so; but they insist on treating the systems their system contains, and those within which their system is contained, as allopoietic. [p. 12]

It is in this sense that I think Varela and Maturana's ideas have ethical overtones, and it is certainly on this issue that Varela and Bateson connect.

By the late 1970s, mainly due to the emergence of ideas such as these, I had become dissatisfied with the existing systems approaches to family therapy. They were extremely control-oriented, and I could not connect them with Bateson's thought at all. It was at this time that I first became aware of the work of the Milan team: Mara Selvini-Palazzoli, Luigi Boscolo, Gianfranco Cecchin, and Guiliana Prata (1978). This group, which formed in 1967, had initially been very influenced by the ideas coming out of Palo Alto, and they became increasingly interested in Bateson's views. They had done their Bateson reading conscientiously and had applied to clinical practice ideas that were, for most people, forbidding abstractions.

The concept of circularity is a case in point. Inspired by the many ramifications of this concept, the Milan team came up with a characteristic style of interviewing (circular questioning), a characteristic assessment process (hypothesizing), and a characteristic therapeutic stance (neutrality) (1980). Their work also embodied what you might call a "circular" structuring of the therapeutic enterprise. Taking the egalitarian implications of the idea literally, they applied it to social relationships within the team. They substituted position for hierarchy, believing that the place you stand (behind the screen, in the room) determines what you can do and see more than your status or degree. And by constantly shifting trainees' places, they showed them that both positions are part of being in an observing system, in a quite literal sense.

The relationship between team and client was also defined as relatively non-hierarchical; again, position defined the difference, not power. Implicit in this treatment stance was a bias against intrusive interventions. The therapist seldom made an interpretation except at the end of an interview and even then it was an opinion, a point of view among many others. A ritual directive might be given but if the family did not carry it out, this was simply accepted as feedback about how the system worked. Thus there was seldom a confrontation or an escalation. The team simply wove any response, even a hostile or challenging one, into an extended hypothesis that was always changing.

This non-instrumental tendency seems close to the way one would deal with other living beings if one believed, as Maturana and Varela do, that they were informationally closed, autopoeitic unities. In this sense, the Milan approach reminds me of the movie *The Extra-Terrestrial*. To try to reshape a family according to one's normative ideas of what a family should be like would seem as wrong in this model as it was for the doctors and researchers in the movie to assume that E.T.'s life system was like our own and would respond in the same way to heart machines and respirators.

The Milan method has continued to evolve in this direction. In 1978, after the original team split up, Boscolo and Cecchin began to take an even less instrumental position, arguing that the circular questioning they were developing was an intervention in itself, and that the team message at the end of the interview was not needed (Boscolo, Cecchin, Hoffman, & Penn, 1987). [As far as I know, Boscolo and Cecchin have been influenced in a more formal and conscious way by the teachings of "second-order" cybernetics than have Selvini-Palazzoli and Prata, who have been researching family systems using a powerful clinical tool in the form of an "invariant prescription". Since this work has not yet been fully reported on, I cannot comment on their current position and hope that they will forgive me if I seem to ignore the significance of their present thinking in this piece.] Second-generation teams in Europe and North America have gone even further. For one thing, there has been a conscious effort to counteract the implicit power imbalance between therapist and family that is set up by having a team that confers invisibly behind a screen. Tom Andersen (personal communication 1985) of Tromso University in Norway is asking the family at the end of the session if they would like to listen to the discussion of the team. If they agree, family and therapist watch while the team, which he calls a "reflecting team", considers different points of view without having prearranged strategies built into the debate. Taking the same tack, Gerry Lane and Tom Russell (1984) of the Institute for Systemic Studies in Atlanta have been limiting their final intervention to a non-judgemental description of the way the problem system works, which they call "circular replication".

More generally, early Milan techniques such as prescribing the sacrifice of the child in the service of the parents were felt to carry too great a negative connotation and have been dropped, as has most of the paraphernalia around "paradoxing" families. These methods seem to be holdovers from the more strategic Palo Alto days. The practice of positively connoting the impasse of a therapist who is asking for a consultation has also proved to create a negative effect and to evoke a power differential between therapist and consultant. In an effort to counteract this problem, Peggy Penn and Marcia Sheinberg (1986) of the Ackerman Institute for Family Therapy in New York have developed a consultation method that takes care not to disempower the therapist. Overall, the trend has been towards dismantling some of the cumbersome technology of the original Milan method and moving towards a format that sets more equality between family and team.

This leads into another consequence of "second-order" cybernetic thinking for therapy. If we abandon the expert-dummy model, we have to throw away the idea of diagnosis as well. We have to see the extent to which a preoccupation with finding the cause and location of a problem in some out-there unit itself contributes to the problem. The emphasis shifts from a concern with the aetiology of the problem to a concern with the meanings that are attached to it. I believe that von Glasersfeld's (1984) constructivist model, with its emphasis on the collective premises that underlie behaviours, can be helpful here. Let me elaborate in the next section.

## STICKS AND STONES

Although it is clear that ideas and behaviours are two sides of the same coin, it makes a difference which category is emphasized in therapy. In family therapy, perhaps because of a reaction against the intrapsychic focus of psychodynamic theory, the emphasis has been on changing behaviours insofar as they are seen as part of a dysfunctional family system. The pendulum seems to be swinging the other way. Mental phenomena have been brought back from a long exile, and ideas, beliefs, attitudes, feelings, premises, values, and myths have been declared central again.

This is where the constructivist view comes in. Von Glasersfeld (1984) holds that we do not "discover" the world-out-there but, on the contrary, "invent" it. Knowledge, in fact, reflects the coupling between organism and environment that ensures its viability. For this reason it is not as important that our constructs *match* items in the environment as that they *fit* sufficiently to ensure survival. For instance, von Glasersfeld says, a bricklayer might begin to believe that all openings in walls require an arch. It does not matter *if* this is true or false; what matters is that in a world where houses are made of bricks, that premise is part of the fit between the builder and his environment.

Paul Watzlawick (1984) compares this concept to a pilot navigating a difficult channel at night. If the pilot does so and gets through safely, he has found a fit. It does not matter if in the morning he looks back and sees that he missed the safer or shorter channel which would have represented a better match. In this view, a miss is as good as a mile. The analogy does not really hold up, of course, in that neither we nor the pilot can ever know "the way things really are". All we can know is the operation of remaining viable.

Here the sophisticated reader may well say: "Wait. Psychological concepts based on the social construction of reality have been around a long time, witness the work of personality theorist George Kelly, the sociology of knowledge of Berger and Luckmann [1966], and the extensive literature on attribution theory [Hewstone, 1983]". And I would have to add: "Yes, and many schools of family therapy subscribe to the idea that the therapist is in the business of altering the client's perception of reality." So what is new?

What is new is the extensive philosophical tradition that von Glasersfeld acknowledges, from Kant and Vico to Wittgenstein and Piaget. I would also add the recent advances in cybernetic biology and cognition that I have been mentioning, which furnish a substrate of scientific research that the social construction theories of American social psychology did not have.

Another difference lies in adding the concept of the observing system. The notion that a therapist must deliberately set out to change the belief system of the client is a common one. The danger is that the therapist will forget about the assumption of fallibility built into the fact that we are all observing systems, and that there is a Heisenberg Uncertainty Principle of Human Relations to which we cannot not subscribe. For a therapist to believe that it is his/her job to know how to change the reality of the client is to overlook the possibility that this opinion is itself a reality that needs to change.

And why should it change? Because the socially legitimized treatment of psychiatric problems is itself a prime example of constructing a social reality. Diagnosis of so-called mental illness, in our society at least, is always pejorative, unlike diagnosis of a biological condition. And here the children's verse "Sticks and stones can break your bones but names can never hurt you" must be questioned. Names, to the contrary, can often maim and sometimes kill. Attributing blame for a distressing condition to a person or group almost always reinforces or heightens that condition. Mental illnesses are indeed mental, in that they are at least 90% made up of blame, or causal attributions that are felt as blame. Many family therapists hold the opinion that nobody can leave the field under a negative connotation. I would add that neither can they change under a negative connotation—at least not easily.

I suspect that this fear of negative connotation has to do with the attributions of blame that are such a signature of problem systems. Blaming processes are ubiquitous forms of mutual causal cycles between humans—witness the scapegoating by such groups of a special member, or the symmetrical warfare between couples both of whom are convinced the other is victimizing them. The politics of family life are intensely connected to the fearsome power of collective attributions because of the threat they pose; one defence against them is to form coalitions that can create counter-attributions, or simply counter-blocs.

In an article entitled "Changing the Family Mind", psychologist George Howe (1984) applies cognitive social psychology to family therapy in just this sense. Howe points out the many moves by family therapists that are directed towards altering or shifting ideas that have to do with perceived responsibility for problems. These interventions work by challenging perceptions of causation (oriented to the past) as well as patterns of expectancy (oriented to the future). Howe cites techniques such as unframing family beliefs, reframing linear beliefs, and moving family members towards positions of shared responsibility and mutual cause. These are all ways to cut into the negative attributions that in their extreme can endanger the life and/or sanity of any person who in this fashion is being thrown outside the social pale.

But it is not enough to stop with a technique of intervening upon intra-family attributions and the politics that support them. If we take our observing system stance seriously, we have to decide that the treatment context is part of an attribution of fault that goes with the territory. It is not for nothing that the phenomenon of resistance is common to all discussions of psychotherapy because it is next to impossible not to experience a request for change—even a self-imposed one—as a statement that something is wrong with one. So how does the treating professional cope with the puzzle that the very operation of offering to change people gets in the way of so doing?

Here is where the entire technology of "paradox" comes in— symptom prescription, restraint from change, positive connotation, and so forth (Hoffman, 1981). They work, I believe, not because the client has a defiant streak that has to be dealt with by indirect suggestion, but because these are all ways the therapist tries to remove the attribution of fault buried in any attempt to elicit change, thus allowing clients the freedom to explore their own alternatives. The danger in using these moves purely as a technology is that the therapist then operates from within a strategic mind-set. The message "this is really to get you to change" will be beamed at the client in all kinds of non-verbal and analogic ways, radiating negative attributions as it goes and obscuring for the clinician the awareness of observing system factors.

Another useful stance in puncturing negative attributions is the assumption that goes with the model of circular organization. If there is no first horse on the merry-go-round, it follows that we cannot isolate a cause or an aetiology for a problem or condition except as an artifact of our own observation. This recursive or "bootstrap" model for describing human systems finds an elegant expression in the hypothesizing process of the Milan Method. What best describes the rationale of this process is von Glasersfeld's distinction between "fit" and "match," mentioned earlier. In a Milan-style interview, there is no attempt to find the "truth," only successive approximations to an explanation that will fit the most amount of data together in the service of a meaningful idea. This collaborative investigation of the problem, whose outcome is merely provisional and hypothetical, takes the place of the usual diagnosis applied by an expert.

A different way of challenging the concept of diagnosis is provided by the Palo Alto doctrine of inadvertent addiction to problem-maintaining behaviour. The group at the Mental Research Institute notes that problems are often kicked off by some chance event, but then, instead of dying out, are reinforced by attempts to alleviate them, as in the famous injunction "Relax" to a nervous person (Fisch, Weakland, & Segal, 1982). Soon—due, I believe, to the negative attribution implicit in this type of injunction—it is the solution that has become the problem. "Relax" becomes equated with "You are bad" and the person injuncted becomes more tense than ever. The Palo Alto group gives us ways to avoid this effect.

I would like to say one final thing about this emphasis on meanings rather than behaviours. Traditional family models have tended to focus on altering "objectively" perceived facets of behaviour: interaction patterns, dysfunctional family structures, and the like. These models stay within an observed system framework. If one moves to an observing system framework, one becomes immediately interested in what Bateson (1972) thought of as *premises*—shared ideas held collectively by family members that are laid down at a deep structure level and operate at a higher level of abstraction than particular behaviours.

However, if one is looking for a premise that would explain the presence of a problem, one has to be clear about the non-objectivity not only of the family's perceptions but of the observers' constructions of those perceptions. A premise cannot always be verbalized but is often expressed through pantomime, so to speak, in analogic actions and in feeling-states. If the observer does put one into words, it is merely a guess, and has no validity unless the family takes it up and confirms it. This gives the development of a hypothesis during a family interview the quality of a construction that therapist and family create together.

Many Milan interventions start by describing a premise ("In this family, it seems that the parents feel that they have to be perfect", "Men are always the protectors of women", "Children feel that their parents are vulnerable", etc.). If a premise falls by the wayside, many subcategories of behaviour may topple, too. It seems to me that reframing has long been used to alter premises, but has not been given that explanation. In the same way, a task involving behaviour change may also hit a premise—witness the Palo Alto strategy of asking a perfectionist to make deliberate mistakes.

The person who is currently doing the most innovative thinking in regard to family premises is Peggy Penn. In her paper "Feed Forward: Future Questions, Future Maps" (1985), she takes a premise and pushes it into a hypothetical future, thus unlatching it from a fixed context and projecting it onward in time, where it is not fixed. The difference between this type of operation and a reframing operation is not always obvious, but I believe that there is much less of a conviction that the therapist is doing something to or for a client in the sense of designing a strategy for change, and much more of an emphasis on creating a perturbation that may or may not have an effect. Thus the Uncertainty Principle of Human Relations is always kept firmly in mind.

## TOWARDS A "SECOND-ORDER" FAMILY SYSTEMS THERAPY

A young architect in a family I had seen once told me that he had led a workshop at a conference and that he had tried to work the way I do. I asked what that was. He said, "Shedding power". I have pondered that phrase a lot since then, and although I don't know exactly what it means, I feel it has something to do with how one goes about influencing people within a "second-order" cybernetic model. You don't, strictly speaking, influence *people*—you only influence the *context*, maybe the only part of which you can control is yourself.

What I am describing here is not a method of therapy but something more like a stance. The new paradigm—the one that Bateson set out in hauntingly eloquent terms—does not specify any particular way of working but contributes a set of guidelines for how we put the methods we do use into practice. From my point of view, then, any therapy that respects a cybernetic epistemology will tend to have the following characteristics:

1. An "observing system" stance and inclusion of the therapist's own context.

2. A collaborative rather than a hierarchical structure.

3. Goals that emphasize setting a context for change, not specifying a change.

4. Ways to guard against too much instrumentality.

5. A "circular" assessment of the problem.

6. A non-pejorative, non-judgemental view.

This does not mean, however, that we do not also live in what Bateson thought of as a Newtonian world of forces acting upon things. Although it is more correct to say that one is always acting within both a "second-order" and a "first-order" cybernetics, I prefer to simplify and say, "Render unto Newton the things that are Newton's". Non-neutral, "linear" attitudes and actions are often (1) necessary, (2) appropriate, (3) what you are being paid for. Coercion, bullying, seduction, and force are time-honoured ways of bringing about results, particularly when fragile bodies must be protected from harm. Of course, sending child molesters to jail or taking abused children out of the home does not alter the recipe for abuse handed down to the next generation and the next. However, the first order of priority is protecting human life and rights. The only rule is to be clear about which hat one is wearing, a social control hat or a systemic change hat.

Another point is that one cannot be neutral and be a parent, a teacher, or a policeman. One has to be free in these roles to say, "This is right and wrong", and to make moral judgements. The Milan group will, for this reason, not include persons in these roles behind the screen as part of the team, and will say, when necessary, "Call the police. Use the hospital. Set up a suicide watch" (Boscolo et al., 1987).

The same thinking applies to social or political reform. The Milan point of view has been objected to by feminists like McKinnon and Miller (Miller, 1978) on the grounds that you cannot attack social injustice without reference to power issues and without giving up "neutrality". I agree. However, this brings up a question: Is there such a thing as a "second-order" feminism, and if so, what would it be like? Feminism, like most activist movements, has yet to take advantage of the insights of cybernetics; in my view it would be immensely strengthened if it did.

Another important reminder is that if neutrality, positive connotation, and systemic thinking become a way of life, the differences out of which systemic thinking arises are inhibited. I know one group that, in the attempt to be neutral and connote everything positively, began to distrust each other and to long for a more open exchange. This is why, during a team discussion, it is important to start with linear points of view and move to more circular ones later.

A "second-order" approach also promotes a high tolerance for difference. Although I work within a Milan systemic framework, I feel comfortable about incorporating methods from other therapeutic schools as long as I can be clear about what I am doing and why. [The term "systemic" (taken from Bateson) was originally used by the Milan team to describe their work. However, it has been adopted by many other practitioners whose work has a cybernetic base. It has also been used by Sluzki (1983) and Keeney (Keeney & Ross, 1985) to encompass structural, strategic, and interactional schools as well as Milan, as in "the systemic therapies."] I work at present with an Ericksonian hypnotherapist in the room, and actively pursue hypotheses with my co-therapist and with the family in a reasonably straightforward manner. Except for training purposes, I find that the use of a team behind a screen tends to make too big a cut between the therapy group and the family group and promotes a power ethic unawares.

More generally speaking, I see the contribution of family theory to date as a kind of Part One of a larger enterprise. It's as though my first twenty years in the family therapy movement were spent in the foothills. The mountain has turned out to be much larger than I had thought. The view from its slopes shows me that the scientific community is moving from a base metaphor clustering around energetics to a base metaphor clustering around cybernetics. Linked to this shift is the move from behavioural to an imaginal framework—Platonic ideas reborn in cybernetic guise.

In light of this framework, the term "family therapy" is rapidly becoming incorrect. It is less and less possible to use a medical analogy for so-called psychiatric problems. These problems fall more into the category of spells—collective illusions that must be dispelled rather than biological or social units that must be healed.

According to this view, a problem is best described as an ecology of thought in which living systems at several levels generally take part.

The future, according to my guess, will see the further delineation of problem systems in their human context, and far less focus on the family, extending the basic position of the Mental Research Institute. In addition, I predict a move away from the highly instrumental "first-order" models, whether we are talking about an overtly directive authoritarian mode or a covertly directive strategic one. Here is where I think the Milan method, with its inclusion of the observing system, has offered a much-needed reform.

The major difference, for me, between Part One and Part Two, is in the general direction of stepping down from the dictum that one must produce a change. The position of the Palo Alto researchers was to challenge the non-directive position of the psychoanalytic establishment. Giving technology a vote of confidence, these pioneers maintained that one should go to a therapist the way one goes to a mechanic to fix a car. Nowadays, this analogy does not seem so tenable.

However, in warning about technology, I do not advocate a Greenpeace family therapy, or some kind of vague family therapy Buddhism. Despite the growing consensus that objective reality does not exist, as long as we have Western science and Western minds we will always be asking: How is it built? How can it change? A virtue of the recent research in the cybernetics of cognition is that it does elucidate "the organization of the living". As we better understand that, we also understand the processes associated with change in these organizations, if only to declare what they are *not*. Chief of the insights coming from this knowledge is summed up in Maturana's radical statement that in the world of the living there can be no instructive interaction. That opinion, more than any other, will probably resonate in the field of systems therapy for a long time to come. It is up to us, now, to find a non-interfering, non-purposive vocabulary for change that respects this way of being organized. We need to think of each other as if we were all E.T.s.

# A constructivist position for family therapy

> Copernicus . . . successfully abolished the egocentric notion
> that the little planet on which we live must be the center of
> the universe. We know that it was a difficult step to take and
> that resistance against it lasted longer than a century. It seems
> that now there is yet another, even more difficult step in that
> direction we shall have to make, namely, to give up the
> notion that the representations we construct from our
> experience should in any sense reflect a world as it might be
> without us.
>
> von Glasersfeld (1987b, p. 143)

Periodically (though not many times in a lifetime) there comes a
shift that is so radically different from one's previous framework as
to qualify as a shift in Gestalt, if not of paradigm. When I discovered family therapy in 1963, I experienced such a shift. I moved

---

From *The Irish Journal of Psychology*, 9 (1988), no. 1: 110–129. By permission.

from the position that a symptom was a property of the individual to the idea that it had to be understood in the context of the family "system". For twenty years thereafter, I studied families with an eye to discerning what interaction patterns or relationship structures were connected with the kind of problems a family therapist might be asked to treat.

In the past few years, I have experienced another shift to a philosophical position called "constructivism" (von Glasersfeld, 1984). Constructivism holds that the structure of our nervous systems dictates that we can never know what is "really" out there. Therefore, we have to change from an "observed system" reality (the notion that we can know the objective truth about others and the world) to an "observing system" reality (the notion that we can only know our own construction of others and the world). This view has a long and noble lineage, from Vico and Kant to Wittgenstein and Piaget.

Experimenting with this view, I am trying to move away from the notion of objectively treatable structures in families. This is not to say that they don't exist; but I now don't think that I or anybody else can know for certain that they do. These are only ideas which a group of observers in a given field, like Tinkerbell's audience, agree to believe in. This constructivist view represents, for me, a discontinuous change from my initial thinking in the field.

There is also a tactical reason for this position. Setting up a diagnostic category as an independent reality is a way to create pathology. For example, the current designers of the third edition of the Diagnostic and Statistical Manual of Mental Disorders (DSM III RL) have created two new official diagnoses: the self-defeating personality disorder (e.g. women who are abused) and the sadistic personality disorder (e.g. those who abuse them). Feminists are already pointing out the unfortunate political consequences of these titles for women. Family therapy has contributed its own unofficial diagnoses implicit in the idea that dysfunctional family structures are to blame for many of the problems of individuals. As a result, we have a group like the National Alliance for the Mentally Ill that has virtually declared war on family therapy.

In view of a general tendency to objectify pathology, the shift I will be talking about goes in a corrective direction. However, it also goes against the majority position in the family field. I should add that I am talking not so much about Europe as the United States, where the majority position has been eminently practical and technological. In the eyes of those family pioneers who emphasized their difference from non-directive individual approaches, the therapist's job was to "fix" the problem the family came in with. The therapist was a sort of repairman—a social engineer.

But if you have a repairman, you have to have something to repair. This is where the family system idea became so doubtfully useful. According to early family theory, the family system, analogous to a cybernetic machine, was said to seek stability by means of error-activated feedback loops (Jackson, 1957). A symptom was described as part of this homeostatic mechanism. Once you have such an entity, it is easy to see it in terms of dysfunction. In particular, family systems that were too rigid were thought to predict for pathology. The assumption was that the therapist knew what a "functional" family structure should be and should change the family accordingly. I accepted this position uncritically for nearly fifteen years. Let me trace the history of my change of view.

## THE "NEW EPISTEMOLOGY"

Around the end of the 1970s, family researchers Paul Dell and Harold Goolishian began raising some important questions about established family theory (Dell & Goolishian, 1979). These authors challenged the idea that the family was like a self-stabilizing machine. It was incorrect, they said, to talk as if a symptom was acting homeostatically to preserve family balance. One part of a given system (the "governor") cannot be said to be regulating another part (the rest) because all elements interact as part of a mutually recursive process. If we saw a homeostatic regulator, this was only something that we, the observers, imposed upon the process.

Following Bateson's systemic views, Dell also attacked family theories of schizophrenia for basing explanations on concepts of linear causality rather than on the non-linear dynamics of complex systems (Dell, 1980). He felt that the idea of treating the family unit was not only misleading but led to a pejorative view of a family whose dysfunctional structure "caused" mental or emotional problems.

Criticisms like these made me feel uncomfortable with the family system idea, the repairman idea that went with it, and the cut between the two. I had just finished my book, *Foundations of Family Therapy* (Hoffman, 1981), and that was the picture of the family therapist that I had drawn throughout. In an effort at self-correction, I wrote a prologue and an epilogue that attempted to point the way to a less control-oriented model, a model that did not place the therapist outside of, or above, the family.

Just before my book was published, I had also met psychologist Brad Keeney. I was intrigued by his sleuthing into the ideas that swirled around information theory, General System theory, and cybernetics during the Josiah Macy conferences after World War II, and impressed with his book, *The Aesthetics of Change* (Keeney, 1983), which placed Bateson's often arcane views into a historical context. Keeney himself was proposing an "ecosystemic epistemology" for family therapy that would stress an aesthetic rather than only a pragmatic position (Keeney & Sprenkle, 1982).

My version of this point would be to say that many of the family therapy models that I myself had helped to publicize went too far in setting the therapist up to control the therapy in a technological sense. Along with Keeney, I believed that the time had come for a push in a different direction. An important influence on my thinking at that time was my first exposure to the authors of the conceptual framework known as "second-order cybernetics".

## "SECOND-ORDER CYBERNETICS"

It was during the summer of 1984 that I attended a Gordon Conference on cybernetics. This gathering was initiated to recreate some of the ambience and excitement of the original Josiah Macy conferences in the 1950s (Heims, 1977). It was organized by cyberneticians Heinz von Foerster, Humberto Maturana, and Francisco Varela and included a fourth contributor to the new thinking, cognitive psychologist Ernst von Glasersfeld. The ideas of these researchers were already percolating through our field. Keeney had introduced us to the thinking of von Foerster and Varela; Paul Dell was heralding the ideas of Maturana in articles and workshops; and Paul Watzlawick had published *The Invented Reality*, a collection of pieces on constructivism that included articles by von Glasersfeld, von Foerster, and Varela (Dell, 1985; Watzlawick, 1984).

These scientists were offering a version of cybernetic theory which they called "second-order cybernetics". Von Foerster, citing experiments on neural nets, held that we actively compute our vision of the world (von Foerster, 1981). It was he who originated the idea of the "observing system".

In a similar vein, Maturana's experiments with colour vision had convinced him that the nervous system is what he called "informationally closed" (Maturana & Varela, 1980). This led him to declare that there is no transmission of images from the outside world to our brain which then prints out a picture the way a camera does. The brain computes reality digitally, the way music is computed on compact discs. This was the basis for his belief that there can be no "instructive interaction" (meaning direct transfer of information) between human beings

Von Glasersfeld added another piece, as I have mentioned elsewhere ["Beyond Power and Control"—this chapter], saying that one should look not for truth but for fit in our attempts to understand the world (von Glasersfeld, 1984). From a constructivist view, it is not possible to *match* our perceptions with items in the environment; what is important is that they fit sufficiently to ensure our on-going viability.

Knowledge is, in this sense, survival, but it is not necessarily a correct depiction of a "world out there". Von Glasersfeld (1979) makes the point that survival only means not fatally colliding with the environment, and depends on a kind of negative knowledge, saying:

> In order to remain among the survivors, an organism has to "get by" the constraints which the environment poses. It has to squeeze between the bars of the constraints.

Along with the idea that all reality is constructed, a distinction was made between cybernetic systems that were seen as machines that could be programmed, and a view of cybernetic systems that could, so to speak, program themselves. Living systems would be in this latter category. Varela contrasted "allopoietic systems" (systems that can be controlled from the outside) with "autopoietic systems" (systems that are self-organizing and self-maintaining) (Varela, 1979). Biological systems are autopoietic. Social or ecological systems, however, do not have the tight coherence of biological systems, and so Varela used the broader term "autonomous" to describe these other varieties. The study of autopoietic or autonomous systems would fairly belong to a "second-order" cybernetics.

These ideas supported a trend away from a belief in an "out there" pathology. If one took the observing system idea seriously, one would have to see therapy as an immersion into a larger system that included oneself and other professionals as well. The therapist would not be able to claim an objective view of structures or sequences in the family that purportedly had to change. One also had to respect the fact that one could never really know what another living entity was, or should be, like.

Gradually, a daunting picture built up of all the comforting concepts that would have to be jettisoned if one took this non-objective view. As I have said, one would have to question the idea of the family system as an entity that could be manipulated. That would be a first-order cybernetics idea. Another notion that would have to be rethought was the idea that one could use standard interventions for standard situations. According to this new position, one might "perturb" the family with hopeful little probes, but the outcome could not be predicted. One would also have to question the idea of objective knowledge—so much for research. One would have to throw out linear causality—so much for aetiology. What would replace these familiar, not to say important, mainstays of clinical practice?

## AN EMPHASIS ON MEANINGS

One idea has been to redefine the target of therapy—which I used to call "the thing in the bushes"—from some kind of behaviour to some kind of meaning. This is what constructivism is all about. In many fields, in fact, we are seeing a shift away from the notion of an objectively perceived reality in favour of what you would call "template theories": the notion that people, tribes, nations, or whatever, build up constructs (embodied in myths, premises, concepts, or belief systems) about the world and then operate according to them. Von Glasersfeld (1979) comments:

We thus redefine "knowledge" as pertaining to invariances in the living organism's experience rather than to entities, structures and events in an independently existing world. Correspondingly, we redefine "perception" It is not the reception or duplication of information that is coming in from outside, but rather the construction of invariances by means of which the organism can assimilate and organize its experience. [p. 40]

In expanding upon this idea, von Glasersfeld (1979) draws upon the "control theory" model proposed by cybernetic engineer William Powers. Powers presents a drawing of a simple cybernetic feedback loop with three stops: a place for some information to come in and be perceived; a place for this information to be compared with some reference value; and a place for modifying behaviour in such a way that new incoming information and the reference value move closer. On the basis of this description, one can say that behaviour controls perception, not the other way round.

In other words, if I perceive that there is a fire, my perception of, say, discomfort is compared to a reference value for comfort. The ensuing gap between the perception of discomfort and the reference value prompts me to behave differently. I call the fire department, or run out of the building, or whatever, with the result that my comfort perception and my comfort reference value move close together again. Such reference values, Powers says, are nested in hierarchies, up a staircase from simple goals to more and more global abstractions.

Bateson's idea of the premise, axioms that he felt were built in at the level of deep structure and inaccessible to consciousness, is another example of a template theory. So is the hierarchy of values of Roy Rappaport (1979), one of Bateson's favourite correspondents. Rappaport holds that individuals, families, and societies develop connected networks of values, ranging from low-level directives such as goals for coordination of muscles, to rules or axioms for actions at a more inclusive level (what men should do, what women should do), to principles at a very general level like "Liberty for All". When you have a middle-level value like "What is good for General Motors is good for the country" elevated to the status of "In God We Trust", he feels that problems will arise.

The templates that govern attitudes or behaviours in a family or individual are of the same character. However, they are usually hard to get at because they are not set down on a little slip of paper like the fortune in a fortune cookie but are expressed in non-verbal ways and remain out of consciousness. A number of family therapists, including myself, are currently studying methods to find the templates that have the most explanatory power in delineating this or that problem situation.

## THE PROBLEM-DETERMINED SYSTEM

Another tendency has been to do away with the concept of the family system altogether. In the mid-1980s, clinicians like Evan Imber-Black (1985) and Luigi Boscolo and Gianfranco Cecchin were beginning to talk about the "significant system" or the "meaningful system", that is, the configuration of relationships and issues around a given problem. At about this time, Harlene Anderson, Harry Goolishian, and Lee Winderman of the Galveston Family Institute came up with the concept of the "problem-determined system" (1986). I had been thinking along the same lines and the way I put it was to say: "The system doesn't create the problem, the problem creates the system."

Anderson, Goolishian, and Winderman placed their concept within a challenge to what they called the "onion theory" of social roles. This theory described society as a series of nested concentric rings. Each layer of the onion—individual, family, network, community—was said to be subordinate to the level above and all had to be managed for the larger social good. This normative theory, which the authors associated with the work of sociologist Talcott Parsons, was felt by them to be responsible for the development of "objectively" determined treatment units such as the individual, the couple, or the family. In place of these units, the authors put the idea of the problem-determined system. This system would consist of a conversation, or meaning system, that included the contributions of the therapist and other professionals in its process.

Getting rid of the family system idea gave me an immense sense of freedom. However, I worried that the term "problem system" would be understood as one more bit of objectified pathology. To be really accurate, one would have to call it "the system that is formed by a conversation about a problem". Thus, I do not assume that there is such a thing as a problem system in the wild, all by itself. It is always something specified by participants and behold-ers.

In musing about problem systems, I am reminded of the folk tale about the young man who steals a magic goose. Anyone who touches this goose gets stuck to it, and anyone who touches that person gets stuck too. Eventually, there is a long line of people running through the countryside all stuck to each other and the goose. This is a good example of a problem system. But the impor-tant shift is to say that the components of such a system are not the individual bodies but the ideas linking them. A problem system is not a collection of people but a network of meanings.

## *THE CONVERSATIONAL DOMAIN*

This perspective is further supported by the conversation theory of Gordon Pask (1976) who suggests that the "psychological indi-vidual" is not bounded by the skin but can also include a dyad or a group. This idea suggests that the analogy of the informationally closed biological unit may not be applicable to communities. In talk-ing of families or therapy groups, we may do better to think in terms of what Varela has termed the "conversational domain".

In describing this concept, Varela states that, "there is mind in every unity engaged in conversation-like actions, however spatially distributed or shortlived" (Varela, 1979). Such higher-order unities, as Varela calls them, are not reducible to the contributions of the individuals. Varela cites Linde and Goguen's (1978) study of a plan-ning session as an example of a conversational domain in which the product was an "alloy" of the participation of the individuals who shared in it.

Varela emphasizes that the observing system for him always means an observer community, never a single person, since we build up our perceptions of the world not only through our individual nervous systems but through the linguistic and cultural filters by which we learn. From this vantage point, therapy is not an occasion where somebody tries to do something to, for, or with someone else, but a meaning process that has a life of its own, independent of the individuals involved.

There is a related observation of my own which has to do with establishing in therapy what I would call a "shared unconscious".

In an interesting sentence, Varela observes that one cannot have direct access to any higher-order unity one is part of. I have recently wondered whether there is any individual unconscious that is not merged with a family unconscious or a societal or cultural unconscious. Whenever a conversation or interactive process of any kind is established between people, a shared consciousness is, in my belief, always forming. Therapy always consists of tapping, or adding to, this underground spring. This argument was another that persuaded me that making therapy too much a matter of rational planning was leaving out a huge part of the endeavour.

## A DIALOGIC SYSTEMS VIEW

A different view of conversations comes from Norwegian sociologist Stein Braten (1984). Braten speaks of social interaction in terms of what he calls "dialogical systems theory". He believes that consciousness can only be present when there is a dialogue between perspectives. Braten explains what he means by referring to the term "cybernetics". He points out that it was adapted from the Greek word for steering or navigation. In contrasting a world-view that becomes monolithic to a posture that admits opposing points of view, Braten says:

> In Plato's metaphor of ship navigation [from the dialogue *Gorgias*], a mono-perspective may be compared to the inability to take cross-bearings at sea, which severely limits the navigation horizon. It means that an apparent dialogue becomes a monologue; that a conversational dyad is turned into a monad, incapable of consciousness since it is unable to allow for the crossing of perspectives. (p. 193)

Carrying this position into an analysis of the post-war economy of Norway, Braten talks of a dialogue collapsing into a monologue or single-minded, linear model of the sort that fascist regimes, in particular, have made so famous. This position has enormous relevance to therapy. According to the models that currently interest me so much, a quest for multiple and differing perspectives is always at the base of the inquiry.

Braten (1987) goes even further and proposes the radical position that we do not come into the world as monads but as dyads. It is a mistake if we break down into an electron spinning by itself. He speaks about the space we each carry by our sides for the Virtual Other. By this he does not mean merely a space for the other person but a space for another view, for the loyal opposition even, or for the Beloved Enemy.

In entertaining these ideas, I thought of Bateson's emphasis on the dualities in nature: the bisymmetricality of the body, our binocular vision, the bicameral brain. I also thought of the sperm and the ovum and the experience before birth of the child linked to its mother. I felt intuitively that, even if that theory of the Virtual Other could be proved to be untrue, I would still want to believe it. I asked Braten during a conversation at a conference if he meant a space for the other the way motorcycles have sidecars. He said, "Yes", and in that way "Sidecar Constructivism" was born—in other words, a constructivism that is not limited to the individual brain.

Braten thus differs with Maturana in that he does not make the individual the unit of autonomy, but the dyad, with its implications of complementary perspectives. He says, "The metaphor for self-reference of the snake biting its tail may fit the [idea of a] dialogue when two such are intertwined" (Braten, 1984, p. 24).

In therapy, the implication of a dialogic point of view is that, when you have a problem system, you usually find that people have become incapable of adopting the perspectives of other people or entertaining a dialogue, in the I–thou sense. Each person has broken down into a monad, so to speak, and it is important to find ways to replace the connections that allow for a renewed sense of the Virtual Other.

## FOOLS RUSH IN

A final piece has been contributed to my argument by *Angels Fear* (Bateson & Bateson, 1987), the book put together posthumously by Mary Catherine Bateson from an unfinished manuscript of her father's. It is a true collaboration, since this daughter has turned the tables on her father by including several metalogues paralleling the ones her father wrote. Needless to say, the characters are still father and daughter, with the difference that this time it is the daughter who is putting words into the father's mouth.

l am indebted to this book for the beautiful way it rounds off Bateson's (father) ideas about transformation and change in complex systems. The two Batesons note that in many areas of the "sacred" it is not efficient or useful for one hand to always know what the other hand is doing. Bateson (father) states that too much consciousness may make impossible some desired sequence of events. Among several examples, he cites the case of the Ancient Mariner (from the poem by Coleridge) who has been cursed after he kills an albatross. His shipmates, to punish him, put the bird around his neck. The boat is becalmed and everyone dies of thirst except the Ancient Mariner, who is left alone in a boat floating on becalmed seas. It is only when he blesses some sea snakes "unawares" that the albatross falls from his neck. Bateson observes that, had he decided to bless the snakes on purpose, he might not have had the same result.

Following the same logic, it may be necessary to build into therapy provision for less deliberate procedures. I used to talk about "restraint from change" techniques. Here, the argument would go that it is the therapist who should be restrained from change. In other words, it may be important to minimize the consciousness of the therapist in pushing for, or strategizing for, change.

## THE MILAN TEAMS AND BATESON

So far, I have been discussing ideas at the level of abstract concepts. I now want to look more closely at the ideas that family therapists have proposed based on their everyday work of struggling with human problems. From my vantage point, the trouble with most of the established family therapy models has been that, with the exception of the Mental Research Institute in Palo Alto, they depend on an objective reality point of view. The only recent approach that seems to be congruent with the new thinking is the Milan method pioneered by Maria Selvini-Palazzoli, Luigi Boscolo, Gianfranco Cecchin, and Giuliana Prata (1978). Let me describe their method before seeing how closely their clinical concepts relate to second-order cybernetics and the tenets of constructivism.

The Milan method was thought of as a kind of research from the beginning. The four team members would meet before the session to discuss preliminary hypotheses about the family. Two of the therapists (later only one) would then interview the family while the others watched from behind a screen. The observers could call in questions or suggestions and, towards the end of the session, would meet with the interviewer to discuss ideas while the family waited. The team would then compose a message which the interviewer would share with the family. The family might be told something about the team's impressions or be given a prescription or a ritual task. Another session would be scheduled for two weeks or a month later.

The work of the Milan group was originally imprinted with a strategic perspective. In the book *Paradox and Counterparadox* (Selvini-Palazzoli et al., 1978), family therapy is represented as a game for high stakes that the therapists try to win. In 1980, Boscolo and Cecchin split off to form a training institute while Maria Selvini and Guiliana Prata concentrated on research. The two women continued to go in a more and more strategic direction, evolving a theory of "psychotic games" that was not very flattering to families. The two men, on the other hand, adopted an overall philosophy that was eminently non-adversarial and non-blaming. I became drawn to their camp for this reason.

The Milan team had the advantage that their method took shape during the ten-year period that began with the publication of Bateson's *Steps to an Ecology of Mind* (1972) and ended with *Mind and Nature* (1979). In their Bateson readings, the Milan team found the idea of "circular causality", a term Bateson used to describe the recursive organization that he felt characterized living forms. The team transformed this abstraction into a number of new and interesting clinical ideas. The article "Hypothesizing–Circularity–Neutrality" (Selvini-Palazzoli et al., 1980) was written just before the team broke apart, and contains a description of these ideas. As I have said previously (Boscolo et al., 1987), the team found a "circular" method of assessing families (*hypothesizing*); a "circular" version of the therapeutic stance (*neutrality*); and a "circular" approach to interviewing (*circular questioning*).

In their devotion to a circular—or, as they began to call it, "systemic"—framework, the Milan team was careful not to establish a linear causality for a problem that a family might come in with. They preferred to describe how elements of the problem system fit together in an interlocking way, one part supporting another, and the whole evolving logically over time. This became the basis for a hypothesis covering not just the person with the problem but the entire constellation of behaviours and beliefs that were attached to it.

They were also careful in their use of language. In an effort to avoid giving the idea that clinical descriptions were other than subjective interpretations, they banned the use of the word "is". Rather than saying, "He is depressed", or, "She is anxious", they would say, "He *shows* depression", or, "She acts *as if* she were anxious". And in their circular questions they would ask for someone else's *ideas about* a behaviour rather than asking a person, "Why do you do this?" or, "Why are you sad?" This was an early adoption of a constructivist position even before constructivism was widely known in the field.

My acquaintance with the Milan team went by stages. In 1978, the team came to the Ackerman Institute for Family Therapy to demonstrate their work. More than anything else, I was astounded by the way they attended to the team/family interface. This was the first time, to my knowledge, that the therapist had been routinely included as part of the problem. For instance, in cases where a therapist came for an "impasse" consultation, an intervention might consist of commending the therapist for protecting the family from change. Both family and therapist might then co-operate in changing very fast. Or a family might be praised by the team for missing a session as a way to indicate that they wanted to slow down the therapy. This practice called into question the frame between family and therapist much as Escher's two hands drawing each other break the artist–subject frame.

Not less impressive to me was the idea of the positive connotation. The Milan group had translated the paradoxical intervention, a way of prescribing the symptom that had become a hallmark of the work at the Mental Research Institute in Palo Alto, into a benevolent rationale for the behaviour of everyone connected with the problem. Not just the problem, but the entire interaction complex, would be positively connoted or prescribed. This technique created a context in which dramatic improvements sometimes took place. The positive connotation, in that it went the opposite way from pushing the family to change, fitted in very well with my later wish to move away from an instructional methodology.

After I saw the Milan team work, I immediately began to experiment with a team myself. However, this method seemed to have different consequences in the United States from those in Milan. From my point of view, the team behind the screen could seem too powerful relative to both the family and the interviewer. The family often saw the interviewer as a servant of the team, going backstage to get suggestions and coming out to deliver messages. Worse yet, the family was left in the dark about the team's rationale for these messages. Because of the use we made of naive "paradoxing", we gave an impression of sarcasm. Sometimes, family members would get so angry they would drop out of treatment.

On the other side of the mirror, I was often dismayed to find myself part of an extremely competitive debate as different team members jockeyed among themselves to find the "bomb" that would blow the family system out of the water. There was a general feeling of being at war with the family and having to outmanoeuvre it. Wherever the Milan team format was accepted in the United States, it seemed to be taken as a way to extend the more and more popular strategic approaches.

However, Boscolo and Cecchin had moved away from the emphasis on strategy associated with the early Milan method. This was demonstrated by their increasing tendency to treat the questioning as an intervention all by itself. The portentous message at the end of the interview was less and less emphasized and the adversarial language from game theory was falling away.

There was also a stronger emphasis on ideas. Instead of seeing everything in a family in terms of manoeuvres, coalitions, and games, the focus was on beliefs, premises, and myths. This shift was in part influenced by Bateson's own constructivist belief that, in living organisms, the kind of abstract premises that have to do with survival are laid down at a deep-structure level. Thus, rather than attempting to change family structures, interaction patterns, and the like, Boscolo and Cecchin aimed at the governing ideas that held many lesser attitudes or behaviours in place.

This development had an interesting philosophic impact. We were at last beginning to see a "conversation" or "discourse" model for therapy replacing that of the "game", which had for so long been such a fertile metaphor for the field. We were also beginning to see the effect of constructivism and second-order cybernetics on the practice of family therapy. The vehicle for these new ideas was, for the most part, the network of what I have begun to call the post-Milan teams. Let me describe this phenomenon.

## THE POST-MILAN TEAMS

These teams began to spring up ten years ago in the wake of the peripatetic Italians. After Boscolo and Cecchin had started their training activities, they were called upon to demonstrate their model in different places all over the world. Offshoot teams took root in a significant number of communities in Europe, Great Britain, Canada, the United States, and Australia. Because of the geographic spread of these newer teams, a practice known as "teams" conferences evolved, first hosted by the Milan Associates in Italy, and then spontaneously erupting in other countries. Because the Milan method was so grounded in Batesonian ideas, and because Bateson shared a common conceptual heritage with the founders of second-order cybernetics, the evolving teams took naturally to a more or less constructivist view.

The Milan model also offered to its offshoot teams a starburst of new techniques. Second-generation teams often founded their whole approach to therapy on one of these techniques. Karl Tomm (1987a) of Calgary University has taken the circular questioning of Milan and made it the basis for an approach he calls "interventive questioning". The same could be said of the work with future and hypothetical questions pioneered by Peggy Penn and Marcia Sheinberg of the Ackerman Institute in New York (Penn, 1985). Penn and Sheinberg have also been using the concept of the premise in their clinical work. My own work has focused on the "positive connotation", reinterpreted as a "logical construction" of the problem and used, not as a particular intervention, but as a total stance. I have been working on this approach with a team in Amherst which includes William Mattews, Mary Olson, Dan Olshanski, and Joanne Christianson.

Another post-Milan idea is the "reflecting team" concept developed by Tom Andersen, Magnus Hald, Anna Margareta Flam, and others in Tromso in the north of Norway (Andersen, 1987). This group has been experimenting with a changed version of the Milan team format, where the team comments spontaneously while the family watches from behind the mirror. The family is then asked to comment on the comments of the team. This powerful idea has extended the "conversation" model for therapy in the direction of a less hierarchical and genuinely recursive dialogue. There is another group that has been closely involved, not only with myself, but with the Tromso group in experimenting with this approach: they are William Lax, Dario Lussardi, Judy Davidson, and Margaret Ratheau of the Brattleboro Family Institute in Vermont (Lax, 1989).

Family therapists like Rosalind Draper, David Campbell, Martin Little, and Peter Lang in London have been exploring the application of the Milan method to social agencies and the public sector (Campbell & Draper, 1985). Nollaig Byrne, Imelda McCarthy, and Phil Kearney of Dublin have been working with families and their attached agencies in an imaginative approach to the meanings of incest (see their concept of the "Fifth Province"—McCarthy & Byrne, 1988). Mia Andersson, Klas Gravelius, and Ernst Salamon, a Stockholm team, have been using the concepts of problem definer and problem definition in their research (1987). Karin Barth and Jarle Raknes in Bergen have been experimenting with and writing about the reflecting team. There are several Milan-style teams in Germany that have interested themselves in a second-order cybernetic approach: among them, Helm Stierlin, and Gunthard Weber's group in Heidelberg and Kurt Ludewig's group associated with editor Juergen Hargens in Hamburg. The Milan Centre itself is producing some outstanding younger systemic researchers, among whom are Laura Fruggeri (Fruggeri, Dotta, Ferrara, & Matteini, 1985), Valeria Ugazio (1985) of Milan, and Umberta Telfner of Rome (Telfner & Ceruti, 1987).

A U.S. team that has been exploring a systemic approach to family violence is the Southeastern Institute for Systemic Studies in Atlanta, founded by Gerry Lane and Tom Russell. They have been working with violent couples, using a technique of playing back the meaning of the problem-system that they call "circular replication" (Lane & Russell, 1987). Two other pioneers who have been applying second-order cybernetics to incest and violence are feminists Dusty Miller (1988), who is now associated with the Brattleboro group, and Laurie McKinnon from Sydney, Australia (McKinnon & Miller, 1987).

There are two groups that did not evolve from the Milan work but represent the new thinking in their own way. One is the team working with Bradford Keeney at Texas Tech University in Lubbock, Texas, and the other is the clutch of people trained over the years by Harold Goolishian and his colleagues from the Galveston Family Institute in Texas. Both Keeney and Goolishian are literate psychologists who have taken the second-order cybernetics path seriously and are extending their interest into the realms of hermeneutics and postmodern anthropology. These are only some of the groups that are building clinical work upon a constructivist position.

## CONSTRUCTIVISM
## AND THE PRACTICE OF FAMILY THERAPY

From the jostle of concepts and clinical innovations I have been describing has come a general style of systemic therapy that merits being thought of as influenced by a constructivist approach. Although what I do as a clinician is different from the work of Boscolo and Cecchin and the post-Milan teams, there are certain commonalities that I will list here, starting with a discussion of therapeutic stance and general philosophical guidelines. Some of this will summarize what I have already described.

*There is no belief in an objective reality.* This sounds as if I am also saying that therefore there is no problem, no bad thing. I am not saying that. On the contrary, I say that problems do exist but only in the realm of meanings. If I learn, for instance, that a child in a family is at risk of violence, I will report it or try to stop it. If the victim is a brain-dead person whose family is deciding to pull the plug, I may decide to remain silent. However, it is my responsibility to consult with my own belief system and/or that of the agency I am working for. I would say that this position carries with it more implications of acting from one's conscience rather than fewer.

The effect of this dictum, however, is, at first, to make one stop dead. One suddenly doesn't know how to "teach" therapy, much less how to "do" it. One loses one's status, one loses one's expert position. An entire Western upbringing can go down the drain; but, after a while, like a person who stays inside a room after being sun-blinded, vision returns, muted, but in some ways more acute. I come back to my old repertory of techniques, but I now put them in quotes. I give interventions and tasks, but they are "ideas about" interventions, or "ideas about" tasks. I use reframings that are no longer reframings but believable opinions. The world is the same, and yet it is not.

*There is a shift in focus from behaviours to ideas.* This follows an overall shift in the field of psychology from behaviourism to an interest in cognition. For family therapy, that means an emphasis on change of inner structures as well as outer structures. However, this is not just going back to the days of individual work. The shift from intra-psychic systems to interactional systems is kept, and there is an interest not only in personal ideas but in collective ideas; in recipro-cally maintained premises; in conflicting reference values; and in what I think of as a "shared unconscious", not easily accessible to the individual conscious mind. Symbols, dreams, stories, trance, are all important linking elements in the meaning systems that humans take part in collectively.

*The problem creates a "system".* Instead of conceiving of the unit of treatment as the "family system", there is no unit of treatment at all. Instead, we see that there is a group of people who are having a conversation about a problem. This conversation is defined as a particular kind of ecology of ideas, one where there are some people who are complaining and (usually) some who are not. If therapy is successful, the conversation ends up being one in which no problem is being discussed. Therapy is, in this view, a narrative or text. There is not the usual cut between the ones who treat and the ones who are treated, because all are contributing to this text.

*There is no such thing as a "God's-Eye View"* (von Glasersfeld, 1984). The therapist does not adopt a "metaposition", to use the term proposed by the Milan Associates. If we ourselves can con-struct reality, we can never find an outside place from which to look at it. However, there is an enormous emphasis on perspective. The therapist tries to allow everyone's private reality to be understood, and tries to "get behind" every person in the situation. This is much like the distinction between the authorial omnipotence of a nineteenth-century novelist like Tolstoy, and the intensely imagined personal worlds evoked by Dostoyevsky. Philologist Mikhail Bahktin has called this view of Dostoyevsky's a "polyphonic" vision, defined as "a plurality of consciousnesses, each with its separate world".

*The therapist sides with everybody.* "Neutrality", in the Milan sense (meaning that the therapist takes no sides), carries an unfortunate connotation. People get upset, saying, "You mean neutral like Switzerland? What about wife battering and child abuse?" Terms like "multipartiality" (contributed by Harry Goolishian of the Galveston Family Institute) or "plurality" (Laura Fruggeri of the Milan Centre) feel more accurate. The theory is that the therapist has to side with everybody, in an effort to find the meaning behind even the most repugnant actions or events.

An interesting point is made by von Glasersfeld in his distinction between "viability" and "adaptation". As I previously said, he notes that our knowledge of the world is a negative one. It in no way lets us know what this world is like, it only represents our success in avoiding collisions. This is very different from saying that our knowledge helps us to adapt. Our behaviours may be very maladaptive, but as long as we don't hit the constraints, we continue to exist. As long as an alcoholic driver does not have an accident or run into the particular environment known as a breathalyser, he remains on the road. Thus, it is possible to look at all beliefs and all behaviours, even those of Adolf Hitler, in the light of how these beliefs or behaviours have stayed viable. This is one of the bases for what I think of as a "logical construction" of a problem.

*There is a relative absence of hierarchy.* The reflecting team, for instance, makes the family a party to the thinking of the team. The status structure built into most family therapy models does not apply here, since not only is the family asked to listen in on the deliberations of the experts, but it is given the last word. In addition, the experts are being asked to discuss the family without having planned what they are going to say. For a therapist used to professional distance and the protection of anonymity, this can be a shock. A related shift is an increased tendency to self-disclosure. In this model, it seems natural to share one's own beliefs, biases, or life experiences, since what one says or does can only be interpreted in the light of one's own subjective views.

*There is much less focus on issues of power and control.* Here I would like to clarify the difference between what one would call "imposed" power and "reciprocal" power. By the former I mean any short-viewed, unilateral attempt to control circumstances without regard to the benefit of the social and natural ecology. This kind of power I believe eventually boomerangs against itself. This is true whether one is talking about control of feeling states, of other people, of weaponry, of agricultural output, of therapeutic outcome, or of any other human domain.

The alternative is a concept of power that acts mutually to enhance the balance of interests involved. However, to achieve this, I have to go against the models of family work I was trained in, which was always to believe I had to win the "battle for control". For instance, if a family cancels a meeting or only a few members arrive, I no longer treat this as a "manoeuvre" to be counteracted, but will try to understand the logic of this action. Maturana says in his theory of structural determinism that living systems do what they must do according to their structure because that is the only thing they can do. In that sense they are always "right". If one thinks like this, one can never experience what other models call "resistance". This is only a name used by therapists who are not getting the results they would like.

*The concept of position.* De-emphasizing hierarchy does not mean that one throws out all distinctions. Images of up and down in this model are replaced by horizontal images like centre and edge. What one can see and think and do depends on where one stands. To get a true sense of the validity of different perspectives, one has to be clear about boundaries. The team behind the screen can see differently from the interviewer in the room, both see differently from the family, and each family member and each individual on the team sees differently from the other.

To keep this differentness is one task of therapy. Thus, in a reflecting team, there is a tendency not to allow team members to arrive at a consensus before reflecting, and to keep the distinction between subgroups. In a consultation, for instance, the consultant, the therapist, and the family are kept separate. The consultant does not treat the "stuck" therapist as part of the family. If the consultant and therapist reflect together in front of the family, they take care not to include the family by verbal or non-verbal communication.

*There is a tendency to inhibit intentionality.* If it is true in everyday life that too much conscious purpose can sometimes backfire, how much truer is it of therapy. Therapy seems to have been devised precisely for those occasions where the conscious purposes of self and others are least helpful, where willpower and rational intelligence and well-meant advice have all failed. I have come round, therefore, to a less change-oriented view, at least in the immediate sense. I am still committed to the goal of change, but not as something that I can control with my technology or my art. The best I can hope to do is to join with the family in setting up a context in which change can come about "unawares".

## SUMMARY

In this article I have tried to paint a picture of a different kind of clinical work which, like a Polaroid print, is becoming more and more distinct before our eyes. This work seems to be evading the term "therapy". It avoids the implication of fixing something that has broken down or is not functioning, and comes closer to being some kind of hopeful discourse. It is, as far as possible, non-judgemental and non-pejorative. It is not control-oriented. It is lateral rather than hierarchical in structure. It is wary of an instructive stance. It shrinks away from an influence that is primarily intentional. It is pluralistic in nature, focusing on many views rather than one. There is no assumption of objectivity or truth.

In my belief, this stance fits closely with constructivist thought. Family systems work has always presented itself as a pre-scientific endeavour. It has looked at living systems with the fresh mind of the artist but without the legitimacy of a scientific frame. Constructivism, being part of the larger enterprise of psychology and the cognitive sciences, offers such a frame. It also offers a less ethnocentric view. There was a time when I believed that we were about to decipher the Rosetta Stone of symptomatic communication. I felt, "This is really science". Now, instead of the image of the ethnographer analysing the language of the natives, I feel like a person who is struggling to understand beings from another planet. My hope is that out of this struggle will come an overarching language, accessible to all.

# CHAPTER TWO

# Joining theory to practice

In the next two pieces—the "Foreword" to Tom Andersen's *The Reflecting Team* (1990), and Richard Simon's 1988 interview with me in *The Family Therapy Networker*—I was focusing on ways to apply my Zen-like philosophical ideals to clinical work. Basically, I was looking for elements of practice that would not only fit within a non-objectivizing and non-pejorative framework but also offer a style of working that was congruent with my "different voice", even though at the time I did not know exactly how the details of that practice would look.

Some aspects of the work of the two Milan men, Luigi Boscolo and Gianfranco Cecchin, were already moving towards this style (Boscolo, Cecchin, Hoffman, & Penn, 1987). I liked their emphasis on questioning as a substitute for interventions and their focus on beliefs instead of structures. However, I was becoming increasingly uncomfortable with the secret discussions of the team behind the mirror and also with the so-called positive connotation, which was often experienced as the reverse.

Another problem for me was what was called the "orgy of negative connotation", in which the backstage team made funny jokes at the family's expense, or aired critical reactions. The rationale was that this ritual served to debrief people of negative feelings. I felt that it merely reinforced these feelings. I was looking for a style that decreased the distance between professional and family that the use of invisible watchers had encouraged from the start.

I finally found such a style in Tom Andersen's (1987) invention of the reflecting team. Andersen had come to the Brattleboro Family Institute, where I was teaching with psychologist Bill Lax and others in his group, and we had all become converts to this brilliant and interesting format. A reflecting team was very different from a Milan-style team in that it exchanged ideas about the family, preferably non-pejorative ones, while the therapist and the family watched and listened. Then the family would be asked to comment while the team watched and listened.

I welcomed this innovation because it answered my prayer for a more horizontal and positive way of working, not only with families but with trainees as well. It was also less demanding. The Milan method required clinicians to come up with messages that were difficult to compose and hard to agree upon. The reflecting process allowed each person to offer their own thoughts independently rather than having to come to a consensus. Along with many other former Milan devotees, I found this shift an enormous relief.

Part of this relief came from the fact that I found myself feeling less and less responsible for the direction of therapy. I began to stop making any kind of presupposition about the problem or trying actively to control what people said or did. But it was hard for me, a well-trained family therapist, to sit on my hands without secretly believing that I would become totally ineffective. I also feared being swallowed up by the family, which strategic therapists had often compared to monsters of the deep. That was when I started imagining that I was a big beach. The waves might come and the waves might go, but the beach (barring hurricanes) would still be there.

I found a thousand and one uses for the reflecting process, as Andersen began to call it. The short "Foreword" I wrote for his book describes the way I used a reflecting format in classroom seminars, supervision groups, workshops, consultations, and so forth. Even when you were talking with a family alone, you could reflect with one family member or a subgroup while the others listened. The women might talk while the men listened, or the children while the

parents listened, and so on. It broke up the therapist-designed interview with a vengeance, because there was no possibility of unilater-
ally controlling the direction of the conversation once this process
got going.

I toyed with guidelines for reflecting teams for a while, then gave
them up because of the risk of ossifying the form. Basically I stuck
with one simple principle: an affirmative and affiliative stance. This
was something that I had got from Virginia Satir; I called it her
relentless optimism. Of all the elements of therapy that I had learned
during twenty-five years of studying other therapists' work, this
was the one that stuck with me most stubbornly. However, in
describing it, I didn't want to use the term "positive"—as in "positive reframing"—because this sounded too much like a little white
lie. It was essential to believe that everyone had the possibility to be
a good person.

The reflecting team offered a supportive framework for that
aim. People talking in front of a family had to abandon the clinical language that was usually used to describe family or individual dynamics. Phrases like "enmeshed family", "over-involved
mother", "projecting", "controlling", and the like were not appropriate in this situation. Thus, the use of a reflecting team was as
much of an influence on the professionals as on the family. For the
first time in the history of psychotherapy, as far as I knew, a con-
straint against this blameful in-house discourse was put into place.

I was also becoming aware of the radical nature of the work that
was being done by Harlene Anderson and Harry Goolishian in
Galveston. Harlene was commuting to Houston to work with Harry
while practising and teaching in Boston where she then lived. Both
of them were questioning the idea of the family system as a unit of
treatment. Soon after I moved to Amherst, I remember having supper with Harry and sharing my idea with him that "the system
doesn't create a problem, the problem creates a system". He and
Harlene had expressed a similar thought in their term: "problem-
organizing, problem-dis-solving system" (Anderson & Goolishian,
1988).

Watching tapes of their interviews at workshops, I was impressed
because I saw that they were pioneering a style that conformed very
closely to what I myself was looking for. In their interviews, they
followed the thinking and feelings of the people they were working

with, rather than imposing their own views. They stayed close to peoples' phrasings, often picking up a word and then offering others that were similar but contained more hopeful options. I called this "ratcheting". Above all, they offered a respectful appreciation of the often strange methods that people used to handle difficulties in their lives. This attitude alone seemed greatly to help the people they saw, who were mostly rejects of the mental health system and labelled ten times over. It also amounted to a profound critique of the system itself.

Harry and Harlene provoked considerable controversy by claiming that they wished to come from a place of "not knowing". At first I resisted this idea. All therapists come into a session with baggage in hand, and I felt that the only thing one could do was to be as conscious of this baggage as possible. Another objection many people made was that Harry and Harlene had enormous expertise and experience in the doing of therapy, so how could they claim to "not know"?

However, the extremely non-pathologizing atmosphere that resulted from their rejection of an expert status was most welcome, and I felt that on this score alone the Galveston group, along with the Tromso group, was contributing an element that I found nowhere else in my field. Thus I found myself incorporating aspects from both groups in my own work.

In 1988, an opportunity to talk about practice issues was offered to me by Richard Simon, who interviewed me for an issue on constructivism in *The Family Therapy Networker*. The title of the interview, taken from a phrasing of my own, was: "Like a Friendly Editor". Harry Goolishian commented later that the analogy of the editor continued the notion of the superior therapist who knew better than the family how its story should go. I agreed that the term "co-editor" would have been better, even though it still implied that the story needed to change. This sensitivity to wording made me very aware that getting out of the old ways of describing therapy wasn't easy. In fact, many of us were more and more coming to the conclusion that the description was the doing; the two facets were inextricable.

In the interview, Richard asked me how my criticism of traditional family therapy compared with the criticisms levelled by feminists. I talked about my own ideas of sexism in family therapy. One example, of course, was the idea that the therapist had to control the therapy. I had found myself more and more objecting to the practice of power therapy, which, like power dressing, seemed to me to be just another example of men's fashions being applied to women. Hierarchy was another example of a concept that originated with institutions led by men. I explained that I was interested in finding a practice that would be congruent with value systems and methods of communication that were more usually associated with women.

Richard also wanted to know how I linked up constructivism as a theory with what I did. I included an anecdote about some work that showed how we construct our reality, not discover it. This view, of course, had long been accepted by many therapists, especially Ericksonians, but their emphasis had always been on the therapist's ability to alter the client's reality; it was not a two-way street. Embedded suggestions and other strategic techniques placed the therapist in the superior position. What I as a constructivist believed was that this view of the therapist as the technocrat of change was incorrect. My reasoning was that since the family was not a machine—that is, that its members were autonomous, self-creating beings—any change would have to be co-constructed. There were a lot of phrases coined at this period with the prefix "co": co-evolve, co-author, and so forth. The idea was to create (sorry, co-create) a more egalitarian pose.

I want to include one story here about Richard's visit to Brattleboro to interview me. He saw a session that Bill Lax and I did with a couple whose son was in trouble at school. It was 100 degrees behind the screen, the interview went on for over an hour, and the wife stayed quiet while the husband did most of the talking. Despite the fact that the session seemed to have been helpful, it was heresy from a structural, not to say feminist, point of view.

Richard was polite after the interview, merely saying that we must have a lot of patience to work like that and wondering why we had not let the wife speak more. We explained that we were being careful not to control the interview unduly, although when the wife finally did come in, we made sure that her contribution counted. Later, when we three went out to a local eatery for supper, Richard told us about a conference he had just been to where Minuchin had done one of his star turns. It was clear that Minuchin was one of his heroes.

As Richard was expounding on what Minuchin had said and done, I noticed that an elderly couple at the next table seemed to be listening. Finally, the gentleman of the couple leaned over. He asked: "Are you by any chance talking about Salvador Minuchin, the famous family therapist?" Richard said: "Yes." The gentleman said: "Well, we were Minuchin's first family when he came to Philadelphia. Our nine-year-old son was anorectic."

I was fascinated, since I had heard about this case from Haley in 1969 before I ever went to Philadelphia. It concerned a boy who had begun to limit his diet, first refusing to eat anything from the animal kingdom, then the vegetable kingdom; the mineral kingdom was all that was left. The father said, "We used to go home and weep— Minuchin was so mean, and made us feel so bad. But he saved our boy's life. Minuchin made me take my boy out to the woods in back of the house and say to him, 'You must eat! I insist that you eat!' And he went back home and started to eat. He's now a successful banker, married, doing very well. He lives right near-by."

It would be hard to describe my reactions. Basically I was thinking, what right had Minuchin to come and invade my evening? Just as I had begun to rid myself of his influence, he had to come back and take over. And then I got irritated at myself. The fact that I felt threatened by a ghost meant that I wasn't so emancipated from Minuchin's shadow after all. Be that as it may, the following pieces will describe the revolution in thinking that finally set me free from the structural views that had become so embedded in my work.

# Foreword to
# "The Reflecting Team"

One could call this a book but one could also call it the description of a new flying machine. When I first heard from the book's primary author, Tom Andersen, about the Tromso team's idea of the Reflecting Team, I was enchanted by its simplicity and stunned by its radical implications. I was once the interviewer in a family where a very angry and drunken father threatened to come back with a pocket full of stones to throw through the one-way screen. It never occurred to me to ask him and his family to change places with the team. But that is exactly what the reflecting team allows people to do.

In this sense, it is a statement that dramatically alters a family's position in relation to the professionals they have come to see. I talk about ways to "put the client on the Board of Directors". One family outreach worker I know invited representatives from a mother's group, whose families had all been troubled by problems of alcoholism or violence, to attend the Annual Banquet of the Board of Directors of her agency. They were asked to critique the services that

---

From T. Andersen (Ed.), *The Reflecting Team* (pp. 7–11). Broadstairs: Borgman Publishing, 1990. By permission.

they had received by recommendation of the court. They did so with great dignity, despite severe stage-fright beforehand. These mothers, many of whom had been sexually abused, and some of whose children had been abused, have now been given a small grant by the agency to put together a Handbook of Child Sexual Abuse for other families like theirs.

The reflecting team is a similar concept. Families do not just experience it as empowering but seem fascinated by the process of eavesdropping on conversations among professionals about themselves. Of course there are rules about using positive descriptions and avoiding competitive or criticizing terms. The comments generally offer new options and descriptions rather than ideas about what is wrong. It is paramount that people do not feel singled out for criticism or blame.

Those of us who began to experiment with this idea found more and more uses for it. I have begun to use a reflecting conversation in my teaching classes, asking small groups of five to discuss some topic or some case, in fishbowl fashion, with the rest of the group listening in. Then the larger group comments back about what they heard. The smaller group is asked to comment on the reflections in turn, or else we can turn back to what I now call a "free-for-all".

Some of my students became upset. They said, "This seems too artificial. What about open and honest communication?" I explained that if you don't set up rules against rivalry and negative connotation, people tend to compete against one another. The talkers in the group, whom I call the "Lions", begin to take all the space, and the "Lambs" get more and more silent. In fact, without interference, most classrooms will become divided into two species, which will soon begin to experience themselves as "smart" versus "dumb".

I also explained that the idea of "open and honest communication" is also an artificial structure, born of humanist psychology in recent decades. In many countries of the world—Korea, Vietnam, Puerto Rico—this type of communication is considered extremely disrespectful, especially in hierarchical relationships. A similar factor that I stumbled on by accident was the shyness or feeling of being pressured that can be produced by direct gaze. I had asked a young woman therapist to present a case in front of a workshop group, and I divided the participants into reflecting teams. I had asked them to talk to each other and not to direct observations to me or the therapist on the platform. Some forgot and began talking to us directly. Then I too forgot. At the end, unable to resist a "final comment", I turned to the therapist and made what I thought was a profound and interesting summary of her predicament. Then I sat back and waited for her to reflect back on what she had heard.

To my surprise, she looked very distressed and confused. She put her hands to her head and said, without looking at me, "I couldn't hear you, I couldn't hear you. When people talked to each other, I could hear, but not when they looked directly at me." She seemed very upset by her reaction, and needless to say I was also upset. But that was a moment I never forgot. I began to see that the protected communication offered by the use of a reflecting team was extremely useful in giving people the freedom to accept or reject a thought or an idea, or even the freedom to hear it.

To offer one more illustration of the versatility of this concept, in a family outreach team I now consult with (People's Bridge Action, in Athol, Massachusetts), we have adapted a reflecting conversation to create what we call a "narrative model" for supervision. Instead of the usual problem-solving method in which everybody fires off suggestions to the person presenting a case, people go round the room in turn, offering associations from plays, movies, stories, their own lives, or other cases. During this improvisatory process, each person has their own space bubble and may take as much time as they want. Interruptions and cross-talk are not allowed, and the original presenter speaks last as well as first. Then, if we want, we can go into the old-style free-for-all. But often the group wants to have another round of reflections, which then build upon each other in a folding-in and layering way, as whipped egg whites are folded into cake batter (apologies to those readers who have never made a cake from scratch). A capacity for metaphor, poetry, and wit emerges, and the group is often surprised by the range of its own imagination. And a useful new idea for working with the case often emerges, although it is never clear how this comes about.

Perhaps the equalization between consultant and client is what most appeals to me about the reflecting team format. Even if people are asked to comment on the reflections but don't, or simply make a few polite statements, an implicit respect to their expertise has been paid. In addition, the professionals expose themselves to the family in quite a new way. I'll never forget a time when I interviewed a therapist about a family in front of the extremely forward-thinking social work staff of a for-profit psychiatric hospital. The social workers were "allowed" to do family therapy but they had little say in the treatment plan for the patient. Here the psychiatrist was King (or Queen, as the case might be) and made all the clinical decisions.

In the case that was presented to me, the therapist described a ten-year-old girl who had become upset during some incident at home and had run off down the street crying. Her mother, acting like a good mother, had become alarmed and had taken her to see a psychiatrist. This doctor, because she was about to go on pregnancy leave, wanted to play it safe and recommended hospitalization. Once in a hospital, another psychiatrist interviewed the child and gave her a diagnosis that automatically mandated a course of in-patient treatment for at least a year. For the next two weeks, as was the rule for hospitalized children, the girl was forbidden to see her parents.

Since I was using a reflecting-team format, I had asked to interview the therapist in front of the parents (the daughter, hospitalized, a year, was not present). I explained that the parents would act as my reflecting team. Although the therapist gave the family high marks for their co-operation and mentioned how hard they had worked on their intensifying marital difficulties, the parents said they felt less optimistic. They blamed themselves for their daughter's condition—especially the mother, who had learnt from the hospital reports that she was considered a "symbiotic mother". The father, after some initial reluctance, told of their intense despair. He said that they were given no information about their daughter's "illness" or about her recovery. They had no idea when she would be allowed to come home, or in what way they could help her if she did come home.

I felt unable to comment but instead told about a time when I thought I would lose one of my own daughters. I said that the idea that one might have harmed one's own child was the worst fear that any parent could have. I also said that just as in sudden crib death, these fears and the feelings of guilt and blame that go with them, could severely stress the parents' relationship. The therapist also commented sympathetically, saying that he had no control over the hospital policy. When the couple left, I joined them in the hall and impulsively clasped the mother in my arms. I was unable to stop my tears, so I ducked quickly into the bathroom to repair my face. Afterwards, I met with the social worker, who shared his frustration at having so little influence over this particular case and gave me his private criticism at the way it had been handled.

What I was struck by was the way the use of the reflecting team allowed the family to comment on, or at least raise some serious questions in regard to, the handling of their own case. As these questions related to differences in the field regarding the diagnosis of mental illness and the treatment plans attached to those diagnoses, it was hard to answer them directly, especially in a private hospital setting. But I thought that if I had gone in and interviewed the family as the outside "expert", as I used to do, I would never have elicited this feedback. The therapist and the social work staff, who were listening in, would not have heard it. And I would not have given the same message to the parents, which was: "Your voices count." The most interesting comment they made, in fact, was when the father said to the therapist: "You have often asked questions, but we have never heard questions being asked of you."

Another feature of the idea of the reflecting team is the rapidity with which people snap it up and use it. It seems to be touching some nerve. The need for guidelines, such as this book delivers, is clear, given the popular appeal of the format and the likelihood that it may be used without sufficient training. Andersen's expansion of his group's initial insights about the "reflecting position", as they now term it, adds many important dimensions to the original idea. The section by Judy Davidson, William Lax, and Dario Lussardi of the Brattleboro Family Institute is an eloquent and thoughtful description of how this format can be applied to a private practice group, not only in therapy but also in teaching and supervision. Finally, Arlene Katz's "Afterwords" is a poetic statement that suggests how one might do a "follow-up" study using a reflecting position as inspiration.

A question people will ask, of course, is: "Is this a new method?" "Is it a new school of family therapy?" At this point, my answer would be "No". It enters the picture at a more general level of abstraction, at a level of therapeutic values and therapeutic stance. It offers a way of demedicalizing a profession that in its many manifestations—psychiatry, social work, psychology, and all the branches of counselling, has been forced to deal more and more with objectively conceived assessments. These assessments have to do with degrees of individual pathology or type of family dysfunction. Labels based on these assessments (often dignified with the term "diagnosis") are often stigmatizing and usually pejorative.

In support of this idea, let me cite the work of Ben Furman, a psychiatrist in Helsinki, who has sent me a draft of a paper called "Glasnost in Psychiatry, Psychotherapy and Related Fields". The paper calls attention to the concealment of information from patients that routinely goes on, supposedly to protect the patient. In addition, clinicians will often discuss cases among themselves in a manner that is prejudicial to the patient, but of course not in his or her hearing. Furman says that this practice, initially designed to protect the patient, often gives implicit licence for what he calls "undisguised blaming". He feels that this is an oppression of the so-called mentally ill by the so-called mentally healthy.

Thus, the idea of the reflecting team is particularly welcome. It comes at a time when many of us in family therapy, particularly those of us who are having to deal with the new emphasis on criminality in families, are finding that we too are being co-opted as a vehicle for "undisguised blaming". The emergence of such formats gives us hope that some correction to this situation may be at hand. For this reason, the publication of these papers is an important event, one that should be welcomed by every practitioner in the family therapy field.

# Like a friendly editor:
# an interview with Lynn Hoffman

*Richard Simon*

Lynn Hoffman is not one for clinical razzle dazzle and instant problem solving. There's even a sly note of pride as she describes herself
as a "boring" therapist, someone whose style is likely to elicit such
comments as, "You must have a lot of patience to work like that". As
she readily acknowledges, she is not likely to spellbind many audi-
ences on family therapy's workshop circuit—or, as she puts it, our
"dog and pony show".

With a dedication rare in a field known for its indifference to
theoretical issues, Hoffman has established a reputation as an illu-
minator rather than a clinical innovator, a student of ideas who
explicates the abstract concepts and assumptions her more pragmatically minded colleagues take for granted. Through a series of
papers examining the enigmas of systems theory and, most notably,
in her book, *Foundations of Family Therapy*, she has brooded over the
fundamental assumptions of clinical practice and served as an intellectual pathfinder connecting family therapy to developments in the
wider scientific community.

"Like a Friendly Editor", an interview by Rich Simon, reprinted by permission
of *The Family Therapy Networker* (September/October 1988).

Since she left her position at New York's Ackerman Institute and moved to Amherst, Massachusetts, in the early 1980s, however, Hoffman's career has taken another turn. Although she has at one time or another been associated with just about every major family therapy approach, she had not found a method with which she was entirely comfortable—until recently. In what follows, Hoffman discusses how her interest in constructivism has led her to discard many of the ideas about systems and change that she once held dear.

Q: *I'm sure it's no secret to you that a lot of clinicians think of terms like "second-order cybernetics", "the new epistemology", "constructivism", as a kind of esoteric mumbo-jumbo that doesn't have anything to do with the real business of helping people. What do you say to people who question whether any of these abstract ideas are relevant to the experience of the ordinary clinician?*

HOFFMAN: My starting point is that even though many therapists have been challenging the idea of labelling people, we've never challenged it in a fundamental enough way. It seems to me that constructivism—or social constructivism as I would rather put it—is just a way of saying that whatever we describe is made up by us. Therefore, we must be very careful about assuming an "expert" position and trying to diagnose or influence the people who come to us for help.

But there's even more to it than that. I think the mistake many family therapists made was believing that once they got beyond an analysis of the individual psyche, they had a "real" description of the world. A description of how a family works isn't any more "real" than other kinds of description.

Q: *Why do you think constructivism has attracted family therapists' attention?*

HOFFMAN: I think we're in the midst of a swing away from a behaviourist orientation towards a more cognitive view. Family therapy began with a focus on changing the way people acted rather than on how they thought about things. Now, within the field and within other disciplines as well, there's a movement towards what I would call "story theories". By this I mean an agreement that we organize the world in little packets of meaning—call them stories, call them parables, call them premises, call them themes. It's as if reality consists of the tales people tell themselves to make sense of the world and to navigate within it. In other words, maybe it's not sufficient to try to change somebody's behaviour. Maybe we have to get to the narratives they are using to make sense of their lives, the metaphors they live by.

Another impression I have is that the entire systemic view on which family therapy is based is coming into question. In our descriptions of social systems, we are moving away from the timeless circle metaphors that represent this view—such as homeostasis, circularity, autopoiesis—to rivers-in-time metaphors, concerned with narrative, history, flow. The cybernetic analogue for human groups, which is essentially spatial, may be on the way out. For me this has meant that I have had to question some of the ideas I was most identified with.

Q: *Why do you think so much of the discussion of this movement seems obscure and hard to grasp?*

HOFFMAN: Well, once you move from a focus on behaviour to one on meaning, you find that it's harder to talk in precise terms. Behaviour is readily observable, ideas are not. You can't see them change. Also, I don't think ideas reside "inside" people the way fortunes reside in fortune cookies. Ideas are more like time flows—they arise in dialogue and are always changing, though sometimes rather slowly. A therapeutic conversation takes advantage of this fact.

## COMING OFF THE MOUNTAIN TOP

Q: *Perhaps you could make this discussion a bit more concrete by describing how embracing a constructivist perspective has changed how you operate as a therapist.*

HOFFMAN: It changed me drastically. I started by asking myself how my work would look if I gave up all ideas of instructing people and stopped trying to take an expert position. And that was like bowling; all my old ideas started to fall down like ninepins. When I was at the Philadelphia Child Guidance Clinic, I found that [Salvador]

Minuchin's managerial style of doing therapy didn't fit me at all. I used to say I needed a Therapy of the Feeble. However, I never did anything about it until now.

The way I have begun to work moves away from the stance of trying to change people. It's much more a matter of sitting down with people to help them tell their story—like a ghostwriter, you might say, or a friendly editor. I might suggest some alternative framings, but it's basically their text. And if what I do together with people works, they start to feel better about themselves and the problem either becomes easier to resolve or else it doesn't, but it stops being seen as a problem.

But let me emphasize that what I do in therapy shouldn't be called Constructivist Family Therapy—it's only my own application of these ideas to clinical work. The things I do haven't changed so much as the fact that I've become more personal and less concealed as a therapist. Individual therapists have always been scandalized by the fact that the therapeutic relationship is the stepchild in family therapy. In my own way, I'm trying to put the relationship back.

*Q: Could you give a clinical example of how you put your philosophical position about constructivism into practice?*

HOFFMAN: Okay. Let me tell you about a mother and young adult daughter who came in to see me three years after a huge quarrel had estranged them. The family had been this little island of three women—grandmother, mother, and daughter—but after the grand-mother died, the mother wanted the daughter to be more available to her. The daughter, who was already living alone, backed off, saying, "I have to live my own life". So they had this big fight and stopped seeing each other. They tried once to see a therapist to settle some things, but quarrelled all over again.

After several sessions of failing to reconcile them, I asked myself whether I really understood their conflict. So I told these two women that I thought I'd been going in the wrong direction. My trying to push them together could have been the worst thing in the world for them.

I also said that I might not be the right therapist for them because my own grown daughters had become estranged from me. I said that for that reason I might be trying too hard to push them together.

I had been feeling more and more indignant with the mother because she was so angry, but when I said that I felt my own anger fall away. The first thing the mother said to me was, "Then why are we paying you for therapy?" A little later, out of the blue, she turned to her daughter and said, 'I want you to know that I don't hold you responsible for my depression after Nana's death." After that mother and daughter had their first positive exchange in three years.

Q: *I'm not sure I see how the case reflects constructivist thinking.*

HOFFMAN: I think because I stepped back and reflected on what "story" of my own could have been influencing me and shared that reflection. In former days, I would have defined the couple as "resisting" me and would probably have thought up some counter-acting manoeuvre. I would not have paid attention to my feelings. I particularly would not have discussed my plight with regard to my own daughters.

Of course, there were some things on the level of technique that you could say were "constructivist". For example, the way the mother and daughter were constructing "reality" wasn't very help-ful, so I offered a different way to construct it that they both felt comfortable with. The problem was still there, but I tried to shift its meaning.

But my stance was very different from former days. When I stopped being an 'expert", I also became less distant and less anony-mous. I will now share a much more private side of myself, and I will admit error if I think I have been in the wrong. So many models of family therapy have kept therapists standing on a mountain-top or hidden behind a screen. I feel less and less comfortable with that.

## CHALLENGING ASSUMPTIONS

Q: *Let's talk about some of the fundamental concepts of family therapy that you are questioning. First of all, you seem to be challenging the idea that the family should be the primary focus of the therapist's work.*

HOFFMAN: Yes. That took a lot of doing because I had been one of the most enthusiastic proponents of the family system concept. Harlene

Anderson and Harry Goolishian have been experimenting with terms like "problem-organizing, problem-dis-solving system". I prefer the formulation that instead of the system creating a problem, the problem creates a system. I say that what I am struggling with in therapy is not a problem but a conversation about a problem. Very often the problem persists but people no longer need to have a conversation about it. That, for me, is the equivalent of a "cure".

Q: *You also seem to be unhappy with the idea that family problems are linked to confusions in the family hierarchy. What's wrong with that idea?*

HOFFMAN: I had always felt vaguely unhappy with the emphasis on hierarchy, but I accepted the idea from organization theory that a functional family has clear boundaries between status lines. I'm not so sure of that now. A family is not a bureaucratic establishment like the Army or the Church. I prefer to think in terms of position and perspective rather than up and down. How does where people stand influence the way they feel and see? In addition, if you construct a dogma as to what is a normal pattern for a family, you implicitly accuse families. That's what consumer groups like the National Alliance for the Mentally Ill are vociferously objecting to. Too many families have felt blamed for the difficulties of their children.

Q: *How would you compare your critique of family therapy with that of feminist family therapists?*

HOFFMAN: I don't hold the position that family therapists should take up the feminist cause and fight for the rights of women. Instead, I prefer to examine how gender-linked ideas bias our clinical thinking. If you start doing that, all sorts of idols go down. One idol that is associated with men's values in our culture is a power stance. In family therapy, there has been this rule that the therapist has to "win the battle for administration" and "take control". It's a top-down power system. First comes the therapist, then the parents, and then the children. I don't agree with that at all any more. If anything, I sit in a family like a big beach and let the waves come and break on my shore. Before, I used to think in terms of families trying to out-manoeuvre me. Therapy became like a military operation—either a

straightforward campaign we had to win, or an underground guer-
rilla war. I don't know which made me feel more uncomfortable.
Women aren't trained to think like that.

Q: So *this is where your emphasis on therapy as a conversation instead of*
*a game comes in?*

HOFFMAN: Yes. If you use the old metaphor of the therapist as someone who is engaged in a "game" with clients, you continue to see
therapy as an adversarial process. I prefer to approach therapy as a
special kind of conversation. As an image for the therapy process,
the metaphor of the conversation feels more accurate to me than that
of a game. A conversation is egalitarian and not especially goal-
oriented, people don't take sides, nobody loses and nobody wins.

## THE DANGERS OF CONSCIOUS PURPOSE

Q: *Within that conversation, you seem to believe that intention and*
*conscious purpose should have a very limited role.*

HOFFMAN: Yes, it's the idea that if you too consciously try to get a
result, you can come in for a nasty surprise. This is in line with the
systems thinking critique of common sense. People who simulate
human systems on computers find that common-sense solutions to
complex problems have widely inappropriate outcomes, usually in
the opposite direction of what was intended. As the group at the
MRI say, the solution becomes part of the problem. Family therapy
drives away consumers who feel blamed by it. Medication and psychiatric labels make emotional illness worse.

I call these "first-order" views. "Second-order" views are one
step removed from the process and allow you to see more clearly
your otherwise hidden influence and how your meddling is making
the matter worse. A first-order view would compare the therapist to
an environmental engineer trying to change the course of a river. A
second-order view would compare the therapist to a white-water
canoeist who is navigating upon the river. A constructivist position
automatically gives you a second-order view as well as a first-order
view. So it's not better, just more inclusive.

A lot of my distrust of too much planning comes from my own experience, too. The more I tried to control therapy from behind the scenes, the more insecure I became because I could never count on things going right. Sometimes they would, sometimes they wouldn't. Part of it was because I was so fixed on making people change. Now that I have given up that goal, I find I am far more effective.

Q: *Isn't there the danger that if we give up our interest in results and our sense of being in charge as clinicians, therapy will become terribly vague and unfocused? It could get hard to tell the difference between therapy and channelling.*

HOFFMAN: Sure. Adopting the constructivist perspective makes it harder to justify clearly what you do or to define a therapeutic outcome. Therapy becomes frankly subjective. But that has an advantage. For a long time, I subscribed to the idea that the therapist should be able to be "neutral", take a "meta-position". This got many colleagues upset because they felt that I was taking a hands-off approach to problems of violence and brutality. A constructivist position gets me out of that controversy because it holds that you can't take a God's Eye View. All you have is an awareness of your own subjectivity. That means that you are always operating from your own value system and/or that of the agency you are working for. I now share these value systems with clients if they have some relevance to the therapy. But always as "my opinion" or "the position taken by the state", not as "the objective truth".

## SWEETNESS AND LIGHT

Q: *It sounds as if in the therapy you do, confrontation has no place. Can you ever imagine trying to break through a client's "denial"?*

HOFFMAN: If you say someone is denying reality, you are judging what their reality ought to be. I don't do that. However, many therapy methods depend on getting somebody to see or do what you think they should see or do. Not only do these first-order methods not work very well, not only are they resisted, but now here are some people saying that we don't have absolutes based on objective criteria that will back these methods up. I get around this problem by saying, "This is my idea of reality. It may not be yours, but it is the best I have."

Q: *What about people who say that your way of working has too much of an atmosphere of sweetness and light?*

HOFFMAN: I think they're right. This is a very low-key way of working, almost Rogerian. People remark on how this shows the family "respect". I'm always surprised by that, as if we wouldn't be trying to show the family respect anyway. And then I remember how miserable my own experience in family therapy has been, how inadequate I felt, and how hopeless. Most parents have a horror of discovering that they have harmed a child, but much family therapy is based on the premise that they have. This thought gets communicated even when it's tacit. To get around that, I think family therapists have to be much more careful than individual therapists. I notice that since I've been working in this more careful way, people I see are apt to say, "I feel more comfortable with you", and they never said that before.

## THE REFLECTING TEAM

Q: *I know that you've become especially interested in an approach called the "reflecting team". How did it originate?*

HOFFMAN: It was developed by a Norwegian psychiatrist named Tom Andersen, who had been trained in the Milan approach. One day several years ago, Tom was supervising a trainee from behind a one-way screen. He kept trying to get the trainee to positively connote what was going on in the family, but the trainee kept going in and saying these negative things. Tom realized that the more he put the trainee in the wrong, the more he was in conflict with his own ideas about positive connotation. What he finally did was ask the trainee to ask the family if they would like to listen to the team behind the screen. They agreed, and the team began to talk about their ideas while the family and trainee listened. Once the family had heard the team's comments, they were asked to comment back. The upshot was that everyone felt relieved. It took the supervisor out of the position of criticizing the trainee, stopped the trainee from criticizing the family, and gave the family a seat of honour at the table. This is a nice example of the kind of work I call "putting the client on the Board of Directors".

Q: *What role, if any, does strategy play in the reflecting team approach?*

HOFFMAN: None, that I know of. I myself don't do strategic therapy any more. I am more and more dedicated to sharing the reasons for what I do with clients. I might come up with a strategic idea, but I will share the rationale for it. And I will talk about my own theory of therapy—how I see problems and what I tend to do about them.

Q: *What about rituals and tasks? Have you given them up as well?*

HOFFMAN: I did when I first began to think this way. Then Gianfranco Cecchin said, "Oh, in a reflecting team you don't give a prescription, you give an 'idea' of a prescription". So I give people the "idea" of a task or ritual. I tell them that whether they use it or not, the information that comes back is what is important. I should add that Tom Andersen's group doesn't use tasks or prescriptions at all. I am still influenced by the models in which I was trained where one offered suggestions and directives. In that sense, I'm not very pure.

Q: *What about losing the privacy of the conversation between therapist and team, or therapist and consultant? Have there been any negatives?*

HOFFMAN: Mostly positives. Obviously, there are some occasions when you can't share your thinking, but much of the time you can. And I am convinced that the practice of exchanging negative comments, clever strategies, and laughter behind the screen, the way I used to do in Milan-style therapy, creates an unconscious climate of distance. The reflecting team is useful because it trains people to use a positive description in talking and thinking about clients. It also counteracts the pejorative language of diagnosis and assessment.

## BENEVOLENT INTENTIONS

Q: *I'm struck with the emphasis you place on benevolence. Why do you make such a point of seeing all motives as so positive?*

HOFFMAN: Well, that has to do with the belief that—in family therapy at least—people find it hard to change under a negative connotation. I sometimes think that 99 percent of the suffering that comes in the door has to do with how devalued people feel by the labels that have been applied to them or the derogatory opinions they hold about themselves.

Q: *These ideas about constructivism and therapy seem to have taken root in Europe far more firmly than in the United States. How do you understand that?*

HOFFMAN: The Europeans, especially what I call the "social justice" countries of Northern Europe, seem to be very enthusiastic about Bateson's ideas and the ideas of some of his colleagues like cyberneticians Heinz von Foerster, Humberto Maturana, and Ernst von Glasersfeld. They have also been heavily influenced by the work of the Milan therapists, Luigi Boscolo and Gianfranco Cecchin. I think the Europeans are responding to the distrust of technology implicit in this group's thinking and the consequent notion that therapy is an I–Thou matter rather than a matter for social engineers. Perhaps they're also pulled by the emphasis on a collaborative relationship in therapy instead of one that makes the therapist the "expert". But I agree with you that constructivism has not had much impact in the United States. It's not in line with American pragmatism and the can-do spirit. The day when there are no more ads in *The Networker* for the tapes of the "Master Therapists" is the day when I will believe that being a "Master" is not an abiding ideal of American family therapy.

# CHAPTER THREE

# The shift to postmodernism

Towards the end of the 1980s, I was beginning to criticize the entire systems model, start to finish. "Constructing Reality: An Art of Lenses" was the result. I had much support from Harry Goolishian and Harlene Anderson, with whom I checked in from time to time. Harry had never really been a systemically oriented person anyway, and his scepticism about the cybernetic model continued to deepen and support mine.

Harry and Harlene were also beginning to question constructivism. Harry pointed out that this view was basically tied in with the biology of cognition and was extremely skull-bound. I thought he was right; examined closely, these ideas had very little to do with what happened in therapy from a relational point of view. For a while, along with Harry Goolishian and Lee Winderman (1988), I had tried to counteract this problem by putting the word "social" in front of constructivism. Then it became obvious that this misrepresented the constructivist position. The nervous system was portrayed by constructivists as "informationally closed" even though it was open from the standpoint of material exchanges with the environment. I had earlier used the image of separate bathyspheres to dramatize this informational isolation, and it came back to haunt me.

Actually, I had overlooked a much more relevant theory which I had confused with constructivism in my ignorance: social construction theory, which was being popularized by the social philosopher Kenneth Gergen (1985). This theory holds that what we know evolves not primarily within the individual nervous system but in the densely languaged give-and-take between people. Maybe both theories are true, but social construction theory is far more applicable to therapy than the other. I would have been much better off if I had started there.

But I am getting ahead of my story. My disenchantment with the cybernetic framework was hastened by being present when Harry Goolishian himself let go of this view. In 1988, during Tom Andersen's "Greek Kitchen in the Arctic" conference, I was on a panel of six so-called epistemologists invited to talk with each other in the presence of an international group of clinicians. The other five were professors from biology, sociology, artificial intelligence, and communication. What they had in common was the fact that they were all interested in a cybernetic framework. I was the only woman, the only practitioner, and the only non-academic person. I felt quite outnumbered and wished particularly that Harry, who was in the audience and was very good at academic debate, were on the stage with me.

I did notice Harry pacing around in a kind of frowning stew, muttering to himself. During our talks in the breaks he might criticize something one of the panellists had said, but it wasn't until the last day of the conference that he came to a conclusion. With a happy and excited air he announced to me: "I have finally figured it out. They are trying to rescue cybernetics from itself. That's why Maturana says that cybernetics is the science of meaning and understanding. But originally Norbert Wiener called it the science of communication and control. It's an engineering concept, and you can't take it out of that frame."

At this point I realized that if I agreed with Harry, and I did, I would have to leave all those fascinating ideas based on systems and feedback loops and systemic wholes. I would also have to leave constructivism behind. There was no way to keep the organism–machine analogies that came out of the marriage of biology with cybernetics. Not even "second-order" notions would help; they were useful in that they included the observer's influence on the observed, but they still put a Cartesian split into the indivisible social process that was therapy. I was extremely unhappy. I wondered how, after so publicly promoting a constructivist position, I could recant without looking very silly indeed.

Harry was not unhappy, because he had discovered the various writings lumped under the increasingly fashionable term "postmodernism". He kept sending me dense computer essays written together with Harlene that reflected a great deal of reading in postmodern linguistics and philosophy, especially the newly revitalized field of hermeneutics. These pieces were dotted with terms like "intersubjectivity" and "the circle of the unexpressed". They were full of references to scholars I had not even heard of. I admit that I was left far behind in the dust, wondering if Harry had struck gold or just gone round the bend.

But I wasn't alone in my wonderings. Postmodernism, whatever that meant, was a small black cloud on the horizon for many of us systemic people for several years. Then it burst with thunderstorm force on the field of family therapy, accompanied by a few lightning bolts from feminists who found that it supported their own views. It is a tribute to the tightness of my own intellectual loyalties that I personally ignored it for so long. I had heard of French deconstructionism and had read a few articles by postmodern American literary critics, but their writings seemed deliberately precious and obscure and I was also put off by their pretentious, self-advertising airs.

I then read an article by Gerald Erickson (1988), a Canadian social worker and feminist sympathizer; it was called "Against the Grain: Decentering Family Therapy". This gave the final death blow to any hope I might have had of salvaging the systemic enterprise. Erickson made three points which got to me. The most upsetting, of course, was a quote from my own writing; it was used as a type example of the kind of fascist thinking that could result from a too-literal application of an ecosystems analogy to human life. If you applied human values to ecology, you had to admit that the much-admired balance of a successful ecosystem was based on some species being more privileged than others. Calling it a system simply obscured the injustice of this fact.

Second, Erickson pointed out the origins of ideas about structures or "systems" that had influenced social theories in the twentieth century. He explained that the notion of "system" originated with the father of modern linguistics, Ferdinand de Saussure (1959). De Saussure reorganized the study of linguistics by introducing two ways of understanding language. The first was diachronic or historical: how a language system evolved through time. The second was synchronic or immediate: if you made a cross-time cut through any linguistic cable, so to speak, and analysed the connections between the elements, you got what de Saussure called a system of grammar. Erickson pointed out that the word system was taken up widely and applied to many other fields. Here I had thought the term somehow came from cybernetic theory, and it came from a discipline that had nothing to do with cybernetics at all.

Finally, using feminist arguments, Erickson took family therapists to task for being blind to questions of power and gender. He pointed out the obvious: if you only looked at the system as a self-enclosed body, you could easily miss the social, political, and historical influences that impinged upon it. The moral was clear: we family therapists had ignored important social questions in our efforts to focus on the systemic properties of the family. While trying to rescue the person from the stigma of individual pathology, we had allowed social pathologies to blossom under our very noses.

This article made me rethink the common feminist objections to family therapy. The systemic idea had already been singled out for criticism, along with terms like "circular causality" and "complementarity". In cases of violence done by men to women, these phrasings suggested that the woman was as much to blame as the man by obscuring her role of victim. Another idea targeted by feminists was the Milan school's concept of neutrality. This posed a more difficult question. While a hands-off attitude in cases of violence or abuse could hardly be defended, there was a counter-problem to consider. Taking sides with any person or group in a family interview could lead to losing the family or, even if they stayed, their cooperation. Most people live within an immensely complex web of loyalties and will often protect an abusive family member even when they themselves are being hurt.

I had no easy answer to this dilemma except to decide to abandon not only neutrality but all aspirations to being "meta" anything. A frankly admitted subjectivity seemed to be a much more tenable position than holding on to supposedly objective values and norms. Another solution was to abandon family therapy entirely in cases of violence or abuse, and this has understandably been the decision of many professionals. If one still insisted on working with relationships, this might mean limiting oneself to families in those grey areas where violence was not a primary issue, or where it had already been dealt with.

With these thoughts in mind, I tackled the hard task of saying good-bye to a cybernetic framework and welcoming the new and far more political postmodern perspective. My "Constructing Realities" article was the result. Here again, a regressive tug got into the very title. "Constructing Realities", suggested by a friendly editor, was an ambiguous phrase, since it might mean that the topic was the strategic art of changing people's realities. In addition, the word "lens" referred the reader back to the sight-bound universe of Western science. I thought later that I should have used the more intimate analogy of voice. However, I let the title go, trying not to be, as Tom Andersen would say, "too different".

# Constructing realities:
## an art of lenses

Believing . . . that man is an animal suspended in webs of
significance he himself has spun, I take culture to be those
webs, and the analysis of it to be therefore not an
experimental science in search of law but an interpretive one
in search of meaning.

Geertz (1973, p. 5)

The terms in which the world is understood are social
artifacts, products of historically situated interchanges among
people. From the constructionist position the process of
understanding is not automatically driven by the forces of
nature, but is the result of an active, cooperative enterprise of
persons, in relationship.

Gergen (1985, p. 267)

I begin this essay by calling attention to a massive challenge to
the mode of scientific reasoning that has dominated our century.
This challenge has crystallized in the term "postmodern", which

From *Family Process*, 29 (1990), no. 1: 1–12. By permission of Family Process,
Inc.

amounts to a proposal to replace objectivist ideals with a broad tradition of ongoing criticism in which all productions of the human mind are concerned. Theory and research in the human "sciences" fall into the category of written texts that can be analysed for their often hidden political and social agendas rather than statements of objectifiable fact.

My own path to discovering this point of view was long and tortuous. Twenty-five years ago I picked up a lens called cybernetics that was lying on the floor of the universe. Cybernetics was the brainchild of Norbert Wiener (1961) and was called by him "the science of communication and control". It described the activity of feedback cycles not only in machines but also in human affairs. From then on, I only saw circles, timeless circles. They seemed to invade every sphere. Influenced by this metaphor, I subscribed to a theory of family therapy in which a symptom was described as part of a homeostatic cycle that stabilized the family. A therapist was a person who had the skills to disrupt that cycle and help the family get to a different place. I never made the mistake of thinking such cycles were good, but I did think there were these hidden arrangements that the family couldn't see.

It has only been gradually and with great difficulty that I have become aware of this lens and what some alternatives are. Social construction theory, preceded by my interest in the related although quite different philosophy of constructivism, have both been crucial to my developing awareness. However, I have now cast my lot with social construction theory for reasons that will become clear below.

Taking a historical view, in the mid-1980s a number of persons in the family field, myself included, fell in love with constructivism. During this time, reports of the work of biologist Humberto Maturana and his colleagues, cognitive scientist Francisco Varela (1980), cybernetician Heinz von Foerster (1981), and linguist Ernst von Glasersfeld (1987a), began to filter into the consciousness of family therapists. This awareness was greatly aided by the publicizing efforts of family theorists Brad Keeney (1983), Paul Watzlawick (1984), and Paul Dell (1989). Research into neural nets by von Foerster and experiments on the colour vision of the frog by Maturana had indicated that the brain does not process images of the world the way a camera does but, rather, computes them like music on compact discs. It would be impossible, therefore, to know what the image was "really like" before it was transmuted by the brain. Maturana talked about placing objectivism in parentheses and, when lecturing, would put a schematic eye in the upper corner of his blackboard. Von Foerster had also emphasized the importance of the observer. It was he who contributed the term "observing systems".

Constructivism as a general view derives from the European tradition that includes Berkeley, Vico, Kant, Wittgenstein, and Piaget. Von Glasersfeld calls his version of it "radical constructivism". He believes that constructs are shaped as the organism evolves a fit with its environment, and that the construction of ideas about the world takes place in a nervous system that operates something like a blind person checking out a room. The walker in the dark who doesn't bump into a tree cannot say whether he is in a wood or a field, only that he has avoided bashing his head.

For a long time, I assumed that constructivism and social construction theory were synonymous. In both cases the idea of an objectively knowable truth was banished. Then I read an overview of the social constructionist position by Kenneth Gergen (1985). I realized that the social constructionists place far more emphasis on the intersubjective influence of language, family, and culture, and much less on the operations of the nervous system as it feels its way along. This view, an American product, has been known in the field of social psychology for a long time and is represented by the work of researchers like George Kelly (1983) with his theory of personal constructs; Berger and Luckmann (1966) with their book *The Social Construction of Reality;* Kenneth Gergen (1985) with his emphasis on the "texts" that create identity; and Clifford Geertz (1973) whose studies have forever banished the idea that knowledge is anything but local.

Basically, social construction theory holds that our beliefs about the world are social inventions. Gergen (1985) says: "Social constructionism views discourse about the world not as a reflection or map of the world but as an artifact of communal interchange" (p. 266). As we move through the world, we build up our ideas about it in conversation with other people. Gergen traces the evolution of this approach to Kurt Lewin's cognitively oriented field theory, which took the idealist side in the European controversy between idealism (the view that knowledge derives from internal constructs) and positivism (the view that knowledge is a representation of facts and events in a "real" world). Departing from both positions, social construction theory sees the development of knowledge as a social phenomenon and holds that perception can only evolve within a cradle of communication.

I initially liked the constructivist position because it implied that all interaction takes place between what Maturana called "informationally closed" nervous systems that can only influence each other in indirect ways. The analogy that came to mind was the attempt to set up a dialogue between different species. This idea undermined the assumption that therapy was a matter of instruction or manipulation of one person by another, who was by definition some kind of expert on how the other person ought to be. But I did not like the idea that people were stuck in a biological isolation booth.

In contrast, social construction theory posits an evolving set of meanings that emerge unendingly from the interactions between people. These meanings are not skull-bound and may not exist inside what we think of as an individual "mind". They are part of a general flow of constantly changing narratives. Thus, the theory bypasses the fixity of the model of biologically based cognition, claiming instead that the development of concepts is a fluid process, socially derived. It is particularly helpful for the therapist to think of problems as stories that people have agreed to tell themselves. Even the "self" may be a story. Janet Bavelas once remarked, "The big deception is the biological package; then people give you a name and you have to take responsibility for it". As Gergen (1985) says, "The move is from an experiential to a social epistemology" (p. 268).

In line with the social construction approach, family therapists like the Galveston group (Anderson & Goolishian, 1988) are beginning to take an interest in postmodern semantics, narrative, and linguistics. This attitude seems to mark a large-scale swing away from the biologic/cybernetic metaphor that compares a family to an organism or a machine. Terms like "homeostasis", "circularity", "autopoiesis", are all spatial metaphors that explain how entities remain the same. Temporal analogies like narratives, histories, and flows assume that entities are always in the process of change.

In my metaphoric shorthand, this shift focuses us on rivers through time instead of on timeless circles. Although you can never say that one metaphor is more "true" than another, I currently prefer the findings of scientists like Prigogine and Stengers (1984), with their idea of "order out of fluctuation", Thom's (1975) catastrophe theory, which offers a mathematical description for discontinuous change, and Gleick's version of chaos theory (1987), which depicts the order to be found in turbulence. I think these models propose a better analogue for describing the shifting trajectories of human groups than do the more static cycles of cybernetic theory.

Obviously, social construction theory is only part of the larger ideological shift that is heralding a new day in family therapy as well as in other human sciences. I could have chosen many other terms like "postmodern semantics", or "critical theory", or "deconstructionism" for the different frame that is now taking shape, but it seemed to me that social construction theory had a time-honoured heritage and was also the most convenient umbrella. Many styles of doing therapy that would otherwise compete can crowd together under its broad rim, as long as their practitioners agree that all therapy takes the form of conversations between people and that the findings of these conversations have no other "reality" than that bestowed by mutual consent. A good analogy is found in the movie *Peter Pan*. An anguished and slowly disappearing Tinkerbell asks the audience to help her: "Clap your hands if you believe in me." Of course the audience—all children and parents—respond as asked.

Thinking this way about the construction of meanings, one can say that even the choice of sensory modalities in psychotherapy is socially derived. A few decades ago, based on the interest in humanistic psychology, the key word was "feeling". The more recent cognitive models have given primacy to ways of "seeing". In the future, I suspect that the growing interest in the metaphor of voice will point to a different way of "listening. "

Be that as it may, this essay was written as an aid to "seeing" differently. And to help me, I rely on three powerful new lenses. One is social construction theory. The next is what I call a second-order view. The third is gender. Social construction theory is really a lens about lenses. The other two are only handmaidens in that they dramatize and shake up world views in their respective areas. All three can be metaphorically applied to psychotherapy. All three represent sets of lenses that enforce an awareness that what you thought looked one way, immutably and forever, can be seen in another way. You don't realize that a "fact" is merely an "opinion" until you are shocked by the discovery of another "fact", equally persuasive and exactly contradictory to the first one. The pair of facts then presents you with a larger frame that allows you to alternate or choose. At the cost of giving up moral and scientific absolutes, your social constructionist does get an enlarged sense of choice. Let me now describe the two "handmaidens": the concept of a second-order view and an awareness of gender.

## *THE LENS OF A SECOND-ORDER VIEW*

This term comes from mathematics and merely means taking a position that is a step removed from the operation itself so that you can perceive the operation reflexively. These views are really views about views. They often make you more aware of how your own relationship to the operation influences it, or allow you to see that a particular interpretation is only one among many possible versions.

For example, when my youngest daughter was in ninth grade, she came home with some "new math" homework and asked for my help. I, who had never managed to master arithmetic, was totally baffled by the new math. I told my daughter that I could not be of use because new math didn't exist when I went to school. She went off muttering, "What a drag to have a mother who grew up in the past". I, however, was determined to bring myself up-to-date and asked a friend what new math was all about. She explained it to me, using the decimal system as an example. It seemed that you could use a system of numbering based on groups of ten, but that you could equally well use any other group: twelve or two would also do. I, who had always thought that the decimal system was engraved in stone, was astounded. I "saw" what new math was about. It was not about a way to do mathematics at all; it was about a new way for me to *think about* doing mathematics.

Another example of a second-order view was the way it came to be applied to cybernetics. The research that led to the science of cybernetics was connected with experiments (with guided missiles and rockets) that had begun during World War II. After the war, a series of cross-disciplinary meetings called Macy Conferences sprang up, attended by researchers from both the physical and the social sciences, and united in a common purpose: to explore the applications to various fields of the new and fascinating idea that both living and non-living entities may be governed by error-activated feedback loops. At the same time, work on computers and artificial intelligence was offering what was known as a "systems" approach to mental processes and the brain.

During the late 1970s, the field of cybernetics underwent a schism. The engineers and robot builders were still in the majority, but a small band of dissidents stepped forward, including not only the late anthropologist Gregory Bateson, but also von Foerster, Maturana, Varela, and von Glasersfeld. Von Foerster proposed a second-order cybernetics as opposed to the first-order cybernetics of the "hard" scientists (see Keeney, 1983). According to this second-order cybernetics, living systems were seen not as objects that could be programmed from the outside, but as self-creating, independent entities. They might be machines, but they were, as von Foerster put it, non-trivial machines, meaning that they were not determined by history nor did they follow any predictive path.

I saw this distinction as a liberation from the models that treated family therapy as purely a matter of behaviour change. A first-order view in family therapy would assume that it is possible to influence another person or family by using this or that technique: I program you; I teach you; I instruct you. A second-order view would mean that therapists include themselves as part of what must change; they do not stand outside. This view allows a whole new picture to appear. For one thing, the very notion of "fixing problems" can be seen to be part of the problem, as the "interactional school" in Palo Alto pointed out decades ago (Watzlawick, Weakland, & Fisch, 1974). Models of family therapy based on an idea of the "normal" family alienate parents who feel blamed by it. The technology of psychiatry (medication, labels) intensifies emotional illness. Attempts to prevent drug abuse only exacerbate it.

J. W. Forrester of MIT (1961) has called this effect the "counter-intuitive principle". In computer simulations of economic systems, he found that common-sense solutions to complex problems often have the opposite effect to what was intended. He believes that this is the result of secondary and tertiary feedback loops that are out of sight of the experimenter. Just as it is widely conceded that we will never be able to predict a weather system accurately, due to its

www.amazon.co.uk

## Invoice/Receipt for

Your order of 22 June 2009
Order ID: 202-2367853-1591102
Invoice number: Doc6N74R
Invoice Date/Date of Supply: 23 June 2009

**Paid by**

David R Crew
27 Fernbank Avenue
Woodlands
Wolverhampton
United Kingdom

Invoice to:
Wolverhampton
WV10 8QN
United Kingdom

| Qty | Item | | Our Price (exc VAT) | VAT Rate | Total Price (exc VAT) | Total Price (exc VAT) |
|---|---|---|---|---|---|---|
| 1 | Exchanging Voices: Collaborative Approach to Family Therapy (Systemic Thinking) | | £22.33 | 0.00% | £22.33 | EUR 26.32 |
| | Hoffman Lynn 185575052X PaperBack | | | | | |

| | | | | |
|---|---|---|---|---|
| Shipping Subtotal (exc VAT) | | | £0.00 | EUR 0.00 |
| Order Total | | | £22.33 | EUR 26.32 |
| Sale order paid by Visa | | | £22.33 | EUR 26.32 |
| Balance Due | | | £0.00 | EUR 0.00 |

Conversion rate: 1.00 (EUR 1.18)

This shipment completes your order.

You can always check the status of your orders or change your account details from the Your Account link at the top of each page on our site

## Thinking of returning an item?

PLEASE USE OUR ONLINE RETURNS SUPPORT CENTRE

Our Returns Support Centre (www.amazon.co.uk/returns-support) will guide you through our Returns Policy and provide you with a printable personalised return label. Please have your order number ready (you can find it next to your Order Summary above). Our Returns Policy does not affect your statutory rights.

Amazon EU S.à r.l. 5 Rue Plaetis, L - 2338 Luxembourg
VAT number: GB727255821

Please note: this is not a returns address. For returns, please see above for details of our online Returns Support Centre.

# Thank you for shopping at Amazon.co.uk!

2eDuMRv7a7Ro/-1of-1//HPMN1 pemem of 4L4Bd56f0b23-18-00/0623-16-48  Pack Type: CMF176

extraordinary complexity, so it seems that the behaviour of human systems will never be predicted either.

As I looked back on my 25 years in family therapy, I realized that most of the models I had trained in or studied were first-order models, which were quite aware of the beauties of intentionality but showed little awareness of its dangers. The distinction between first-order and second-order views allowed me to consider what a therapy would look like that allowed for, counteracted even, the extremely instrumental tendencies of my earlier training. This idea, which I shared with Harlene Anderson, Harry Goolishian, and others of the Galveston Family Institute, pushed me away from the notion of "the system creates the problem" to the equally valid view that "the problem creates the system". Anderson and Goolishian (1988) went even further in specifying that a problem system was always a linguistic system, and that problems do not have an objective existence in and of themselves, but only through conversation with others.

## THE LENS OF GENDER

I also became stunningly aware of gender bias in psychological research. Carol Gilligan's *In a Different Voice* (1982) impressed me enormously. Her research questioned the world view associated with male value systems, especially the emphasis on independence, autonomy, and control, and showed that women contrastingly tend to value relationship and connection. In our own field, recent books like Carter and McGoldrick's *The Changing Family Life Cycle* (1988) and Walters, Carter, Papp, and Silverstein's *The Invisible Web* (1988) challenge many foundational theories of modern psychology and psychotherapy: developmental schemes based on studies of male maturation but applied to all humans; biases built into the family life-cycle concept that take the heterosexual but patriarchal family as the norm; devaluation of qualities like dependency and caretaking that are usually associated with women. Family therapy theories have only just begun to be sifted for gender bias, and already terms like "over-involved mother" or "enmeshed family" are coming under attack.

One particular school of family therapy that is being challenged by feminist family therapists is the Milan version of the "systemic" model (Luepnitz, 1988). Feminists particularly object to terms like "circular causality" or "complementarity" to designate the reciprocity of elements in a relationship between a man and a woman. They say that, in the case of an unequal or abusive relationship, the use of these terms can mask both the responsibility of the man and the vulnerability of the woman. Luepnitz (1988) singles out a quote from my *Foundations of Family Therapy* (1981) in which I say something to the effect that, just as the individual must fit within the family, the family must fit within the community, and all must fit within the larger ecology. I wrote that in the mood of happy mysticism that too much reading of Bateson can induce. It sounds to me now like a particularly offensive kind of ecological fascism whereby the individual may be sacrificed to some greater good of the whole. Of course I repudiate it, as I imagine Bateson would.

I believe, however, that Bateson would agree with me that the early emphasis on power and control in family therapy can be seen as a case of gender bias (see "Beyond Power and Control"—chapter one, this volume). Bateson objected to Haley's (1976) use of the metaphor of power and to the central part it played in his theory (see Sluzki & Ransom, 1976). Bateson (1979) used his own peculiar terminology to attack the power concept by calling it a myth or an "epistemological error". As a result, he has been accused of saying that power does not exist. I think he meant to say that he did not agree with a philosophy of therapy that recommended a power stance for the therapist, but wished to avoid moralizing because he saw that that would be to take a power position in turn.

At this point I would like to turn around and include an argument against taking Bateson's view too seriously. Social activists are apt to feel more comfortable with structural models of family therapy than systemic ones because they at least recognize power as a factor in human affairs. As in fighting fire with fire, it may be necessary at times to fight power with power. Dell's (1989) recent treatment of the issue of violence makes a distinction between the universe of scientific explanation, into which issues of personal responsibility and moral judgement do not enter, and the world of human experience—a world of description in which people feel and speak of being victimized. The weakness of Batesonian systemic views is that they offer no language in which to describe experiential events.

Dell (1989) also points out a fact that the above controversy has obscured: that Bateson felt as strongly as Haley that the use of power to control other people was pathogenic, except that he preferred to describe this ugly practice as an error of thinking rather than an error of action. Clinicians more often agree with Haley. They are often brought face-to-face with the necessity to "do something" about a criminal or quasi-criminal situation in a family and, in that case, they often have no choice but to fall back on reformist linear models that have arisen in response to the recent focus on wife battering and child abuse. An exception is the attempt to use a low-key and non-pejorative systemic approach to domestic violence by teams like Peggy Penn and Marcia Sheinberg (1988) at the Ackerman Institute for Family Therapy in New York, or Gerry Lane and Tom Russell (1987) in Atlanta, Georgia. Both groups have reported successful outcomes, although not in all cases.

Experiments like these question the belief, central to structural models like Haley's, that the therapist must always take a hierarchically superior stance. Many women, and men too, feel uncomfortable with this position and do better with a style that is less authoritarian. Many schools of therapy, both individual and family, carefully avoid a power-based stance and seem to have equal success. In fact, the "resistance" that power-based therapies seem to encounter often disappears when gentler tactics are used. As a result, practitioners of these gentler therapies have begun to claim that resistance is an artifact of the way therapists present themselves rather than a trait of a mule-like family.

There is another problem with structural models. Since they derive in part from organization theory, they tend to uphold a normative bias in favour of status lines, which are by definition unequal. A family is said to be dysfunctional if the generation line is not enforced. But families are not necessarily structured like the Army or the Church, any more than a therapist need be a general or a pope. Here again, one finds an implicitly patriarchal value system at work. As feminist critics of family theory like Virginia Goldner (1988) have pointed out, looking only at the generation line can easily obscure the gulf of inequality between the domestic roles of husband and wife.

For me, the main importance of a gender lens is that it exposes established assumptions and mores in psychological theory that have come to be taken for granted, and which are detrimental not only to women but also to men. Gilligan's *In a Different Voice* (1982) has been much criticized for taking what Rachel Hare-Mustin (1988) has christened an "alpha" view. This view is said to support female "differentness", like the separate sphere of domesticity for women idealized by Victorian writers. Hare-Mustin contrasts this position with a "beta" view: the belief that men and women should be treated alike. A "beta" view seeks to abolish the power differential between men and women and comes out strongly in favour of women's rights.

It seems to me that Gilligan may be putting forward a third view, which is that *both* men and women need to be able to choose the "different voice" that has been derogatorily assigned to women. She is talking about a more balanced cultural repertoire for both genders. For that reason, I prefer to call her position "gender-sensitive" rather than "feminist". In my own therapy, I find that this distinction has helped me to avoid imposing my own definition of "the problem" on a family while still remaining faithful to an ideal of justice. I also have another worry. In seeking to declare war on gender-linked ideas or structures in families, feminists may create another set of labels for mental pathology to add to the ones we already have, and a new kind of "expert" to tell families how they ought to be.

Let me end this section by saying that I feel particularly uncomfortable with the message that family therapists who do not use their skills to fight against the oppression of women are not politically "correct". Having been brought up in a world of Marxist artists, I am particularly allergic to this kind of idealism. Another problem is effectiveness. I sometimes despair that a feminist family therapist can do very much to change sexist family attitudes by working at the micro-level of the particular family. These attitudes will probably yield only to social policy enforced by political action. However, the feminist position is invaluable as a kind of consciousness-raising beamed at other therapists, and it has certainly made me take another look at hitherto sacred texts in family theory and challenge the hidden injustices they often perpetuate.

## *THE ROSETTA STONE FALLACY*

As a way to illustrate some of the ideas I have dealt with in this essay, let me include an anecdote that describes a gestalt shift of my own. This particular case concerns my dawning awareness of the implications of a postmodern view for systemic therapy. My story begins not with family therapy but with literary criticism. Recently I discovered deconstruction theory, a school of literary criticism that has busied itself with dismantling an earlier school called the "New Criticism". I used to be a "New Critic" in my college days. That meant that I believed that a poem or a novel possessed a hidden structure of meaning—a kind of symbolic architecture—that only the critic had the skills to discern. The author's social and political beliefs, the genre he or she chose to write in, and his or her culture, history, and gender, were unimportant compared to the Grail to be found within the text. It was agreed that the author was less able to know what that symbolic structure consisted of than the critic. And, of course, the ordinary reader had no notion of it at all.

I was thrilled when I stumbled on the family research the Mental Research Institute was doing in the 1960s because I saw that I could use the New-Criticism template that I knew so well. The idea of a "cybernetic system" in which a symptom was embedded was heaven-sent because it offered a metaphor that exactly fit my idea of a hidden structure of meanings. I used the analogy of the Rosetta Stone for the work of the pioneers at the Mental Research Institute. They were decoding the Rosetta Stone of pathological communication, and I was going to help them do this.

Twenty-five years later, I was beginning to alter my ideas and to feel that it was time to leave "systems", in particular "family systems", behind. It has only been recently, however, on reading an article attacking the systemic view by Gerald Erickson called "Against the Grain: Decentering Family Therapy" (1988), that I realized my Rosetta Stone analogy was a myth that had some harmful consequences. The impetus for Erickson's critique was a movement that for some reason had entirely escaped my attention: the deconstructionist challenge to the New Criticism of my college days. I don't want to go into a description of this movement except to say that it had the effect of bringing literary criticism back into the larger context of politics, biography, and history. This movement has also, according to my prejudiced reading, been responsible for some of the most self-dramatizing posturing that literary criticism has seen in a long time.

But to get back to my story: Erickson argues, as the deconstructionists do, that the idea of the "system" was first introduced by Ferdinand de Saussure (1959) who founded structural linguistics. De Saussure proposed that one could discern an organized set of rules for language that not only accounted for its evolution *across time*, but also for its coherence *at any moment in time*. Whereas previous linguistic theory had emphasized the lengthwise historical development of language, de Saussure's concept of "system" added the idea of an organization of rules for grammar in a timeless now.

De Saussure's use of the term "system" became part of a contagion of ideas. Many other social and psychological theorists either used this term or alternated it interchangeably with "structure". Freud, an early structuralist, had already contributed a psychic version in his theory of the ego, superego, and id. Psychologist Jean Piaget had posited "structures" in the cognitive development of the child. Anthropologist Levi-Strauss, whose name is virtually identified with the structuralist movement, had applied this idea to anthropology, finding "structures" in kinship terminology and in the myths of primitive societies. Noam Chomsky uncovered the "deep structure" of what he called "transformational grammar". Talcott Parsons built a theory of normative role structures for the contemporary family. And the New Critics founded an entire culture of literary criticism in analysing the "structure" of a novel, poem, or play.

Erickson, using the same arguments that the deconstructionists have used against structuralism, suggests that it is time to dethrone family therapy. More exactly, he is questioning Batesonian systemic concepts. And I think he is right. When the general systems theorists and the cybernetic theorists came along in the 1950s, they found the systems paradigm ready to hand. All the cybernetic people had to do was to match up general systems theory with the concept of the servo-mechanism, and it was ready to go. That has been the analogy informing family theory for several decades. It has been the "metaphor we live by" in our field.

However, as Erickson points out, in some ways it is a limiting metaphor. It gives the therapist, as the one who analyses the hidden system of communication, enormous power. Primitive peoples cannot be aware of the complex system of grammar that informs their utterances; neither can the family be aware of the system of rules that governs their "pathological" communications. The imputation of ignorance to the family and all-knowingness to the therapist is inevitable. The therapist becomes a kind of Master Interpreter that leaves him or her in charge of the field by *definition*.

As a result, a style of therapy has come about that is founded on a necessity for distance that only compounds the professional distance already bequeathed to psychotherapists by the medical model. The therapist, under these circumstances, is operating from an alien set of assumptions. Since most of these assumptions (both in family therapy and in individual therapy—let's be fair) are blaming and judgemental, they have to be disguised. So you get the growth of a language to describe emotional or behavioural "pathology" which hides the unflattering nature of the description: "symbiotic" mother; "passive–aggressive" father.

In family therapy, the same kind of descriptive phrases abound: "dysfunctional family", or "psychotic games". In addition, family therapy has often presented itself as an adversarial model. Thus, you get terms like strategies, or moves in a game of chess, or manoeuvres and counter-manoeuvres. This position seems to increase the morale of the therapist or the team, even though the family may be totally unaware that they are being considered in such a pejorative light. The result is a hiatus in the connection between therapist and family that has been enormously limiting for the field. It has certainly scandalized individual therapists and added to the difficulty individual practitioners and family-systems practitioners have had in trying to evolve any kind of common language, let alone rapprochement.

Another disadvantage of the systemic model has been the banishment of politics. The New Critics outlawed the emphasis of a previous generation of critics on the historical, social, and political context of the literary work. In the same way, cybernetic thinking has tended to distance family therapy from such concerns. Social issues are felt to be external to the work of therapy, which focuses mainly on the family as a "system". Systemic therapists include the therapist in their assessment, and sometimes a Milan-style team puts itself in as part of a final message; but, for the most part, the team stays behind the screen in a God-like position, intervening from time to time to rescue the hapless interviewer from being "inducted" into the family, and handing out opinions to which the family has no chance to reply. Other professionals may be included in the therapeutic hypothesis, but they tend to be grouped with the family as potentially harmful to the therapy if they are not handled with care. Issues of race, class, and gender have been nearly invisible to the systemic therapist, as latter-day activists are strongly pointing out.

Another objection to the systemic view has particularly focused on the Milan model's stance of "neutrality". Feminist family therapists point to situations in which there is violence or abuse, accusing the systemic therapist of taking a hands-off position. The Milan group defends its position by saying that handling violence is the job of a "social control agent" and not that of a therapist. Nevertheless, this criticism has highlighted the blind spot of a systemic view. This view, as I have said, asserts that everyone participates in a mutual-causal pattern of behaviour that eventuates in the violent episode, and therefore it cannot assign responsibility in cases of violence.

In writing this essay, I am not trying to resolve the above dilemma. For me it defies easy answers. My main interest is to call attention to the tacit assumptions about psychology or psychotherapy that are grounded in our training or in the less conscious ideas that can be placed under the heading of "folk psychology". Anthropologist Steven Tyler (1978) says that ethnographers go into the field with their eyes "bandaged with texts". Therapists also have their eyes bandaged with texts, although it is easy to be totally unaware that this is the case. I have found my three concepts—social constructionism, second-order views, and gender—invaluable in helping me become more aware of my own texts. As a result, I have widened my old view of systemic therapy to include a stance that emphasizes equity as well as connectedness, and subjective experience as well as neutrality. I now work very differently from the way I did five years ago. And I expect to work differently in another five years.

What intrigues me most right now is the idea that the cybernetic-systems metaphor can be fruitfully replaced by a postmodern, anthropological one. The consequences of using this model is to make us all what researcher Judy Davis (1988a) calls "accidental ethnographers". This role is the opposite of the visiting expert who, using informants and private schemas and observations, puts together a structural analysis of the "ethos" of the tribe. The postmodern therapist comes into the family without any definition of pathology, without any idea about what dysfunctional structures to look for, and without any set idea about what should or should not change. Together, while talking, interviewer and family may come up with some understandings or ideas for action that are different from those the family may originally have had in mind, and also different from those the therapist may originally may have had in mind. (Despite my wish to believe that the new-style therapist must come from a position of "not knowing", I cannot believe that a therapist can go into a session with *no* ideas in mind, and I strongly feel that it is better to be aware of these ideas than not.)

Another effect of being an accidental ethnographer is that there may be no final message or prescription but merely another date to meet. And when the group does meet again, if it does, something is different or is not different. Obviously, this issue is peculiarly vital to a therapy group, since the therapy conversation organizes around a complaint and the ethnographic conversation does not. But the two kinds of conversation resemble each other in the sense that there is no assumption of a hidden pathological structure in the subject that can be assessed according to "objective" standards. The therapeutic interview is a performative text, as the postmodern jargon has it. This text will take its shape according to the emergent qualities of the conversation that have inspired it, and will hopefully create an emancipatory dialogue rather than reinforce the oppressive or monolithic one that so often comes in the door.

Acknowledging the influence of Anderson and Goolishian (1988), whose ideas have been a bellwether for my own, I propose using a postmodern interpretive framework as a banner under which our experiments in co-constructing therapeutic "texts" might take place. In therapy, we listen to a story and then we collaborate with the persons we are seeing to invent other stories or other meanings for the stories that are told. "Family Therapy: Part 1" seems to have found a temporary ending in that the cybernetic paradigm may have run its course. What would "Family Therapy: Part 2" look like? Would it be called "family"? Would it continue to include the word "system"? What would happen to the term "therapy"? I am joining several other people in using the phrase "systemic practice", but other possibilities will undoubtedly present themselves.

Just as several decades ago a nascent family systems theory had the good fortune to profit by the excitement eddying about the study of circular feedback loops or cybernetics, it now has the chance to profit by another revolution, this one in the humanities and human sciences. The postmodern interpretive view proposes metaphors for our work that are derived mainly from criticism and the language arts. Since therapy is an art of conversation, these metaphors are closer to home than the biological and machine metaphors we have been using. Their particular strength comes from the fact that they are non-objectivist and, at the same time, socially and politically sensitive. In the context of this shift, I am asking you to imagine what a new and different story about "Family Therapy" might be.

# CHAPTER FOUR

# Definitions for simple folk

A nd now my river, or rather the journey I am taking on it, comes to a stop and I rest on the bank while I try to construct a map for my position. Since postmodernism is new territory for both me and most of my colleagues in family therapy, I feel some obligation to construct a bridge. This bridge would take us from the engineering universe of cybernetics to the diverse encampments of a more language-oriented world.

In the course of my inquiry, I looked into postmodernism (Kaplan, 1988), poststructuralism (Poster, 1989), critical theory (Held, 1980), deconstructionism (Berman, 1988), the discourse theory of Michel Foucault (Cooper, 1982), hermeneutics and narrative theory (Messer, Sass, & Woolfolk, 1988), social construction theory (K. Gergen, 1985), and feminist positions on postmodern theories (Nicholson, 1990). I will offer my own explanation of these concepts from the point of view of their relevance to family therapy.

First of all, the word "postmodern" seems to be a catch-all term for a change in the zeitgeist that has been taken up by many persons in academic and non-academic fields here and abroad. Similar terms would be "classic" and "romantic" as applied to the literature or painting of the eighteenth and nineteenth centuries. In fact, "romantic", "modern", and "postmodern" are labels that some postmodern critics use for the cultural periods of the last two centuries and the one to come. I had often wondered what would replace "modern", and think that "postmodern" is at least logical, if a bit of an anti-climax. The book that was most useful to me in explaining this sequence was Kenneth Gergen's *The Saturated Self* (1991).

A term related to postmodernism, which at times is used inter-changeably with it, is poststructuralism. In general, both post-modernism and poststructuralism are anti-positivist in nature, attacking the assumptions of objectivity that characterize the West-ern world view and especially the claims of modern science. In fact, postmodernists reject any position that consists of a "totalizing truth", an "ideal discourse", or any other endpoint theory. This position has been helpful to family therapists like myself, who be-lieve that applying notions of scientific certainty to the fields of modern psychology and psychotherapy is harmful to peoples' health. Diagnosing and treating peoples' problems as if they were medical events may be one of our greatest contemporary mistakes.

But poststructural thinkers have gone further and challenged the twentieth-century idea that hidden structures abide within human groups and their productions. This insight could destroy most of the social research establishment, including the part of it that is invested in family systems theory. The idea that systems and structures are merely convenient inventions casts doubt upon the entire systemic enterprise. I found this shock very hard to get over, especially as I had invested twenty-five years in the concept of the family system and had expected to believe in it forever.

However, there has been a great clearing of the decks as a result of this upheaval. Postmodern and poststructural thinking has allowed us to look afresh at all prized or sacred writings and to "deconstruct" them. The purpose behind deconstructing a text is basically one of political emancipation: by laying bare the relations of domination and submission embedded in the text, one (hope-fully) weakens its power to oppress. The French literary critics of the 1970s (Leitch, 1983) were brilliant at doing this and have inspired many academics in the United States to emulate them. It is remarkable how many citadels of thought (the writings of Marx and Freud and Nietzsche, to mention only a few) have been pulled down by an assiduous application of this method in one or two decades. Feminist critics have been given wings by the French deconstructionist movement, and feminist family therapists have profited by it too.

Although French and German intellectuals did not often intersect, there was a similar movement in German philosophy before World War II, called "Critical Theory" (Poster, 1989). Adherents of this stance like Max Horkheimer and Theodor Adorno attempted to adapt the ideals of the Enlightenment and the dreams of Marx to a more general view of social emancipation. The movement continued to develop after the war and was known as the "Frankfurt School". A major difference between French deconstructionism and German critical theory has been that the French seem to enjoy the process of deconstruction for its own sake, whereas the German theorists see it as advancing the cause of social justice. The activists within family therapy have found in critical theory a source of support perhaps even more useful than deconstructionism.

Of all French postmodern theorists, the social historian Michel Foucault stands out for the clarity and originality of his writings (Rabinow, 1984). In fact, he seems to be a movement in himself. Foucault, who died recently, analysed what he called the "discourse" of modern institutions: medical, legal, educational, and so forth. In Foucault's vision, the forms of bureaucratic government that appear so rational and benevolent are actually a kind of surveillance, constraining the life of the ordinary citizen.

But even though these arguments had a left-ward tilt, Foucault did not advocate revolution; instead, he pushed for a kind of informed resistance to these faceless regimes. Thus he remained an ambiguous figure, more political than many of his deconstructionist literary colleagues, but less so than his more Marxist counterparts. For an inventive and original application of Foucault's ideas to therapy, see Michael White's  blueprint for transforming people's problems into the forces of oppression and therapy into a resistance movement (White & Epston, 1990).

Another strand in the complex cable of postmodernism is narrative theory (Sarbin, 1986). This movement takes the position that there are no events that we can apprehend objectively; all we have are stories about these events. A number of revisionist psychoanalysts, as well as family therapists, have found it useful to apply narrative theory to their work (Spence, 1982). They like the suggestion that the therapist helps the client construct a newer and more hopeful story rather than excavating some buried truth. Narrative theory hits at the heart of pathological history therapies and gives new hope to therapists who, like myself, wish that all deficit models could be locked up in a closet and never come out.

On the other hand, there are some flaws built into the idea of turning all therapy into stories. First of all, it is too easy; you can make anything into a story, and the fashion is sweeping the field. But worse is the temptation to label the stories of the people one is seeing as poor and ill-formed, needing the help of the therapist to make them more coherent. This version of narrative therapy has been supported by a number of psychoanalytically oriented therapists. One of them writes: "The analytic listener needs to help [the client] discover behind the coping and make-do version of his tale an increasingly authentic one" (Wyatt, in Sarbin, 1986).

A more collaborative use of a narrative format is being pioneered by a group I consult with, People's Bridge Action. They have substituted "sharevision" for "supervision" and use a narrative process similar to that of an AA meeting. Both problem-solving and back-and-forth dialogue are tabled, and participants are given protected space in which to offer images, tell stories, share personal experiences, or offer consolation to their friends. At the end, the original presenter has a chance to respond. A format like the reflecting team is another way to incorporate a narrative mode, whether in therapy, consultation, or teaching.

The revival of hermeneutics, originally the art of interpreting the Bible, is another offshoot of the interest in literary forms. There is a large body of literature on this subject, much of it applying to individual therapy (Messer et al., 1988). The most eloquent spokespersons for this view in family therapy have been Harlene Anderson, the current director of the Galveston Family Institute, and the late Harry Goolishian, its founder. They and their group have done more than anybody else to create a story-based approach that is innocent of pre-judged plans or theories. As they say: "We come from a place of 'not knowing'."

Somewhere in this aggregate I must find a place for the postmodern ethnographers (Clifford & Marcus, 1986). Their innovations in the theory and method of research interviewing have set the stage for changes in family therapy interviewing as well. In my later essays, I discuss the shift from a top-down model of interviewing, where the interviewer behaves like a colonial official, to a more horizontal one, where the interviewer actively refrains from imposing any theory or outcome. Conflicts of meaning often arise during an interview conducted in a top-down way: for instance, when a medical doctor interviews a patient about his earache and the patient wants to unburden his soul, or when a woman hears her story interpreted according to the researcher's theory and does not see it that way at all.

Finally, what about social constructionism? This movement originated with a group of English and American social thinkers whose roots were in social psychology and anthropology. As set forth by one of its chief proponents, Kenneth Gergen (1991), it is a subset of postmodernism that takes as its battle-cry: "An End to Essences". Essences—things as they really are—are believed in by most modern thinkers and by many past ones too. The Mind and the Self would be good examples of essences. Social constructionists feel that such beliefs are the product of interactions between people and do not exist on their own, any more than a myth exists outside the telling of it in a certain time and place. Concepts of foundational knowledge are also challenged. Along with postmodernists in general, social constructionists reject any position that sounds like a final theory or a grand design.

A central part of social construction theory lies in the meaning given to the word "social". Essences may not exist as ideal forms off by themselves, but they exist in a very lively fashion in the social realm where language, action, and meaning intersect. French deconstructionists like Jacques Derrida contribute an interesting illustration of this idea (Berman, 1988). Literary critics of the past assumed that there was a meaning situated in any text. The French postmodern critics deny that any such meaning exists. Each interpretation has to be considered a unique and local product of the interaction between the reader and that which is read.

Therapists who support a collaborative approach will find this opinion appealing. The most common method in our field is for the therapist to assess the dimensions of a problem and then to offer an insight or prescription that will resolve it. But this method may be based on a misapprehension. Perhaps there are no problems, in the usual sense, to look at and therefore no solutions. Believing this, I attend to the continually changing activity that goes on between all of us who are involved, not to the supposed dynamics of the family or the mind. My hope is that from this activity new and more useful meanings will evolve.

However, not every family therapist accepts this view. The major split in our field right now is between a politically active position, and a less judgemental, relativistic stance. In family therapy, this split shows up most clearly in the conflict between feminist therapists who work with oppressed or abused persons and who see reality in terms of force and mass, and social construction therapists, who believe that reality only exists within the meanings we give it. The former have intensity and moral certitude on their side. The latter have more options to choose from. Since the arguments of each side are correct from the point of view of each side, it is difficult to decide between them.

This discussion leads to a consideration of the choices feminists have made in relation to postmodern thought (Nicholson, 1990). Feminists have allied themselves with or differed from the positions I have been describing according to their private philosophies. Political feminists have often chosen critical theory as a base or marched under the banner of deconstructionism; feminist researchers and historians have tended towards a narrative or postmodern ethnographic stance; feminists researching gender-linked behaviours have preferred social construction theory and deconstructionist tactics. The controversies between postmodernism and feminist thought have provided some of the most fascinating reading in our field (M. Gergen, 1988).

This section ends with an acknowledgement that postmodernism as a movement is as diverse as a floating Sargasso Sea. Any attempt to map it is doomed to fail. My hope is that the impressions I have given are seductive enough so that people will continue to read and think about it on their own. I am also hoping that I will live fully into the twenty-first century, because then I will know whether this postmodern movement is the wave of the future or merely a minor ripple. If it is a wave, I will have the happy feeling that my boat, my personal *African Queen*, has not backed up into the rushes of some marsh but has made it to the open sea.

# CHAPTER FIVE

# A reflexive stance

L eaving my island and embarking once more on my river steamer, it felt clear to me that a postmodern framework supported my vision of a different voice for family therapy. It was also extremely useful for another project I had: to challenge the clinical discourse of the field. A medically minded mental health establishment and a medically minded public had begun to locate, describe, and normify every facet of human thought and behaviour. There seemed to be no community that did not have its trauma, no family that was not dysfunctional, no woman who was not co-dependent, and no activity from love to work that could not be thought of as an addiction.

To this psychologized outlook was added an ever-lengthening list of negative terms for people who were really in trouble. And for every new problem that came to light, a new industry sprang up to treat it. The uncovering of family violence, this most hidden of our social ills, had been long overdue, but solutions were elusive and sometimes seemed to compound the original horror. Given the increasing confusion, I felt it was high time to "deconstruct" psychiatry, psychology, and the proliferation of psychotherapies that had grown up around them, including family therapy.

Thus I started to see Bateson's contribution to psychotherapy in a new light. The writings of social construction theorists like Kenneth Gergen seemed to be reviving ideas from Palo Alto: an emphasis on communal and intertwining histories rather than tunnel-view individual histories; an interest in relational events rather than internal events; and a shift from personal narratives and life scripts to the meanings people produce in concert with one another.

These critics of psychological concepts increasingly tended to ask questions like: Are the emotions we distinguish common to all peoples or are they socially constructed products of a certain time and place? Is the self an internally arrived-at concept or is it a social artifact? What about the idea of developmental trajectories? Does the personality of the individual or the life cycle of the family really go through predictable stages like a plant, or is there room for chance and accident as there is in evolutionary theory?

In my piece "A Reflexive Stance for Family Therapy", I joined the attack on these sacred cows of modern psychotherapy. I ended with one last sacred cow, bigger than the others: the idea of the colonial therapist. I began to look closely at the discourse of family therapy and the relations of power that characterize the relationship between the professional and the family. Therapists, like old-style ethnographers, often behave like colonial officials and "practise down" in their work with people. How could we learn to "practise up"? I felt that even therapists who worked on behalf of the poor and oppressed could end up in the position of colonials without meaning to, and the more idealistic they were, the more likely they were to fall into this trap.

At the same time that my theories became more heretical, the search for a different voice for family therapy continued to haunt me. I began to put together formats and analogies for representing and teaching this new style. Strictly speaking, too much emphasis on how-to was not congruent with the stance, but there was a part of me that loved to link the abstract with the concrete. As the poet William Blake had said: "Eternity is in love with the productions of time." And so I looked for what I called training wheels, or temporary structures that would hold the shape together until the mould could be broken and thrown away.

One concern was the interview itself. There needed to be some way to be more horizontal with people, some way to make listening to them more important than changing them, some way to divest oneself of the sort of professional identity that had created the thera-pist-driven session. Such changes would require a different kind of interviewing style. In a book by Eliot Mishler (1986) on postmodern research, an interviewer called Marianne Paget was describing her attempts to interview women artists in such a way that she did not silence them. In her efforts, she deliberately held back from sound-ing too sure of herself, had no interview schedule, and left long silences in the conversation so that the people she was talking with might come forward with their thoughts.

This discovery made me hope that the interviewing that I found myself doing, which felt so groping and confused, might be going in a good direction after all. After a consultation I recently did in Buenos Aires, my psychologist colleague Dora Schnitman gave me some interesting feedback. She said she saw an unusual pattern in my consultations. Instead of the comic-strip balloons over each head denoting linear, directed dialogue, she noticed that people would talk in a far less sequential way and for unpredictable lengths of time. She said that if she had to describe what I was doing, she would say that I used "opening questions" rather than circular ones.

Dora also said that another view of power appeared in my work. Instead of a fixed attribute belonging to designated people, it was more like a floating ball of light. It might appear in the hands of one person and then reappear over the head of somebody else. This serendipitous motion would make it possible to substitute the lateral concept of centre and edge for the vertical one of hierarchy. Presumably, whoever held the floating ball of light would be at the centre for that moment. I was pleased with this idea, because I had always felt that the term "empowerment" was extremely con-descending, with its implication of somebody higher giving to somebody lower.

I also began to take more seriously the use of what I was calling "associative forms": anecdotes, analogies, jokes, material from one's own history or from poetry, novels, or plays. If one is trying to break loose from a problem-solving approach, the content of the interview becomes different as well as the style. The reason for using meta-phors, for instance, is not because they help you to insert suggestions in the unconscious of a client, but because a metaphor hardly ever implies that people are doing something wrong. Advice or problem-solving always does. How often has a trainee received useful and well-meant suggestions, only to answer "Yes, but"?

This interest in associations also links up with the constructionist idea that all we have in the social realm are stories. Because of the popularity of narrative theory, ideas about stories are extremely prevalent these days. Unfortunately, there is a tendency for this theory to be co-opted. Therapists love word logics that can be equated with expertise: for instance, how to find the "ideal narrative" or the "best story" to express the authentic self of the person undergoing therapy. If the quality of a story needs a therapist to determine whether it is authentic, the customer had best beware. On the other hand, eliciting and offering open-ended stories with no rules about interpretation, and no best or worst, can be surprisingly helpful.

Thinking in this way, I began to create some simple rules for how to be with people. Listening came to seem more important than talking; helping people be more eloquent came to seem more important than being eloquent myself. Most of all, I had to challenge myself constantly to let go of the trapeze, in the faith that another's hands would appear and catch me

I put most of these observations in my "Reflexive Stance" article. And yet I was still unsatisfied. The word "reflexive" seemed too abstract, too connected with mathematical theory, but I couldn't come up with one I liked better. I was also unsure about social constructionism. It took away a lot of what I objected to in psychology, but it didn't put anything in its place. This was the point at which Harry died, and it was as if I had lost the pilot of the boat. I felt stuck in the reeds and unable to see over the tops of them to find out where I was.

I got one last letter from Harry, dated August 2, 1991. He was talking about the debate between those who see therapy in terms of conversation and narrative and those who say, "How can you leave out the person?" He wrote: "I sometimes think of this question like I do the reality/relativism question. It is the wrong question, the wrong metaphor, and it needs to disappear." With this comment, he himself disappeared, leaving me not only to ponder the meaning of his loss, but to wonder what to do with his message.

# A reflexive stance
# for family therapy

During the past five or six years, a view has emerged among a small sub-group of family therapists that offers something different enough to qualify as a new approach. This approach is more participatory than others and less goal-orientated—some would say it has no goals at all. It enrages some people; others applaud. It is represented by a few groups here and abroad, notably the Galveston group (Anderson & Goolishian, 1988), the Tromso group (Andersen, 1987), and the Brattleboro group (Lax & Lussardi, 1989), although its adherents are growing. Having been one of the people groping towards this something, I have also been struggling to name it. But so many streams of ideas are flowing together into a larger tributary that it is hard to find one common ancestor.

In certain respects, our present dialogue is congenial to the movement known as postmodernism—with its implication that modernism is now dead and new perspectives are in the making.

From S. McNamee & K. Gergen (Eds.), *Therapy as Social Construction* (pp. 7–24). London: Sage Publications, 1992. By permission.

Without overstating the matter, one could say—that many adherents of postmodernism have taken on the project of dismantling the philosophical foundations of Western thought. Sometimes the term "poststructural" is used as if it were synonymous with postmodern. A poststructural view of the social sciences, for instance, challenges any framework that posits some kind of structure internal to the entity in question, whether we are talking about a text, a family, or a play. In family therapy, this has meant that the cybernetic view that sees the family as a homeostatic system is under attack. Because postmodern and poststructural ideas were originated by people in semiotics and literary criticism, it is becoming increasingly common in talking of social fields of study to use the analogy of a narrative or text.

Within this context, a number of family systems people like Harlene Anderson and Harry Goolishian (1988) have defected from the flag of cybernetics and have adopted the flag of *hermeneutics*. Hermeneutics, referred to with self-conscious grace by some of its adherents as "the interpretive turn", is a recently revived branch of textual interpretation. For family therapists who have espoused this view, the feedback loops of cybernetic systems are replaced by the intersubjective loops of dialogue. The central metaphor for therapy thus changes to conversation, reinforced by the fact that the basic medium of therapy is also conversation.

For me, a more useful approach is located in social construction theory (Gergen, 1985). Although many persons, including myself, have frequently confused this theory with constructivism (von Glasersfeld, 1984), the two positions are quite different. There is a common ground in that both take issue with the modernist idea that a real world exists that can be known with objective certainty. However, the beliefs represented by constructivism tend to promote an image of the nervous system as a closed machine. According to this view, percepts and constructs take shape as the organism bumps against its environment. By contrast, the social construction theorists see ideas, concepts, and memories arising from social inter-change and mediated through language. All knowledge, the social constructionists hold, evolves in the space between people, in the realm of the "common world" or the "common dance". Only through the on-going conversation with intimates does the individual develop a sense of identity or an inner voice.

In addition, the social construction theorists place themselves squarely in a postmodern tradition. They owe much to the textual and political criticism represented by the *deconstructionist* views of literary critics like Jacques Derrida (1978) in France and deriving from the neo-Marxist thinkers of the Frankfurt School (Poster, 1989). One must add to this intellectual context the writings of the brilliant French social historian Michel Foucault (1975), who has brought the term power back into prominence with his examination of the way relations of dominance and submission are embedded in social discourse.

Due to these influences, we are seeing a revolution in the social sciences: worse yet, a challenge to the idea that students of society ought to call themselves scientists at all. Social researchers like Kenneth Gergen (1991) and Rom Harré (1984) are overturning foundational ideas in modern psychology and sociology. Feminists have joined the attack, finding in the arguments of the postmodern thinkers, especially the theories of Foucault, ample ammunition for their insistence that the very language of therapy is biased against women. And feminist sympathizers like Jeffrey Masson (1990) have made a compelling case for the notion that psychotherapy began as a treatment designed to subjugate women who objected to the way they were treated.

There have been similar explosions in anthropology and ethnography. Ethnographers James Clifford and George Marcus (1986), for instance, take a participatory posture in regard to the people they study, finding in the stance of traditional anthropologists an unconscious colonial mentality. Their critique has profoundly influenced the nature of the research interview and, by extension, the clinical interview as well. The implications of all these challenges to the corpus of beliefs called psychotherapy are mind-boggling. In order to explain in detail what I mean, let me describe five sacred cows of modern psychology and the arguments of their critics, many of whom belong to the social constructionist camp.

## FIVE SACRED COWS OF MODERN PSYCHOLOGY

### Objective social research

The social constructionists not only challenge the idea of a singular truth, but doubt that there is such a thing as objective social research as well. They charge that we cannot ever really know what "social reality" is, and that therefore traditional scientific research, with its tests and statistics and probability quotients, is a pious hope if not a downright lie. This claim, if accepted, would obviously threaten the status quo in the mental health profession.

To take only one example, health insurance coverage in the United States for emotional problems is only forthcoming if these problems can be described as biological illnesses. The diagnosis industry is at the heart of our reimbursement system, yet such diagnoses—and the supposedly scientific studies they are based on—are often questionable and flawed. One has only to think of the DSM Ill category that has recently been invented to characterize women who abuse themselves or cannot leave abusive relationships: Self-defeating Personality Disorder. In a similar category is the diagnosis of Post-traumatic Stress Disorder. This diagnosis evolved because it fitted the flashback problems being experienced by Vietnam veterans, but it is now being used to cover any persons who had a trauma in the past.

My historical sense tells me that now is not a good time to state thoughts like the above, due to the present economics of mental health. In times of crisis, arguments over territory and legitimacy become intense, and we are seeing a rush to define treatable conditions, establish correct ways of treating them, and invent newer and better outcome studies. Never was the idea that reality is socially constructed more evident, but at the same time, never has it been so unwelcome. At the same time, never has it been so necessary.

### The self

Kenneth Gergen presents a compelling case for the "social construction of the self" (1985) rather than assigning to it a kind of irreducible inner reality represented by words like cognitions or the emotions. Early family therapists were also wary of the idea of the self. They tended to believe that the ideas a person held about his or her self would only change when the ideas held by the people close to this person changed. Twenty years ago, having discovered the family field, I engaged in a project to disappear the individual. Actually, I only replaced the individual unit with the family unit. What was needed was a shift away from structure and a view of the self as a stretch of moving history, like a river or stream.

Accordingly, I came to think of the self as the Australian aborigines think of their "songlines" (Chatwin, 1987). Songlines are musical roadmaps tracing paths from place to place in the territory inhabited by each individual. A person would be born into one of these songlines but would only know a section of it. The way the Aborigines extended their knowledge of a particular songline was to go on periodic "walkabouts", allowing them to meet others living far away who knew a different stanza, so to speak. An exchange of songlines would become an exchange of important knowledge. These songlines would also be tied to the spirits of different ancestors—animals or plants or landmarks—who sprang forth in the "dreamtime" before people existed. A person might share an ancestor with people who lived in an entirely different part of the territory.

The beauty of this myth is that it presents a picture of individual identity that is not within the person or any other unit. Instead, it consists of temporal flows which can be simple, like a segmented path, or complex, like a moiré pattern, but which are realized by singing and walking. The mix of ecological and social understanding afforded by this practice is impressive. I offer it as a poetic example of the social construction of the self.

## Developmental psychology

Social constructionists are the first, to my knowledge, to have questioned the idea of developmental stages. Gergen (1982) offers an extremely cogent argument against developmental theories. He speaks of the danger of assuming that there is any universal standard by which humans can measure their functioning, and states that the whole idea of the normal lifespan trajectory is seriously deficient:

it is becoming increasingly apparent to investigators in this domain that developmental trajectories over the lifespan are highly variable; neither with respect to psychological functioning nor overt conduct does there appear to be transhistorical generality in lifespan trajectory. . . . A virtual infinity of developmental forms seems possible, and which particular form emerges may depend on a confluence of particulars, the existence of which is fundamentally unsystematic. (p. 161)

Gergen's words echo the idea, put forth by Prigogine and Stengers (1984) and validated later by Chaos theory (Gleick, 1987), that when a system has moved too far from equilibrium—that is, passes over some choice point where a change of state may happen—an element of the random enters in. The trigger event that is operating at that choice point will determine future development, but exactly which trigger will be operative is unpredictable.

In the same way, according to evolution theorists like Stephen Gould (1980), species develop discontinuously and not progressively. A species will evolve slowly according to the interplay between its gene pool and its environment, but at any point some sudden change may take place, like a meteor hitting the path, which will suddenly provide a new trajectory. Then a whole species may die out and a new one take its place. From the work of researchers like these, it becomes harder and harder to argue that within the human personality or within any human group a predetermined and optimal development path can be discerned, and that the failure to achieve this path spells a poor outcome. Yet current psychotherapy practice is to a large part predicated on some version of this idea.

### The emotions

Rom Harré (1986) has challenged the belief that emotions exist inside people as discrete traits or states and that they are the same all over the world. Many peoples have no knowledge or record of the emotions we subscribe to; the *idea* of the emotions is comparatively recent even in our own history. Social constructionists view them as just one more part of the complex web of communication between people and do not grant them special status as interior states.

This view has an antecedent in the writings of family therapists. Haley (1963) long ago attacked repression theory, which states that repression of emotions at some early stage could produce symptoms in later life. A version of repression theory now underlies many assumptions of folk psychology: I refer to the widely believed idea that to be healthy one has to "get in touch" with one's anger or grief. Not expressing your feelings is held to be as dangerous as not eliminating body waste, and many mothers automatically worry if their offspring seem to be holding in their emotions. In fact, the mental health profession has made almost a fetish of this stance in the case of community disasters like floods or adolescent suicides. In the past, people went to one another for comfort, but now there is a perceived need for a professional mourner (often a social worker or a psychologist) to help whole communities "work through" their emotions. The results of not doing this is said to doom people to live with horrific after-effects, defined vaguely as any kind of psychic or somatic disorder.

## Levels

Inspired by this kind of questioning, I have begun to wonder about the idea that there are hierarchical layers of structure embedded within human events. For instance, there is the superficial symptom versus the underlying cause; there is the manifest content versus the latent content; there is the overt communication versus the covert. A very widespread belief of General System Theory is that the natural world is represented by Chinese boxes, one within another, and the more inclusive are more influential than the less inclusive. What if none of these ideas was true? What if all these levels, layers, and nests were nothing but sets of different factors influencing one another, all equal to one another, but singled out by us, described by us, and given hierarchical standing by us?

The work of communication researchers Pearce and Cronen (1980) illustrates my point. They divide communication into layers, much as Gregory Bateson (1972) used Russell and Whitehead's Theory of Logical Types (1910–13) to classify messages, but they propose many more layers than he did. Basically, they analyse communication in an ascending order of inclusion (revised from time to time): the speech act, the episode, the relationship, the lifescript, the family myth, the cultural program. They maintain that although the higher levels exert a strong (contextual) force downward, the lower levels also exert a weak (implicative) force upward. Thus, a baby's crying (speech act) could be the context for an offer of feeding (episode) on the part of the mother. Or it could just as well be the other way around.

Where I differ from Pearce and Cronen is that I don't think we need the concept of levels at all. It is enough to think of each category of communication as a possible context for any other category. Which is stronger or higher depends on which one is defined as context for the other one at any given time. This idea greatly appeals to me, because I have been struggling for years to find a way to do without the idea of hierarchies of communication.

\* \* \*

So much for the five sacred cows. I would like to consider next a super-sacred cow, the nature of the professional relationship itself. To do so, I will call on the metaphor of the colonial official, a metaphor bequeathed to us by the postmodern ethnographers and increasingly used by family therapists as well.

## THE COLONIALISM OF MENTAL HEALTH

For me, the most serious challenge to the field of mental health follows the postmodern argument that much "normal social science" (as these theorists are calling the Western belief in objective social research) perpetuates a kind of colonial mentality in the minds of academics and practitioners. The postmodern ethnographers that I have mentioned point out that many ethnographic researchers in the past have "studied down", that is, have chosen to study a less "civilized" society than their own, or a group seen as limited in respect to ethnic culture or social class. Similarly, a number of researchers in the field of mental health (Kearney, Byrne, & McCarthy, 1989) now argue that " normal psychotherapy " perpetuates a colonial mentality in the minds of its practitioners. To continue with the analogy, the resulting activity could be then called "practising down".

The French historian Michel Foucault (1975) has much to say to us here because of his extremely interesting work on discourse, and particularly the institutionalized kind of talk and writing that is shared by people in a group, a field of study, a profession like law or economics, or an entire country or culture. Being also interested in the mechanisms by which a modern state establishes its rule, Foucault studies the shift from a designated person or persons monitoring the relations within a society to the *discourse itself* shaping these relations. Once people subscribe to a given discourse—a religious discourse, a psychological discourse, or a discourse around gender—they promote certain definitions about which persons or what topics are most important or have legitimacy. However, they themselves are not always aware of these embedded definitions.

For people involved in the practice of mental health, Foucault's (1975) ideas about the disciplinary use of the "confessional" are absolutely intriguing. He makes the point that in the Catholic practice of confession, just as in the psychoanalytic practice of free association, the subject is persuaded that he or she has some deep, dark secret—usually sexual—to hide. However, if she confesses it to the proper authority, she can receive absolution, "work through" the damage to the psyche, or whatever. This unacceptable secret, this "original sin", has been accepted by the unsuspecting person as the deepest truth of his or her own heart, and once believed, the idea continues to exert its power of subjugation.

The shift in concept from benign therapist to oppressive professional is one that, fair or unfair, is implied in this view. However, one need not therefore assign blame to a person or group. "The patriarchy" is not just a collection of males who are dedicated to oppressing women (although it can be perceived as such); it is a way of experiencing and expressing ideas about gender that are cultural givens for both sexes. A corollary of this idea is that therapists of all kinds must now investigate how relations of domination and submission are built into the very assumptions on which their practices are based.

As a result, a new kind of consciousness raising is beginning to take place that does not exempt Marxist therapists because they are champions of the poor, or feminist therapists because they are defenders of women, or spiritual therapists because they follow an other-worldly ideal. These therapeutic discourses can contain the same colonial assumptions as medical approaches. They can all embody oppressive assumptions about personality deficits. They can all offer the client a saviour to help them. Spiritualist views about therapy are apt to use the word healing, harking back to shamanistic traditions, while medical views use the word curing, but they both place the client in a submissive place.

* * *

This completes the theoretical part of my essay. I turn now to clinical applications of some of the ideas described above. I will describe some reflexive formats, which, because they allow for an alternation of the expert position, interfere with the usual professionalization of the therapeutic enterprise. I will also focus on the postmodern shift in interviewing methods and talk about changes that are affecting the therapeutic conversation itself.

## A GROWING DIS-EASE

About ten years ago, I found myself increasingly haunted by the paradoxes of power that beset the traditional methods of family therapy. They all seemed based on secrecy, hierarchy, and control. Even the modulated versions, represented by many Ericksonian practitioners, and the very respectful approach of the Milan Associates, still kept the client at a distance and did not share the thinking of the clinician. There was a good historical reason for this. From its inception, family therapy had a one-way mirror built into its core. The professionals were the observers, the families were the observed. There was never a two-way street. Most first-generation family therapists seemed to support the idea of therapist control, whether exerted openly or secretly. I didn't know which I liked least, pushing clients directly to do what I wanted them to do, or going underground and getting them to do what I wanted them to do under false pretences.

During this time, what began to happen in my own mind was a shift towards a more collaborative premise. I had read Carol Gilligan's *In a Different Voice* (1982) and had been struck by the idea that in making moral choices, women felt the need to protect relationships while men are more concerned with what is "right". Connection seemed to be more highly prized by women than order, justice, or truth. This was only the first of many insights that came to me from work that represented what is now being called cultural feminism.

While I did not wish to move back to what we used to call "chicken soup" therapy, I began to have doubts about the distance between clients and therapists built into the family systems field. This represented a major shift for me. I had been one of the systemic faithful, and believed that family patterns in the present constrained and maintained the symptom. The machinery of pathology did not reside "in" the individual but rather "in" the family. My aim in therapy was to disrupt or alter that machinery. Thus, there was no need to develop any more of a personal relationship with people than was necessary to keep them from dropping out of treatment.

As I began to search for my different voice, I became increasingly uncomfortable with this technocratic coldness. Actually, I never entirely bought it. When unobserved, I would show a far more sympathetic side to clients than my training allowed. I would show my feelings, even weep. I called this practice "corny therapy", and never told my supervisors about it. But within the past few years I began to feel, "Why not?" Others, like the researchers at the Stone Center in Wellesley, were making empathy creditworthy again. I began to talk with other women and found that they too used to do secretly what I did and also had pet names for this practice.

I also allowed myself to be influenced by my own previous experiences in therapy. Perhaps I was unlucky, but my encounters with clienthood had usually humiliated and intimidated me. At the very least they reinforced an idea of myself as a poor human being. Partly in reaction to these experiences, I started to look for ways to make clients feel more comfortable. Where appropriate, I would share stories from my own life. I would openly assume responsibility if the client had a complaint about the therapy, rather than treating it as evidence of resistance. I insisted on asking about expectations of therapy the client might have, and invited questions about my own work. If I felt stuck, especially if it seemed that a personal issue of mine were getting in the way, I would throw that idea into the conversation, which often did wonders to move things along.

In addition, I began to see few hierarchical distinctions except those afforded by the difference between positions in a lateral sense. In other words, centre and edge replaced up and down. The attempt to honour where people stood and how they saw things became a constant reminder that participants in therapy had their own expertise. A value was placed, thereby, on a participatory experience validated by the expression of many voices, rather than by a reliance on the voice of an expert.

At many points, my evolving position outran my ability to translate it into practice. I continued to "think Zen" but couldn't always figure out how to "do Zen". Then a colleague from Norway, Tom Andersen, came up with an amazing yet simple idea: the reflecting team (Andersen, 1987). The expedient of asking the family to listen while the team discussed the family and then asking the family to comment back suddenly changed everything. The professional was no longer a protected species, observing "pathological" families from behind a screen or talking about them in the privacy of an office. The assumption of normal social science, that the expert had a superior position from which a correct appraisal could be made, went crashing. For me, at least, the world of therapy altered overnight.

## THE WORD "REFLEXIVE"

In trying to verbalize what I was experiencing, I found that I was turning increasingly to the word reflexive. This word has been applied to communication theory by Cronen, Johnson, and Lannamann (1982) in their idea of reflexive discourse, and to systemic therapy by Karl Tomm (1987b) in his category of reflexive questioning. However, I do not wish to elevate reflexive into another piece of jargon. In *The Random House Dictionary* the word is defined quite simply as "the bending or folding back of a part upon itself".

A picture synonym might be a figure eight, which is the sign for infinity and which I saw as an advance on the old idea of the circle or spiral. You had a place for the inner dialogue of persons as well as an intersection representing the forum where they met and spoke. And the figure suggests a moving trajectory when placed in the context of social discourse, congruent with the new emphasis on narrative in the human disciplines and flow in the physical sciences.

Applying the concept of reflexivity to relationships, one could use the ideal of partnership. To me the word implies that there is an equity in regard to participation even though the parties may have different positions or different traits. I have taken this last notion from Riane Eisler's book, *The Chalice and the Blade* ( 1987), where she presents a partnership model for human societies. An example she gives of this kind of equality is the Olympic Games of the Mycenaean Empire, where men and women competed in jumping over the horns of a bull.

Abandoning attempts at finding a title or a symbol, one might say that the formats that are most characteristic of this new approach all "fold back upon themselves". The developments around the reflecting team, the use of reflecting conversations and reflexive questioning, the prevalence of "co-" prefixes to describe a therapeutic conversation ("co-author", "co-evolve"), indicate a preference for a mutually influenced process between consultant and inquirer as opposed to one that is hierarchical and unidirectional. In particular, this approach calls into question the high-level status of the professional.

## *MAKING THE EXPERT DISAPPEAR*

My first introduction to the non-expert position was when I first began to watch interviews by Harlene Anderson and Harry Goolishian of the Galveston Family Institute. Their approach has significantly influenced my own, but there was a time when I simply didn't understand what they were doing. I knew they believed that directive therapy models were pathologizing, but their own interviews were so non–goal-oriented that they seemed to do nothing and go nowhere. Their interviewing methods were equally unorthodox. The therapist might talk to one person in a family for a whole session, shocking persons like myself who had been trained in a structural approach. Always looking for the right pigeonhole, I called this new style "imperceptible therapy".

Indeed, the hallmark of the Galveston group is a kind of deliberate ignorance. When they describe what they do or how they teach, they state that they come from a position of "not knowing". This often irritates people who watch them work, because it seems so clearly not true that they "don't know". Their position, however, fits with postmodern ideas about narrative. In relating narrative theory to therapy, Gergen (1991) has observed that traditional therapists believe that there are "essences" in the human experience that must be captured in some kind of narrative and offered to clients in place of their old, illusory narratives. Going in, the therapist already has some idea of what these essences are.

Postmodern therapists do not believe in essences. Knowledge, being socially arrived at, changes and renews itself in each moment of interaction. There are no prior meanings hiding in stories or texts. A therapist with this view will expect a new and hopefully more useful narrative to surface during the conversation, but will see this narrative as spontaneous rather than planned. The conversation, not the therapist, is its author. This, I think, is the sense in which the Galveston group uses not knowing.

Not knowing in this model is often accompanied by "not talking" or not talking in the usual way. A good example is the interviewing style developed by Tom Andersen, Anna Margareta Flam, Magnus Hald, and others in Norway. Their questions or comments are marked by tentativeness, by hesitancy, and by long periods of silence. Often, the voice of the interviewer sinks so low that it is difficult to hear. They tend to begin their sentences with "Could it be that?" or "What if". At first I thought this strange way of talking was due either to their difficulties with our language or else a cultural difference that came from the well-known modesty of the Norwegian personality. This turns out to be untrue. The interviewing method embodies in a most graphic way the deliberate immolation of the professional self, and the effect on clients is to encourage both participation and invention.

Let me end this section by saying that the idea of reducing the status of the interviewer is also a postmodern one. I recently read a collection of studies of research interviewing edited by postmodern researcher Eliot Mishler (1986). In one of his chapters he looks at the methods of Marianne Paget, herself a researcher, and quotes her description of a project in which she asks women artists about their own creative process:

> Reflectively examining the form and quality of her questions, which were not standardized and predetermined by an interview schedule, [Paget] observes that they often have a hesitant and halting quality as she searches for ways to ask about what she wants to learn; they are formulated and reformulated over the course of the interview. She suggests that this way of questioning may allow for and encourage replies that are equally searching,

hesitant and formulated in the process of answering; that is, she creates a situation where the respondent too is engaged in a search for understanding. Paget refers also to the significance of her silences for how her respondent comes to tell her story in her own way, noting that at many points, for example, when the respondent paused, she remained silent when she "might have entered the stream of speech". [pp. 96–97]

## THERAPIST NARRATIVES

There is above all a reflexive loop between professional and client that includes the therapist's own working philosophy. Social constructionists hold firmly to the idea that there are no incontrovertible social truths, only stories about the world that we tell ourselves and others. Most therapists have a story about how problems develop and are solved or dis-solved.

Ben Furman, in his unpublished paper "Hindsight—The Reverse Psychology of the Therapist", challenges this idea when he says that first we find a hypothesis, then we base an intervention on it. He says that the reverse is usually the case. *We go in with an intervention already in mind and then come up with a hypothesis that supports it.* For instance, if a therapist uses a psychodynamic framework, she will assume that her job is to help someone work through a trauma of the past and will therefore look for a narrative that shows a developmental deficit. Or a family therapist may believe that problems are related to improper hierarchies in the family structure and will propose altering coalitions between members who are in different generation lines. There are many such examples of therapist narratives.

I was playing with this idea in relation to Pearce and Cronen's levels of communication, mentioned above, which they divide into speech act, episode, relationship, lifescript, family myth, and cultural program. Each of these levels can be viewed horizontally, that is, as contexts for one another. A particular sequence between two people can be the context for a child's temper tantrum or it can be the other way around. The segment of communication a therapist most characteristically focuses on will tell us more about the therapist than about the family.

To cite instances, some therapists, like the Milan Associates, go after what they see as a family myth. Others target the individual's lifescript. Still others go in at the level of the speech act, reflecting back a word used by the client and racheting it bit by bit towards one that opens up more possibilities. I saw a videotape of Goolishian and Anderson speaking with a client who had been viewed as a "young bag lady" and who spent much of her time sitting in a dark closet. During the conversation, the woman changed her complaint from a "boredom sensation" to feeling "unhappy" or "depressed". This was one of the events of the session that made it possible to alter the description of the client from a "crazy" person to someone who was suffering from being alone.

Considerations about which level of communication a therapist goes in on can explain some conflicts in the field. Take the objection raised by feminist family therapists to systemic practice. They feel that in cases of battering, seeing the couple together absolves the man from responsibility and blames the woman. This view is congruent with going in at the level of the *episode*. In this context, the violence is wrong and must stop. The woman should not be seen together with the man lest it be implied that she is as responsible for the battering as he is. But if one goes in at the level of the *relationship*, which is what systemic therapists do, then one sees the interlock of behaviours over time. This view may empower the woman to be able to do some things differently; at the very least it relieves her of the title of victim.

Of course, no level is more true than the other; it is just that a different solution to the problem falls out of which one is focused on. It may be that the episode level will supersede the relationship level because stopping the violence takes priority. There are also feminists who prefer going in at the level of the cultural program, saying that to treat the woman as a person who needs therapy is to remain apolitical and to inadvertently support the status quo.

## ASSOCIATIVE FORMS

But the danger in any scheme that divides up social interaction is that we too often choose one category and then start to believe in it. We need a method that prevents us from making such a choice except as intention and context cause us to do so. In therapy, one way to build in the requisite doubt is to set up a situation where a plurality of stories is encouraged and associative formats keep meanings unfixed. This is happening all over now. It is striking how many therapists are showing a new interest in reflecting modes, associative modes, and metaphoric modes of doing therapy.

Tom Andersen, for instance, often uses images to describe people's views and actions. I am thinking of an interview of a couple, one of whom was Buddhist and the other Christian. During a team reflection, Tom offered an image of "two beautiful smiling suns". He followed this idea with an incantation that went: "Let go the sun, let rise the sun." To my literal mind, he was suggesting that a solar system with two suns might have a problem, and indeed they did seem to be locked into a struggle of wills. Now, I know that I am only imposing my own understanding. According to a follow-up, the couple merely remembered the interview as being very useful and did not comment on the symbolism at all. The reflection stayed ambiguous, allowing the couple to associate to the images according to their own views.

I, myself, encourage people to play with stories, and will offer some of my own to push the idea along. I admit that my stories tend to be positive and transformative, meaning that I try to turn what is experienced as a difficulty into something that contains some hope. Often, in the New Age community where I live, the idea of karma comes up. I might then describe a couple's problem as a "karmic issue" and suggest that it might have to do with a dilemma that did not get resolved in past generations, if not past lives. For good or ill, they have the opportunity to work on it with each other. If they are successful, the children of the next generation can move on to a new challenge.

This playing with associative forms—stories, ideas, images, dreams—has always been part of therapy, but only now has it had a foundation in one of the descriptive human disciplines, which is what I take social constructionism in its widest form to be. As I continue to check in with the work of persons who are experimenting with these newer models, I am struck by the emphasis on linguistic play, and wonder if we are not seeing a new *Gestalt* for systemic consultation. The Galveston group is currently using the term "collaborative language systems" approach; Gergen has suggested "narrative therapy"; I and others have been using the word "reflexive". Yet other terms are undoubtedly being tested out, as the social and linguistic process that forms new fields of study wends its way through time.

## AN ETHIC OF PARTICIPATION

In ending, I would like to return to the contribution of the postmodern ethnographers. Clifford and Marcus (1986) take the idea of the transcendental or objective observer and replace it with the idea of a collaboration in which no one has the final word. Implicitly, the nature of the conversation changes. In their words:

> Because postmodern ethnography privileges "discourse" over "text", it foregrounds dialogue as opposed to monologue, and emphasizes the cooperative and collaborative nature of the ethnographic situation. . . . In fact, it rejects the ideology of "observer–observed", there being nothing observed and no one who is observer. There is instead the mutual, dialogical production of a discourse, of a story of sorts. [p. 126]

Statements like these suggest that an ethic of participation rather than a search for "the cause" or "the truth" is now emerging as a central value of social thought and action. Applied to therapy, this would put our goals in a frankly political light. But I would resist the idea that we should espouse a new kind of Marxism. Even in espousing emancipation, nobody has the corner on what the ideal discourse should be or which social problem is the most pressing. In general, our aim should be a critical stance that favours becoming aware of the power relations hidden within the assumptions of any social discourse, including critical discourse itself. Thus, not just our theory but our practice should reflect an awareness of hidden power relationships. It is not sufficient simply to stop blaming women or to empower ethnic groups. Activism, especially in a "good cause", runs the risk of reinforcing the illusions of power of the professional herself.

Here I return finally to the dangers of professionalism. Masson (1990), as I have said, questions the elevated status of the health professional. He quotes from *Profession of Medicine* (1972) by medical sociologist Eliot Freidson:

It is my own opinion that the profession's role in a free society should be limited to contributing the technical information men [sic] need to have to make their own decisions on the basis of their own values. When he preempts the authority to direct, even constrain men's [sic] decisions on the basis of his own values, the professional is no longer an expert but rather a member of a new privileged class disguised as expert. [Freidson, 1972, p. 382]

I respectfully agree with that statement, except for the use of the word "men" to represent all people. As Masson points out elsewhere in his book, the subjects of the early versions of the talking cure we call psychotherapy were mostly women, and still are. In a free society, women as well as men must have access to the thinking of the persons they consult, in order to prevent "professionals disguised as experts" from making their choices for them. The reflexive, reflecting, and reflective formats I am addressing in this chapter go part of the way to make this possible.

# CHAPTER SIX

# "Kitchen talk"

My next to last article, originally named "Kitchen Talk", is based on a series of presentations I did in five cities across Australia in the summer of 1992. It has been published in the proceedings of the 1992 Australian and New Zealand Family Therapy Conference held in Melbourne. This piece was an account of a quite literal journey, informed by the invisible journey of my thought and work. As I moved on, the script kept changing, and the final version is only a version. However, I kept the parts that were successful.

To begin with, I decided to use one-liners instead of a theoretical outline at the beginning of my talk. Some of these were funny, some just poetic, but they all made some point that had to do either with my philosophy or with my practice. Putting on a postmodern head brought with it the wish to rely on stories and images rather than intellectual disquisitions.

Second, it seemed important to make even more than before out of the way that my life and my work had intersected. In my presentations, I included anecdotes of my early life as a wife and mother, as well as of my meetings with the men and women pioneers in family therapy who had influenced me throughout my career. This was not for touchy-feely reasons but because I wanted to stay close to the idea of standing within personal experience and speaking subjectively rather than taking the usual objective stance of scientific papers.

Finally, my focus had changed from postmodernism to women's issues. I was becoming increasingly aware of the literature on "the ways women work" and felt that this research gave all of us, men and women alike, alternatives to the dominant male-oriented models. There were now books and articles not just on women's different development (Miller, 1976), but on women's value systems (Gilligan, 1982), women's management styles (Rosener, 1990), women's ways of learning and teaching (Belenky, Clinchy, Goldberger, & Tarule, 1986), women's career paths (M. C. Bateson, 1990), how women write (Heilbrun, 1988), how women do research (Mishler, 1986), feminist oral history (Gluck & Patai, 1991), how women connect and converse (Tannen, 1990), and women's ways to spirituality (Anderson & Hopkins, 1991).

The work on research interviewing turned out to be a topic of very great interest for me. This practice had been enormously influenced by feminists who believed that taking oral histories was a way of helping women become more emancipated. The feminist ideal of a more horizontal style of interviewing came together with the postmodern injunction against treating the informant as an object, producing a different kind of interviewer and a different kind of interviewee.

Family therapists like myself realized that a new kind of family interview was needed too. The old ways were based on keeping control of the session, asking leading questions, and shaping people's actions. Like the medical interview, the family therapy interview had been modelled on an expert/non-expert framework. The Galveston interview style was the first intimation most family therapists had that something non-expert was even possible, but for a long time it was experienced as so different from established methods that it was ignored. I wanted to put forth a rationale that would connect this style with a larger social shift, one with both feminist and postmodern overtones.

Another concern that informed this paper had to do with the reason I used the title "Kitchen Talk". I had become aware of a new explanation for why women and men have such different styles of communicating. Feminist psychologists, as I have said, indicated that women valued connectedness more than the transmission of information; they would even sacrifice truth to protect relationships. Their explanation was that since women's psychological development differed from that of men, they would of course relate differently.

But there was another possible reason for this difference that had to do with styles of communication. In a paper (submitted) by family therapist Mary Olson, I learned about a book by linguist Walter Ong (1982) which dealt with the evolution in Western culture from an oral to a literary tradition. Olson cited Ong to make a connection between women's "different voice" and the fact that they had only recently been admitted into the world of literacy. In the past, they depended on face-to-face encounters in which talking and hearing were paramount. This was a valuable idea for me because it offered an alternative reason for women's apparent preference for intimate and relational ways of communicating. I felt that I could talk about a historical straitjacket for women that was reversible, rather than a developmental one that was not.

This perspective got me out of the fight between feminists who said that women should not only be equal to men but more like men, and feminists who felt that women should celebrate and capitalize on their differences. I include much in "Kitchen Talk" that is oriented to a women's ways position, but join Olson in suggesting that the different voice of Gilligan has in great part been assigned to women by history and is not an inalienable trait.

There was also much in "Kitchen Talk" that I took from previous pieces. I reemphasized the idea of the different voice and suggested some ways of working that embodied this difference in the interview. I continued to underline my objection to a colonial stance for therapy and offered ways to counteract the sense one often got of a professional feudal system. Even though many of my ideas in this piece repeated those in previous pieces, the emphasis was more on practice than it had been earlier. I was sorry about the overlap, but hoped that this kind of repetitive gravestone-rubbing would produce a more complex picture.

My editors asked me to include here some sense of the way in which the people who came to my workshops across Australia influenced me, as well as how my presence affected them. I present two brief anecdotes that I hope will answer that question. It helps to know that my way of conducting a workshop these days is never to go in and do a consultation with a family in the usual expert position, leaving the therapist on the side. Instead, I sit and talk with the therapist with the family present, later asking them to comment on our conversation.

In Australia, the therapists I spoke with never brought in a family, so I would ask one or two participants to be family stand-ins and reflect back in an as-if fashion. I would also ask groups from the audience to reflect on what they had heard. This usually worked out, but sometimes the audience was so well trained in clinical language, which is usually derogatory, that the therapists and as-if family members would feel hurt and put down. When this would happen, I felt in a most awful bind. If I told the participants they were wrong, they would feel criticized. If I did not tell them they were wrong, the therapist and the as-if family members would feel criticized. Yet my whole idea was to exemplify a method that would not put anybody down.

During one workshop, which occurred after a previous workshop where a therapeutic team felt very criticized, I listened to a reflecting team analyse the therapist and family in terms that were clinically impeccable but full of suggestions about what was wrong with the family and what the therapist ought to do. I felt drowned in dismay, and my poor therapist looked both gloomy and stoical, as if he had known this was going to happen all along. So I took a flying leap into the situation and suggested that I sit in with each group and ask them questions myself. Luckily, there were only three groups of four apiece.

I asked each person in turn to tell me something that they appreciated or found unusual in the conversation they had heard. They responded with very different comments from the first round, comments that highlighted small but relevant aspects of the therapist's work and that were often interesting and surprising. Nobody repeated anything that had previously been said. Then I went back to the therapist and waited for either a joking comment or a defensive one. To my surprise his eyes filled with tears and he said: "Today is my birthday. I am forty years old. I just bought my first house. When my supervisor asked me to take part in this exercise I agreed, thinking, 'This is going to spoil my birthday'. But on this particular occasion I have heard comments from colleagues that were kind, sensitive, and I hope accurate, and I cannot thank all of you enough."

We were all of us moved, of course, and I was also astonished, because I had felt that if I took too instrumental a part in forcing compliments, so to speak, they would not come across as sincere and so would have an opposite effect. For whatever reason, this format worked, and so I have used it ever since, often telling this very story beforehand.

Another tremendous impact the experience in Australia had upon me was the inclusion of the Aboriginal, Maori, and Pacific Island peoples in a family therapy conference that I attended in Melbourne. There were many politics and strong feelings around issues of inclusion and influence to which I was not privy but could only guess about. However, the opening and closing ceremonies, which were organized by the "first peoples", changed the nature of the conference for me and made it a somewhat mystical experience.

Let me explain. I had to give a short address just before the end of the final day. Sensing tensions, I picked up off the platform a branch of eucalyptus left by a Maori spear dancer and put it on the podium like an olive branch. I found myself thinking out loud about how in Australia the family therapy community was lucky enough to have the first peoples with them. I also mused about how this family therapy community was still small enough to be a family, rather than an increasingly commercial establishment as in our country. This meant that there were not only strong loyalties, but many splits, as in a real clan. But luckily there were balancing elements: the first peoples represented a feeling for continuity and the ancestors; the later settlers brought with them an appreciation of what was original and new.

But now the strange thing happened. Towards the end of my talk, referring to the importance of community, I felt impelled to remind everyone not to forget the grandparents. It was an odd circumstance. While thinking that morning what to say, an image haunted me: in my mind's eye, I saw the elderly father of one of my childhood friends floating dead in a neighbour's pond. When this drowning happened, I was no longer living in that community, but what I was told was that after this man's wife, whom he dearly loved, died in a nursing home, he had got up early in the morning, dressed in his best clothes, hat, cane and pince-nez, which I always remember along with his neat grey goatee, and drowned himself. This memory of an event I never even saw was so vivid that I decided to share it and to say that we must treasure our very old ones and never leave them alone.

My vision seemed macabre to me, and also unexplainable, so I put it out of my mind. But after the conference had ended, one of the organizers came to me and asked me if I knew that Geoff Goding, a founding father of family therapy in Australia, was very ill. I had noticed that he had not been at the conference but I did not know why. I read recently in the *Journal of Australian and New Zealand Family Therapy* that he has since died.

This event, and its aftermath, reconnected me to the days when our own family therapy community in the United States was so small that each of us was precious, and any loss or rift wreaked havoc in the connected enclaves. Now it has become so huge that when eruptions happen in one enclave, few people in the others feel a ripple. Perhaps this is why I felt so at home in Australia; for me it was like going back to a 1950s childhood.

# An account of a presentation called "Kitchen Talk" from the 1992 ANZ conference

Instead of a theoretical framework made of the usual building blocks called concepts, I decided to start my presentations in Australia with a series of one-liners. I like one-liners because they are what I call "meanings in a fist". I also wanted to introduce some ideas from the welter of confusion known as postmodernism, but I didn't want to go into a huge disquisition on the matter. The one-liners give the gist of it. Using one-liners instead of a theoretical framework fits with the postmodernists' distrust of what they call "normal social science". I also invented a new acronym, PMFT, for Postmodern Family Therapist.

One reaction to my presentation at the Melbourne conference was: "I feel as if you had pulled the rug out from under me and then left me holding a plate of fairy cakes." I had not heard about these cakes, which turn out to be little party cakes covered with pink and

From *Proceedings of the 2nd Australian and New Zealand Family Therapist Conference*, Melbourne, Australia, 1993. By permission.

141

white icing. I liked the rug idea because it was close to my intention, but I was not so sure about the fairy cakes.

So when I gave this talk as part of workshops in other places in Australia, I tried to clump my one-liners into categories that related to some ideas that family therapists could use. This shift is an example of the changes that took place as I gave my presentation in city after city across the continent. I liked to think that my workshops themselves were a rolling conversation with Australia. So here are my one-liners, sorted into clusters.

*Cluster One*:  PMFTs do not believe in an "out there" reality that can be objectively ascertained, certainly as far as the world of relationships is concerned. Instead, our ideas rest on a bedrock of conjoint subjectivity. We decide upon moral or social agreements or we challenge each others' values and rules, but in either case there is no outside final judge as to what is right or what the meaning of any given event must be. Some other ways to say this are:

- Like the peasant in the old story, first we shoot holes in the fence, then we paint the bullseyes around them.
     (Anthropologist Clifford Geertz)
- I have a seashell collection. I keep it scattered on beaches all over the world.
     (Comedian Steve Wright.)

*Cluster Two*:  PMFTs like the idea of the "hermeneutic circle", a process of continual change through exchange. One example might be this: meanings are influenced by conversations between people, then mutate within the individual mind, then re-influence the common conversation. Example: my rolling conversation with Australia. Other examples:

- The mind fits the world and shapes it as a river fits and shapes its own banks.
     (Writer Annie Dillard)
- Speech exists to bring about that without which speech could not happen.
     (Composer Herbert Brun)
- Society prepares the crime; the criminal commits it.
     (Chinese fortune cookie)

*Cluster Three:*   PMFTs believe in what has been called the "common world"—the intersubjective space in which people are linked through language and social actions. Some PMFTs believe that this web or net is synonymous with a collective or shared unconscious. Here are some statements that express this.

- Taking someone out of the family is like mending a net by removing one of the nodes.
     (Anonymous)
- The problem is not in finding the chief's horn but in finding a place to blow it.
     (African proverb)
- The Copernican Moment: when you realize that your beloved no longer puts you at the centre of the universe.
     (Husband in a family therapy interview)

*Cluster Four:*   PMFTs are not happy with polarities and binary positions like true/false, good/bad, body/mind. They want these dichotomies to go away because they obscure connection and chop up the universe.

- The opposite of a shallow truth is false. But the opposite of a deep truth is also true.
     (Physicist Niels Bohr)
- Definition of Conflict: All the points of a circle fall away and only two points remain. Resolving it is to bring back the circle.
     (Colleague Shuli Goodman)

*Cluster Five:*   Syllogisms in Grass. This rather mystifying term was coined by Gregory Bateson to describe cause by association rather than logic. PMFTs like association causality because it is less apt than linear causality to point the finger. Steve Wright is a master at association causality:

- I have a friend who is a radio announcer. You can't hear him speak when he goes under bridges.
- I was Cesarean-born. You'd never know it, but when I leave a house I go out through the window.

## ONE-LINERS FOR FAMILY THERAPY

My next set of clusters has to do with ideas that can be applied to therapy. I don't know whether they are postmodern or not, but they do challenge traditional fashions.

*Cluster One*:   PMFTs who do family therapy are less certain about claiming results for their models, especially when, like me, they have been doing just about as well no matter what model they have used. I began to think that maybe if I stopped trying, I might still do pretty well. These statements seemed to support my thought:

- Psychotherapy is an undefined technique applied to unspecified cases with unpredictable results. For this technique, rigorous training is required.
  (Victor Raimy)
- Negative Capability, that is, when a man is capable of being in uncertainties, mysteries, doubts, without any irritable reaching after fact and reasoning.
  (John Keats)

*Cluster Two*:   These variations on the above introduce a rationale for a less active posture:

- A man stands alone and cannot sing. Another man sings with him and the first man can also sing.
  (Martin Buber, *Tales of the Hassidim*)
- Don't get mad at me—I'm not trying to help you!
  (Colleague Graham Disque)
- Don't just do something—stand there!
  (Old saw)

*Cluster Three*:   People are more apt to stumble on solutions when they feel that they are basically good people, and these solutions are usually the most successful.

- Positive description is like looking for the windows rather than the walls.
  (Anonymous)
- The mind is most convinced by the reasons it can itself discover.
  (Writer Paul Watzlawick)

Finally, there is a saying for which I can find no niche, but it made a big impression on me at the time, so I will include it anyway. It came from a fortune cookie which I got when my ex-husband and I were struggling towards a divorce.

• You are doomed to be happy in marriage.

Perhaps this one is merely support for the belief that there is a mystical intelligence that throws riddles at you until you figure things out. I did get divorced, but after fifteen years of solitude met an 82-year-old Irish writer and happily remarried. The doom came true!

## MY GENEALOGY

After giving my one-liners, I decided to talk about how I came to the theories and practices that I am going to be telling you about. Michel Foucault, the brilliant French sociologist, would analyse the "genealogy" of modern institutions in order to challenge the impression that they had fallen from the sky like Moses' Tablets and were therefore beyond criticism. It is similarly very helpful to start by focusing on what Tom Andersen has called "the history of the idea to come here".

So I usually go back to my beginnings before I became a Family Therapy True Believer and talk about when I was a confused, unhappy wife and mother of three young children. I followed my theatre professor husband from campus to campus, each move making me feel like one of those cotton shirts that gets smaller each time you throw it in the wash. Through pure accident, I was asked to help a social worker called Virginia Satir complete a book on something I had never heard about called family therapy. A few months later, *Conjoint Family Therapy* (Satir, 1964) came out, and to my surprise became a hit.

That was it. I saw Virginia work from behind a new-fangled thing called a one-way screen, and I read a book by Jay Haley called *Strategies of Family Therapy* (1963) that was actually written in plain English, and I was hooked. In fact, I begged Jay to let me work on a research project with him. It was a series of interviews with other family therapy pioneers, like Carl Whitaker and Don Jackson, and I became even more impressed.

Next I followed my husband to New York and found a job with Dick Auerswald, who was running a Great Society community mental health program in a clinic on the Lower East Side. He was using another idea that was totally new to me: "ecosystems". After the director of the new Crisis Unit, psychiatrist Richard Rabkin, explained to me what this term meant, I wrote a number of stories about Auerswald's ecosystems way of working.

When Auerswald's program collapsed, along with the Great Society, I went back to school (the forward-thinking Adelphi School of Social Work) and got my MSW. Then on to Philadelphia, where I got to watch Salvador Minuchin's dramatic work with children with dangerous childhood conditions like anorexia nervosa, and Harry Aponte's respectful work with minority families. My next stop was New York, where Olga Silverstein, mostly known as the Wonder Rabbi, asked me to join the Brief Therapy Project of the Ackerman Institute of Family Therapy. You could say that I hobnobbed with the great.

However, this had its down-side. What my teachers did with such ease, I utterly failed at. For some reason I always felt clumsy and at sea; unable to look like an expert, let alone feel like one. I used to say to myself, "Oh for a Therapy of the Feeble", but basically I knew I didn't have the "Right Stuff". As friends of my family in the artist community on the Hudson where I grew up used to say: those who can, do; those who can't, teach. My mission in the field was to be the chronicler of the exploits of others.

## SOME NEW IDEAS

This dismal prediction changed only gradually. As I have described in earlier articles, after Gregory Bateson died in 1979 I began to realize the ideological split between himself and Haley. Bateson disapproved of the control idea that Haley and others had made central to family therapy. I found that I sympathized with this view. I was also following the thinking of Harry Goolishian, who had become a kind of North Star in my sky. Harry was criticizing the cybernetic engineering model that had come to dominate the field. Like me, he preferred to think about human events in terms of rivers and flows rather than circles and loops. We both agreed that these metaphors were all wrong; it wasn't a question of damming up a river but learning to canoe on it.

When I read Carol Gilligan's *In a Different Voice* (1982), this slight volume of research acted as a kind of epiphany for me. I suddenly saw the sexism of the models of family therapy in which I had trained. There was nothing wrong with them, it was just that they represented only one voice, the dominant voice in our culture. What would family therapy in a different voice be like? Applying Gilligan's ideas, I surmised that it would value connectedness more than autonomy, and interdependence more than control. I also realized that a move from one sensory modality to another was at stake: from the dispassionate "gaze" of the modern scientist (Foucault, 1978) to the more subjective "voice" that has been used to describe an epistemology for women (Belenky et al., 1986).

At this point, I realized that the voice model provided a better fit, not only for me but probably for other women and men in the field as well. From a friend who had attended a workshop on Geo-Justice, I heard that people were comparing the militant Christian song "We Are Climbing Jacob's Ladder" with another called "Sarah's Circle", which sounded like a sort of peaceful round dance. I didn't know "Sarah's Circle", but another came to mind: "Here We Go Round the Mulberry Bush." There was a whole other way of life out there that seemed to represent a different kind of energy. Family therapy might have room for a feminine energy as well as the male energy that had provided such a motor for the field.

I welcomed such ideas because I found that I didn't want to do the masculine types of therapy that I had worked so hard to learn. Basically, I was unhappy with the managerial, adversarial, and secrecy-laden characteristics of family therapy as it had evolved. Instead, I wanted to define a style that demystified the process, emphasized connection, and encouraged people to develop their own stories instead of accepting the ones fed them by the professionals.

However, my ideal of a feminine energy ran smack into the ideals of the political feminists who had emerged as a major force in family therapy. These activists were not pleased by any position that sounded too much like the Victorian notion of a woman's sphere, separate but inferior. I was in agreement with them. Why sponsor a

Women's Auxiliary of Family Therapy? The Gilligan research clearly linked the "different voice" with some of the new research on the different developmental path of women. I felt that this research might be just a new version of the idea that biology was destiny—a new version of the idea that women were uniquely qualified for the profession of changing bedpans.

## "CONVERSATION" AND "TEXT"

What rescued me from my dilemma was a paper, "'Conversation' and 'Text': A Media Perspective for Therapy", by family therapist Mary Olson (submitted), based to a large extent on *Orality and Literacy*, by Walter Ong (1982). Ong's book takes the position that groups where oral communication is paramount have one kind of consciousness, and those where books and writing are as central another. For Ong, literacy is tied to authority, which leads to hierarchy. Orality sets a more horizontal and inclusive tone. Thus, he says, literacy divides, where orality connects.

This division had far-reaching social effects. For centuries, men (or some men) had sole access to the world of books, whereas women were limited to face-to-face communication. Olson, picking up this point, makes an important tie between the "different voice" described by Gilligan and the oral consciousness described by Ong. Influenced by Olson's analysis, I saw that developmental factors might not be the only explanation for this different voice. Could it also be a historical–cultural accident that many women seem so comfortable with the arts of intimacy, connection, and accord? Could it also be that "voice" is not necessarily tied in with gender at all? In many cultures, the web of harmony is valued over individualism, and this applies to men and women alike.

This amounts to saying that women are not *by nature* unsuited to the competitive styles of men. When you listen to or read the productions of many women who have learned the language of the academy, the adversarial tones of debate we are used to hearing from men are right there, no problem. What is a problem is that there are also many women (and men too) who don't enjoy this style and who either stumble around in it or don't even try.

Perhaps they won't have to. One aspect of an oral consciousness is a commitment to the "mother tongue", to plain-speaking, to kitchen talk. As a result of the postmodern critique of the Western academic canon, there has also been an effort to use ordinary language in speeches, articles, and other professional communications. Unfortunately, some of the most well-known postmodern thinkers have produced the most obscure and ornately self-conscious prose in cultural history. PMFTs like myself are trying to resist being seduced by this fancy terminology, which is even worse than the cybernetic terminology of yore, in order to go back to the plain English that Haley popularized so many years ago.

However, I don't want to romanticize the oral tradition. Our world is now irreversibly based on literacy. The "different voices" of women, indigenous peoples, artists, or any other groups that have kept their oral base are precious, but orality must add to, not replace, literacy. This is why I have pushed women friends in the family therapy field to write and am beginning to ask the people I see to collaborate with me on articles. My friends at a small agency called People's Bridge Action in northern Massachusetts are training mothers of sexually abused children to use media, not only for writing about their stories but for making video movies about their lives. Giving people the tools of production can suddenly transform a group of survivors sharing their feelings to a force for change in the community.

## THE COLONIAL THERAPIST

This brings me to the second important discovery along my groping path, and one I have written about before: the colonial stance of the modern professional. In reading some of the postmodern literature on social research, I was struck by the trend towards horizontality within academic fields that had heretofore been quite elitist. Ethnographers like James Clifford and George Marcus (1986) were beginning to question the idea of "studying down". Why not "study up"? Why must anthropologists always do research on people of a lower social status? Phrases like "primitive peoples", "blue-collar workers", "the savage mind", betray the inherently snobbish view of social science researchers. It is the same with therapists. What about family therapists "practising up" instead of "practising down"? When have we ever dealt with people who were not "less than": less well-behaved, competent, orderly, satisfied, sane?

Dublin researchers Kearney, Byrne, and McCarthy (1989) have made good use of this metaphor of the colonial therapist. McCarthy, in an introductory manifesto entitled "Colonial Sentences and Just Subversions", comments on the parameters of normality that have been set by a white, male, Western elite and says, "Such affiliations, consciously or unwittingly affirmed, colonize the majority of therapy's subjects and proscribe their invalid sub-versions of the dominant reality. Abuse is perpetrated in the name of love."

These objections must be seen within a wider framework. There is an on-going effort known as Critical Theory that has aided the postmodern movement in dissecting the sacred texts of the modern age. Not only have giants like Marx and Freud been under the knife, but many other social thinkers as well. Abstract theories in all fields continue to be examined to see what relations of dominance and submission are hidden between the lines.

Along this line, I have found the thinking of the postmodern social philosopher Michel Foucault (Rabinow, 1984) to be immensely helpful. In works that every student of society should read, he has shown that power has an unequivocal relationship to knowledge—that, in fact, the two go hand in hand. His studies of the institutions of the modern "scientific" state—the penal system, the judicial system, the hospital system—are models of analysis for what he calls "the micro-fascism of everyday life". This type of oppression is all the more insidious in being tied to influences that do not come from any single ruler but are embedded in language and practices that we take for granted from the day of our birth.

The success of Critical Theory in toppling the gods of yesterday has emboldened a number of other postmodern social researchers, including Kenneth Gergen (1991), to express strong objections to "ideal narratives", "totalizing discourses", and "grand designs". All truth positions have been placed in doubt, and instead the questions are asked: Whose truth? To what uses or purposes can it be put? What interests does it serve?

Along with this view goes a distrust of what is being called "normal social science", with its reliance on so-called objective social research. The assumptions of research interviewing have come under particular scrutiny, and a new kind of interviewing is emerging that does away with pre-set hypotheses or interview schedules. Instead, the interviewer sets up no plan, deliberately using a hesitating, wondering style that will hopefully encourage the person interviewed to tell her story in far more detail than she might otherwise have done.

Needless to say, this iconoclasm has been a boon for feminists, who have used it to challenge the intellectual precedence of men along with the schools of thought they historically represent. As a result of their efforts, a number of previously unquestioned premises in modern psychology have gone crashing. One is the assumption that the development of the child is tied to a need for individuation. Such ideas, say the feminists, come out of studies done by men on men. Another recent challenge has been posed to questionable developmental studies by mostly male "experts" about the importance of infant–mother bonding (Eyer, 1993); these claims are not only unjustified but have made a generation of mothers guilty for life.

However, there is a sharp difference between feminist activists who are committed to a clear, political position, and postmodern thinkers who are committed to distrusting such positions. This is particularly a problem in feminist family therapy circles. If we do not have a belief in "out there" realities, like men's fists in women's faces, how can we be good therapists, let alone good persons? The split has been addressed by feminist writers Nancy Fraser and Linda Nicholson (1990), who have given us one attempt to supply a bridge between feminism and postmodernism, saying that post-modern-feminist theory should "tailor its methods and categories to the specific task at hand, using multiple categories when appropriate and forswearing the metaphysical comfort of a single feminist method".

I would agree with this statement if the idea of adapting one's methods to the specific task at hand would at times mean *not* forswearing a feminist point of view. In many cases of violence and abuse, a non-compromising position is the best one to take. In others, a less judgemental stance will have a better outcome. The main point is to have a flexibility of choice.

## APPLYING A DIFFERENT VOICE

So what would a less "colonial" family therapy look like, a "therapy in a different voice", a therapy that exploited its oral context? Let me list my ideas of what would make such a therapy look different.

1.  There would be no more "superior therapist story" based on professional texts. Instead, there would be more emphasis on drawing out people's own stories.

2.  There would be respect for the loyalty fields all people are embedded in, even if it meant putting aside one's own loyalty to an overarching belief system.

3.  There would be no more talk of meta-positions. Instead of taking a God's Eye View, biases, opinions, and subjective views would be openly expressed.

4.  There would be an impatience with abstruse, text-derived language, even when talking with or writing for colleagues.

5.  There would be an increasing reluctance to use hidden teams, one-way screens, and one-way messages.

6.  There would be a move away from therapist-driven questions that constrain people's responses according to the therapist's theory or push the interview in a particular direction.

7.  There would be less secrecy about the professional process and far more sharing. We would try to let people hear what we are saying about them, as when we use reflecting teams in front of families. Also, unless there are good reasons not to, we would report to them what has been said behind their backs, or even tell them beforehand when we are going to talk about them.

8.  To the extent that the mental health bureaucracies allow it, there would be a ban on what I call "clinical hate speech". I am talking in particular about diagnostic categories that become linguistic straitjackets. The "dis-" words should also be discouraged: dis-ability, dis-order, dys-function, dis-ease. Hardest of all to get rid of would be the technical terms the trained clinician uses in conversations about families in case conferences or in corridors.

    As an example, here is a list of terms that appear in descriptions of people seen as victims of incest: powerlessness, loss of control; low self-esteem; denial of reality; dependence/vulnerability, feelings of defectiveness, intrusion, violation, loss. Even if true, the constant repetition of words like these makes a negative universe for the self that often perpetuates its own reality.

9. There would be a move away from deficiency models that influence therapists to "practise down", towards competency models that inspire them to "practise up". Without exception, all schools of modern psychology offer explanations of emotional or mental difficulties as if they were analogous to disorders of the body, except that people are not blamed for disorders of the body whereas they are blamed for disorders of the mind.

10. Finally, taking a page out of some ideas of Kenneth and Mary Gergen (1986), there would be a move away from the normative ideas about maturation and growth upon which most developmental psychology is based. The Gergens question the acceptance of a narrative of development from childhood to adulthood to old age, where value is assigned only to the middle or "adult" stage. Were it not for the cultural values of the psychologist, an accidental trajectory might be equally acceptable, as it is in narratives of evolution.

Let me digress to explain my own version of this idea. I call the concept of the development of the psyche the "vegetation metaphor". The psyche (or soul) is said to have a genetic blueprint like a simple animal or plant, with stages of growth, life-cycle transitions, and the like. If a stage is left out, or a traumatic event distorts the growth process, not only the twig but the whole tree will be bent. The ancients thought of the soul using a different analogy: fire, or air. What would abnormal air be like? Can there be dysfunctional fire? Never mind, the developmental analogy has been useful because it has allowed a profession to come into being that decides what is or is not normal in human existence and how to make it more normal if it is not.

## TRANSLATING THEORY TO PRACTICE

The above are some of the trends that seem to fall out of a postmodern approach combined with overtones of cultural feminism and some elements of social construction theory. However, I do not reject the more instrumental approaches in the family therapy field. My belief is that each innovation in family therapy has been "perfect", in the sense that no other result could have taken place given the innovator's background, placement, populations worked with, and problems that came in the door. I still use much of what I learned from these amazing pioneers. Even though the stance I use may seem non-directive, there is nothing in it that says I should not give people concrete tasks and interpretations as long as I make it clear that I am only giving the "idea of" a task or interpretation. I will explain more about the "idea of" below.

Another proviso is that many of the methods I will be describing are already familiar to practitioners who have learned them from other approaches to psychotherapy, or have done them on their own for years.

1.   Collaboration is perhaps the most important hallmark of this approach. I have taken to asking families or couples to be my part-ners-in-crime, so to speak; giving them control of the use of any materials, written or taped, to a far greater degree than heretofore; telling them that I will rely on their knowledge about their own family as I rely on mine about families in general, and stating right out that I would like this to be as equal a partnership as possible. Of course, with court-mandated families, all one can do is share the dream of partnership and wish that there would be some way in which it could become a reality. Through teaching people the use of media like video and desktop publishing, some groups are begin-ning to make this dream come true.

2.   Another central idea is that of an affirmative framework. This is not the same as a positive connotation, which really disguises a very negative opinion indeed. All the same, I think therapists were influenced by the positive connotation to think and speak well of people because it felt hopeful. Other practitioners who believe in hope are Virginia Satir with her relentless optimism, Steve de Shazer with his solution-focused work, Michael White with his unique out-comes. The only quarrel I have with these styles is my preference for a less managed kind of work. The field is already tilting towards managed care and managed lives at an alarming rate, and I think some of us should lean the other way. However, I have to concede that in doing so, I have to do some managing myself.

In describing this affirmative framework, I talk about my Three A's: Affirmation, Affiliation, and Appreciation. There is enough blame and bad feeling around the standard therapy process to counteract any possibility that one will be too Pollyanna-ish. In fact, I firmly believe that most of therapy consists of removing obstacles—the walls—and pointing out the hopeful factors—the windows. People will often find the doors on their own. To give people some experience of this idea, I will ask small groups to comment on a case that has been presented, limiting their remarks to appreciations of what they have heard. It is amazing how hard this is for therapists to do. And it is amazing how many presenters believe in being told what they did wrong—after all, that is what supervision is all about. It is only after you directly ask people to say supportive things, and they do, that the amazing usefulness of doing so becomes apparent. I got this idea from the Milan men and I have expanded it to say that "Nobody can (easily) grow, change or leave the field under a negative connotation".

This does not mean that I never criticize anyone or anything. If someone is involved in violence or criminal activities, of course I will call in the authorities, or maybe they will already have been called in. I do not work in the field of violence and abuse directly, but I do consult with the staff of the child-protection agency that I mentioned previously, People's Bridge Action. Together we have tried to find a way to create a supportive cradle of hearts and minds that would help the staff—a group of young idealists who go out alone to people's homes—to cherish and nurture each other. In this particular group, I have not seen a case of "burn-out" in six years, despite one of the most discouraging environments in Massachusetts, which is a discouraging environment as a state. In my opinion, the fall-out from this cherishing has energized not only the staff but the people they see to revive and give hope to an extremely depressed community.

This still brings up the question: What about the grey cases? Where incest is only suspected or a man has temporarily stopped beating a woman? Or the abuse is verbal and psychological? What about what one could call white-collar violence? White-collar abuse? These are the situations I see that severely test my model. Fortunately, I find that in these gray cases, which are admittedly not court-referred, my non-confrontational approach is appreciated and makes the difference between a family or couple that walks out and one that stays.

When this model fails, I have invented a sort of "private citizen" position, which I take when "being a therapist" is not working. I will give you an example. An educated young mother and her husband had come in because he had thrown a heavy book-bag at her. This was the only time he had physically hit her in fifteen years, but she had said then that she would leave if he hit her again. When he did, she found that she was unable to leave because now they had three children. She felt powerless, angry, and discouraged. Her husband then brought up a new fact, perhaps to justify himself, which was that for the last few months they had had separate bedrooms. She agreed that her sex drive had deserted her. He offered three reasons for this, each one deriving from her. She kept agreeing with him.

I was moved to make one of my citizen's protests. I told her that when I was a young wife, I had similar problems with sex, and that I too took all the blame. I said that through my later work with families, I had found a number of other reasons for this difficulty. For instance, if there is a hidden conflict between a couple, sex will often be the first thing to go. This led to a different conversation, and, for whatever reason, the couple started to have a sex life once again. But my point is that instead of talking from a position of moral certitude, I used an example from my own history. Thus I avoided "practising down".

3.   Another important idea is openness. Michael White has called upon therapists to be transparent, but I would go even further and say that they should be forthcoming. This means that we should include families or individuals in our consultations or case conferences as routinely as possible. If we must talk about them behind their backs, as is so frequently done, we can ask permission first and bring ideas back if so requested.

Part of my own effort to be forthcoming is that I try to make clear my philosophy of therapy, how I think problems arise and how they are solved or dis-solved. I will share the rationale for a suggestion or task. For instance, if I give a "paradoxical instruction", I will explain how it is supposed to work and ask for the family's reaction to the idea. I will also share my understanding of the constraints upon me:

what the State or my own values or beliefs allow me to do or not to do.

I will share life-stories of my own if they are relevant. As I said above, I will sometimes intrude strong personal opinions or moral positions. If I feel troubled about the process or "stuck", I will share that too. I find it a waste to siphon off such difficulties to a supervisor or peer group but will ask the family to help me with it—this often unsticks the process like a charm. I will be at pains to take responsibility for an error or complaint. If something unacceptable to me is continuing to occur, I may threaten to stop the therapy. That is always a judgement call: whether it is better to struggle along, hoping for a change, or to quit the field.

4. "Bearing Witness", "Giving Comfort", "Being There". These non-specific but highly important activities have mostly been left out of family therapy's lexicon of practice. Of course, there is a whole category of suffering under Acts of God, but there are differences of opinion about what is helpful in such cases. Often, no sooner is a community hit by a catastrophe than mental health persons are sent in to help the stricken group "work through" feelings of anger or grief. But this is only based on a theory of one school of psychotherapy, the idea that unblocking repressed emotion brings about relief. Sometimes it does not. "Regressing" people back to a painful past so that they can re-experience their trauma may stick them there and make them suffer even more.

One alternative is to offer the state of attention referred to above: "Being There". Just letting people talk themselves out is well known to be helpful. Also, I deliberately try to give comfort, through expressions of sympathy, sharing of similar experiences, or even touching people on the shoulder as one would a friend. This is almost the reverse of what I was trained to do as a family therapist. I am not looking to do away with all boundaries, but the distant position I used to take in the face of justifiable grief or anger seems incredible to me now. Finally, when we hear stories of unbelievable horror, all any of us can do is bear witness to the enormity of what has happened. I feel that offering recipes for emotional disaster control in the face of such events is in the same category as telling a person who has just escaped death, "Relax".

5. Less active interviewing. The old theories of family therapy produced a highly managed interview: the therapist was expected to act and the family to react. The move away from ideas of domination by the professional, which is what postmodern theory seems to support, has produced a far less interventive interview. Harry Goolishian, who had started to work non-managerially before anybody else did, used to send me tapes of his interviews. I found them boring, inscrutable, and without purpose. Unwilling to be unkind to an old friend, I told Harry that I thought his way of working should be called "imperceptible therapy." In my PMFT reincarnation, I too do "imperceptible therapy". I too have found that this way of interviewing has struck my own colleagues as boring, inscrutable, and without purpose.

The odd thing is that I have not found this style any less effective than other methods I have used. A better way to put it is that in my previous, super-active phase, my efforts were often ineffective, but such was my belief system that I never paid any attention to this fact. Why, if the outcome seems to be no better, do I continue? Because this way of working is not only more comfortable for myself, but the people I see say so too. And there is a sense of justice in exchanging a top-down model of interviewing, where the interviewer always has the advantage, for one where the input is more equitable.

Thus, I no longer follow a plan based on a therapeutic "text". I listen to the family more. I let people who need to talk do so. My previous theory was that people who "dominated" an interview were trying to control me; now I see that they could just as well be suffering from fear or anxiety. Part of being willing to let people go on and on, despite the injunction against this in traditional family therapy, is an increased respect for the value of "listening" on the part of the people who are silent.

6. More active listening. This is the other side of the coin of less active interviewing. I leave extra silences after people finish, offering space that people can use to revise or extend the same thought or offer a second one. At the same time, with my eyes I check the people who are not talking; they need to be attended to, too. If a reflecting team is being used, the job of the interviewer becomes even more that of one who elicits and facilitates. The interviewer makes no formal interventions, except to check for meaning and

sometimes to invite someone who would otherwise never speak to come in. Questions that are themselves mini-interventions are rare.

The quietude needed for keeping so inactive is hard for the formally trained family therapist to endure. One aid might be to imagine sitting on your hands (or literally to do that). I also imagine that I am a big beach; waves will come and waves will go but the beach will still be there and maybe some new shells or stones will be added. Tom Andersen uses another technique: he times the rhythm of his breathing to that of the person he is talking to. The whole process is a kind of trust game: you let go of the trapeze in the faith that somewhere there is another trapeze, or pair of hands, waiting for you. And, as I have said previously, there always is.

7.  Less emphasis on interventions. The old requirement for accurately designed interventions has lost its strength. The new idea is to keep the conversation going until the complaint that the conversation addresses no longer exists or has faded away. This will happen, we believe, if we address the need for a more affirmative environment and convince people that they are being heard, not only by us, but by other family members. You could say that this is a therapy more about hearing than speaking.

Thus, the end of an interview will often not consist of an interpretation or task, but address the question of if and when to meet next. However, if the complaint has intensified, or if people demand that something be done, I don't disappoint them. I will offer some ideas they might talk over. Sometimes this is a simple piece of advice, sometimes a paradoxical task. If the latter, I will explain the purpose behind telling people to do something on purpose and often tell the family where I got the idea. The idea of "the idea" is an interesting one, as you will see below.

8.  "The Idea Of." Just as we don't see "family dynamics" but "an idea of" family dynamics, we don't see an intervention but "an idea of" an intervention. This position comes out of what has been called "social construction theory". According to the experts on the subject, this theory only means that most of what passes for social reality is something people have agreed upon together through the medium of language and social exchange.

This idea of "the idea" is very liberating. It makes us very willing to talk about our theories of therapy; to offer thoughts and suggestions and to explain where they came from; to take strong moral stands and to explain how we came by them too. My "idea of" violence, arrived at in consensus with other people, to say nothing of the legal institutions of the state, is that it should not be. Therefore I will act in accord with that idea and invoke consequences of some kind. The outcome of the belief that we construct our own reality is that we have to take a strong personal stand against the neutrality of nature, which seems not to care whether we destroy ourselves, our planet, or our relationships with each other.

9.  Reflecting Formats. These practices present one remarkably simple way to begin to escape the top-down, one-way requirements of being a professional therapist. They are also a good way to show people who have known nothing else but top-down, one-way formats that there is something else out there. I think that in time, like training wheels, the formats will wither away, but they are useful now. They have transformed my supervision work, my teaching, my consulting, and my workshops. Due to the more horizontal relational structure I encourage, most of my groups turn into "home-rooms" where people can find emotional sustenance and a non-competitive environment. They need it to face the mini-feudal system which is a school, an agency, or a job.

The main difference is that in whatever hierarchical capacity I am cast—therapist, teacher, consultant, or workshop leader—I can now trade places. Even if I am working alone with a family, I can ring many changes on this format. I am always asking different groups in the family to change places: asking children to reflect while parents listen; women to reflect while men listen; first families to reflect while second or third families listen. If I am with a co-therapist, we will reflect while the family listens. Then the ones who have been the listeners get to talk while the talkers listen in turn.

10.  Stories, Images, and Analogies. This is becoming such a hackneyed category that I hesitate to include it, but I want to point out a difference between thinking of stories as ways to give "embedded suggestions" and stories as ways to give hope and elicit

creativity. The Ericksonian twist on stories is that they get into people's unconscious minds when they aren't looking and so can't be resisted. This method is excused because the therapist is not only benevolent but wise; he knows how to exploit the client's positive resources towards the best possible goal.

I have a different rationale for stories and metaphors. The interpretations or explanations that therapists are trained to give out are often experienced as insulting; after all, clinical jargon evolved to say something a person would hate to hear if it was said straight out. For instance, you might reflect in a team about a person seeming "fragile". That is a way to say "bad person" in disguise. If you were trying to set up an atmosphere of hope, neither the word "fragile" nor any other clinical term would cross your mind. Instead you might say that a person or a couple remind you of a box wrapped for mailing and stamped all over with "Handle With Care". You might wonder who sent the package, what its contents are, what its destination might be, how long it will take to get there. This sort of thing is hard to interpret as negative.

I do sometimes come out with a metaphor that I wish had stayed inside. I once said unthinkingly to a very nice couple that they reminded me of two neutered pets. Luckily they thought it was funny, and also true. And much depended on the fact that we had built up an atmosphere of trust. But it does seem that any kind of metaphor, because it is such a prism of complexity, is less threatening and easier to hear than a clinical interpretation.

11. Postmodern Writing. Even my writing is changing. A colleague in Amherst, Judith Davis, and I devised a paper about a family situation in which she was the interviewer and I was on a reflecting team (see chapter seven). Our article started with a brief rationale for not writing the usual academic paper; that is, we didn't start with an introductory theoretical background. Then came "Judy's Story", which detailed her experience during the four interviews she had with the family. Next came "Lynn's Story", in which I did the same. We sent the resulting manuscript to the three family members, and they sent back short comments on both the experience of working with us and on our write-up. Finally, our editors sent us a few final questions about the whole experiment and Judy

and I provided provisional answers. We are waiting with trepidation to hear what the reactions of our readers will be.

## END THOUGHTS

In my workshops across Australia, I had tried to set up experiences of reflecting conversations based on the more collaborative, open, and horizontal principles that I have detailed here. My talk in Melbourne did not put flesh on such very abstract principles, so hearing about them might well have been like fairy cakes that would disappear just as you put them in your mouth. However, out in the field, I did struggle with the intractable human questions raised by my approach.

This ends the account of my presentation in Melbourne, which started my trip. Since my talk changed with each new city I travelled to, and since I didn't keep my original notes, this is more of a cumulative account of the presentation I ought to have given in Melbourne. I only hope, as in the sieve-like feeding mechanism of the humpbacked whale, that the seawater got screened out and the nutritious plankton remained.

# CHAPTER SEVEN

# Trying to write
# a postmodern text

My own private voyage continued after I left Australia but the next lap of my travels was of a different nature. By this time I felt that I was somewhere near the mouth of the river, and I got out to visit a family in a village, so to speak, on the edge of the delta. The story of that family, "Tekka With Feathers", was composed by myself and Judith Davis in collaboration with the family in 1992. It represents an effort to demolish the idea of the case history as a text. The authors are not authors, the narrative is not a narrative, and the story will never have an end. Read on and you will see for yourself what happens when one takes one's theories seriously in writing up a case.

"Tekka With Feathers" is one of the chapters in Steven Friedman's 1993 book, *The New Language of Change: Constructive Collaboration in Psychotherapy*. Tekka was a twenty-year-old college student who had just come out of hospital. She and her mother and stepfather wanted help in getting her off medication and planning what to do next. Judy Davis was the interviewer for the four family sessions, and I was on a reflecting team for the last two, together with Brian Lewis and Bill Lax. We were all consciously trying to explore a collaborative approach.

First of all, the interviewing style was basically non-intrusive. The interviewer did not shape the discussion, except to elicit ideas about what people were concerned with and clarify impressions. She made few general comments. Occasionally she offered a question that implied change, as when she asked where Tekka would like her Recovery Doll to be in the future, but such questions were rare. In general, there was no purposeful exploring: someone made a remark about a grandmother, but it was not followed up. Neither was there an attempt to look for causality. However, Judy shared personal dilemmas of her own, and sometimes her feelings shone (or leaked) through.

The team, which always had a lot to say, flooded the family with ideas, images, interpretations. We expected that certain kernels tossed out by the team would be picked up by the family and expanded: the thought that for parents every child was a hostage to the universe; the idea that this therapy was only one experience among many; a general amusement at the thought of Tekka turning into a bird.

A certain bonhomie-on-the-edge evolved between the family and the team. The family became very involved with us, as we did with them, at one point asking us to come back in to clarify a point. Despite the one-way screen, there was very little distance and we all seemed to become contagious to each other. Judy and I especially picked up the heartache and worry under the joking; we had been too close to similar situations in our own lives.

Let me go on to the format of the piece. The idea for writing it came from discussions between myself and Judy. We wanted to find a "different voice" for a case study. To that end we decided to use our own voices rather than an impersonal academic voice and deliberately sacrificed the mandatory theoretical introduction. In order to create a "reflecting history", we asked the three family members to comment on our comments. Our editors couldn't resist and jumped in too.

Using a narrative mode, we started with "Judy's Story", in which Judy gave her perception of what happened during the interviews. Then we migrated to "Lynn's Story", in which I described my experience on the reflecting team. Somewhat arbitrarily, I added some of the pet ideas I was immersed in at the time. Stage three consisted of comments by each family member on their experience with us and on our written comments. Finally, the editors of the book added a few questions. In answering, Judy and I again used our own voices and in general tried not to answer as a mutual blob.

The format of the piece was self-consciously horizontal and devoid of the usual structuring. The contributors were deliberately not separated into experts and non-experts. Another difference was that the narrative, like the conversation it described, had no beginning, middle, end. It started when the family first came in and ended when Tekka went away for the summer. Finally, there was no attempt at coherence, no effort to impose a meaning on our meandering results. I became very conscious of the need to interpret the process and tie it up with a nice neat bow. I am amazed that we were able to refrain from that. Perhaps that is what I am doing now.

The main problem with publishing this piece, which we had agreed to do before we wrote it, was that we had no indication that things would turn out well. We wanted to offer an antidote to the usual miracle tales that only appear after the case is a certified success. However, we were quite aware that we were taking a chance in writing about a situation where there were dangerous elements. Our work, being unorthodox, placed us on a firing line. At one point during the following winter Tekka hospitalized herself briefly, and even though she handled the whole episode well and got through it, her parents were understandably anxious. So were we when we found out about this event after the fact. However, Tekka's mother was in touch with Judy from time to time, and at one point she asked if they could come in again, but they never did.

We were therefore very happy that following winter when we found out that our young heroine had completed a stunningly original sculpture show as a graduation project. She asked Judy and myself to the opening. She looked beautiful, her hair was cut short in a pageboy bob, and she was wearing a yellow silk tunic and pants and a yellow cap with a feather in it, like a boy in a Russian fairytale. Her mother told us that the two of them were getting along better than ever before. But it was the exhibit itself that amazed us. I was truly awed by the prodigal invention and busy provocative humour of Tekka's work. I thought all over again how much richness and depth is lost when we see a person in therapy and have only their clinical portrait to go by.

The one thing I would have liked to change was to ask the family to comment yet one more time on our production, so that they and not we would have the last word. However, perhaps our invitation to Tekka's sculpture show was another way for that to happen. Tekka and her family were clearly in the centre, and Judy and I were happy to stand at the edge.

# Tekka with feathers:
## talking about talking
## (about suicide)

*Lynn Hoffman & Judith Davis*

## INTRODUCTION

This is a story about an encounter with a family at the Brattleboro Family Institute.[1] It is told by Judy Davis, who was the interviewer, and added to by Lynn Hoffman, who was a member of a reflecting team[2] (Andersen, 1990). The story is commented on by members of the family, who read our version, and further expanded through answers to questions from the editor.[3]

We understand this experience not as a coherent story, but as a fragment of a less tidy process. The narrative view, popular in psychotherapy nowadays, implies that therapy is like a story, with a *beginning* (recently hospitalized daughter and distraught parents come in for a consultation), *middle* (they engage in a conversation with therapist and team), and *end* (in the process they learn how to talk differently to each other so that daughter no longer needs to know herself or be known by others as "strange"). Our view is that

From S. Friedman (Ed.), *The New Language of Change: Constructive Collaboration in Psychotherapy* (pp. 345–373). New York: Guilford Press, 1993. By permission.

therapy is more like a canoe trip on a river. It starts when we "put in" and ends when we "put out". There is no necessary structure to the events at all except the ones we invent ourselves. Thus we can only claim to present some disparate points of view about an experience in this family's life and in our own lives as they intersected for a few hours over time. Our hope is that in putting these several versions down on paper we will be, as Mary Catherine Bateson (1992) put it, "surprised into new learning".

What seems most different about this work is that it is not attached to outcome, even though it represents an experimental approach. For the most part, family practitioners write up cases and show videotapes of experiences that went well. This case leaves some doubt, and certainly the opinions of the participants vary significantly on that score. However, our idea is to model a new kind of openness in having even controversial work scrutinized by the family and by the wider clinical audience. The family here, being unusually informed consumers, were well able to provide their own comments at a level of critical attention seldom found in studies of this sort. It is we as professionals, our work, and thinking that are at issue here, not the lives and problems of the people in the family.

## JUDY'S STORY

### The first session

Before we met them, all we knew about the family was that the 21-year-old daughter had just been released from a psychiatric hospital. She was being brought to the institute by her mother and stepfather. They had been referred by the mother's friend, a graduate student in a family therapy program: "If she were my daughter, that's where I'd go."

At Brattleboro we were working with a "reflecting team" approach, an idea pioneered by Tom Andersen (1990) and his colleagues in Tromso, Norway. Since I had been wanting more experience in the role of interviewer as contrasted to that of reflecting team member, it was agreed that I would be the one to work in the room with the family. The therapy team met weekly to explore the notion of separating the therapist's traditionally intertwined tasks of inquiry and comment. What we were questioning was whether such separation of functions—where the interviewer's role was simply that of eliciting or making room for the family's stories while the team did whatever commenting was done—would open more space for new ideas. So my head, as I entered the waiting room to greet the family, was filled with thoughts about *not* reflecting, about being in the conversation as non-intrusively as possible, about following ideas rather than offering new ones. We were also interested in the concept of the "unsaid"—the possibility of allowing for thoughts that were not chosen because other thoughts had come to the fore.

Sarah and David, the man with whom Sarah had been living for 11 years, greeted me graciously but with obvious anxiety. Sarah's daughter, Tekka, a beautiful university art student, remained seated on the couch, hungrily eating a yoghurt and drinking from a large bottle of spring water. The most striking thing about Tekka was her hair. Long and strawberry blond, it was piled high on top of her head and cascaded down around her face in a combination of curls and matted dreadlocks that were interspersed with beads, bits of coloured ribbon, and feathers. Dressed in a tie-dyed jump-suit with a fingerless black glove on one hand, and her nails painted with black polish, Tekka looked, to me, both exotic and exhausted.

Our first meeting was taking place on the day after Tekka's release from the hospital, the day after her twenty-first birthday. She had signed herself into the hospital (and was then kept there against her will) for two weeks following a Spring break that had culminated in her attempting to walk into or through the side of a subway car. She described the hospitalization as a nightmare that included thorazine, isolation, and a sense that her parents had betrayed her by not getting her out and by not helping her refuse medication. Tekka was now back at school but was still on lithium. When I asked the family why they had come, they all said they wanted help getting Tekka off the medication safely. They wanted another way of dealing with whatever was going on, a way that didn't involve drugs. I saw the family four times over a period of a month and a half.

Early in our first meeting, I learned that Sarah was a music therapist. She had divorced Tekka's father when their daughter was 6; she described him as alcoholic, violent, and possibly manic-depressive. David was a teacher who described his ex-wife as "a certifiable schizophrenic"; their 25-year-old son had been hospitalized four years earlier for depression and suicidal thoughts. Almost incidentally, we learned that Tekka had been married for two years to Fredrico, a young man from Italy. They had been separated (apparently amicably) for over six months, and Fredrico was now attending school in another state.

Tekka described herself as a recovering drug and alcohol addict. David volunteered that he had also stopped drinking some years ago and that he still attended AA meetings. In the 1960s, he had "done drugs" and was once in "an induced paranoid state for three, four, five days". Continuing the description of the past in ways that pointed to their identification with Tekka's pain, Sarah added that when she was her daughter's age she too had gone through a difficult period. "I wasn't hospitalized, but I did leave school and I was very depressed."

Exploration of ideas about the subway episode revealed Tekka's explanation that "things had gotten too good". Although she could "stay grounded" during the school year, when she went on spring break, she "let out" more than she could handle. It was her first vacation on her own, and it was a kind of "vision quest". It was Tekka's thought, however, that her recent behaviour was not much different from that of her usual self, "only a little more so". Tekka's mother disagreed, although hesitantly. It was her sense that Tekka had "really lost contact with reality".

It was all I could do to resist the impulse to explore this avalanche of intriguing statements. But as I remained quiet a conversation took place here between Tekka and Sarah about what they each thought was "scary", a word Sarah used to describe her feelings about Tekka's behaviour. The conversation revealed a long history of conflict between Sarah, who saw herself as inadequately trying to protect her daughter, and Tekka, who saw Sarah as trying to "break" her strong spirit. Both agreed, however, that there had been less conflict between them when Tekka was married. During that time Tekka seemed to fight more with her "protective" husband than with her mother. Indeed, Sarah and Tekka had become closer during that period.

It seems important to mention here that our conversation throughout this and subsequent sessions was marked—despite the seriousness of the content and the differing opinions—by a surprising amount of good humour and a kind of laughter that was rather bewildering to me. It was as if the family all shared the same private joke, or at least all relieved tension in the same way.

### Team reflection
### (Bill Lax and Randye Cohen)

Towards the end of the session the family and I switched places with the team and listened as they talked about what they had just heard.

The reflections included comments on the amount of concern and humour the family demonstrated, and on the possible role of the hospitalization: was it to signal for help or was it Tekka's way of taking care of herself? Bill wondered where Sarah got her idea about being inadequate, of not being able to speak up. "Is she dealing with messages from *her* mother?" he mused. Randye, on the other hand, was curious about the paradox of things getting "better and better" in Tekka's life and getting out of control at the same time. Both were interested in Tekka's plans for the summer and the family's plans for this therapy. "In other words", said Bill, "how do we draw the boundaries around even this?"

### Family response

When the family returned, it was clear that their primary concern was the immediate future and getting Tekka off the medication. They took the name of a psychiatrist with whom the institute worked and scheduled a second appointment for the following week.

## THE SECOND SESSION

Early in the morning of the second appointment Sarah called the institute, sounding very upset. Tekka had missed the bus to meet her parents, and the family would not be able to get to Brattleboro on time. Since our schedules permitted it, the appointment was reset for later that morning (only Bill, however, would be available to represent the reflecting team).

Much of this session was devoted to the meanings each family member made of Tekka's having missed the bus. For Tekka, it was a simple act of having misread the schedule. For Sarah, it meant that Tekka wasn't capable of being responsible for herself and reinforced her idea that there was a lot of "old stuff" between them that hadn't been resolved. Tekka interjected here that she'd been wanting to talk about this old stuff but that her mother kept getting "hung up on the *way* of talking, and then it's too late. I had to have a psychotic state to get here."

In response to David's explanation of what had happened during spring break (Tekka had had "an overload of energy"), Tekka talked about having known the limits of her depths (alcoholic blackouts) but not the limits of her highs, and it was those highs which she was exploring during the break. She admitted that the hospital was more than she'd "bargained for" and was worried now that anything she did would make her mother think she was crazy.

When the conversation turned to plans for the upcoming summer, Tekka talked about buying and living in a school bus on Cape Cod. When Sarah expressed her concern about these plans, Tekka became angry and recalled an essay she'd written in high school. It was about feeling paralysed between being "responsible" and being a "rebel." Either choice was a "giving in". Even today, she went on, she was struggling between these two ideas of herself. "Who do I want to be right now?! I am being responsible. I'm making wise choices for who *I* am. But *I am not you*", she said to her mother. Here Sarah acknowledged that perhaps she was over-involved but at the same time wondered if she should, in fact, be taking even more responsibility. "Maybe my responsibility as your mother now is to make decisions for you, to be responsible for you even though you are twenty-one." "How?" asked Tekka, challengingly. "I don't know", answered Sarah. "It scares the shit out of me."

## Reflections
### (Bill Lax)

Bill came in and talked with me while the family watched from behind the mirror. Our talk was about issues of responsibility and about changes over time for a child and then for a 21-year-old woman. Bill wondered aloud about who (or who else) should be in the conversation. "Who should be talking to whom and how much?" He also commented on his changing perceptions of the family: the parents did not seem as "timid" as they had been the week before. "Maybe they're somehow less scared of Tekka now. After all, she *is* a strong woman. 'Don't ruffle my feathers!'"

I was grateful for Bill's questions and for his perception that something had changed. That view and his joking about his feathers felt, to me, somehow encouraging.

## Family response

When the family returned, Tekka resonated to the comment about who should be in the conversation. "I *do* want to choose who I talk to", she said. "I don't want to say, 'Fuck off,' but it would be easier. Too often I try to please everyone. I'd rather say 'Fuck you' and see what would happen." "And who else would be in the conversation?" I asked. "Lots", she answered. "My father, his mother. Big family intervention. But not necessarily right away."

Sarah responded to the comment about being less timid. She agreed with Bill and talked about a conversation she and Tekka had had after our last session, which both agreed felt very different: "less timid, and nice".

## THE THIRD SESSION

Our third session, one week later, began with talk about a phone conversation Tekka and her mother had had during the week. Tekka had called to say that she wanted to cancel the appointment because she had so much school work to catch up on. According to everyone, Sarah "freaked" at this idea, and handed the phone to David. In her conversation with David, Tekka was able to figure out a way to make the meeting and still get to her work. In describing that discussion, Tekka talked about wanting her mother to be less reactive and more objective, "more like a friend than a mother". It was, she said, easier to talk to her stepfather than her mother at this stage of her life.

T:  My mother can be objective before and after a conversation, but can't step out and look more clearly [while] in the conversation. I can't talk about what's going on; I begin checking out the dynamics of what's going on and that becomes the conversation.

J:  So there's a different response with David?

T:  It's easy for me to be more mature.

As a teenager, Tekka went on, she'd felt forced to lie to her mother a lot. She always wished she could tell her mother the truth about where she was going and what she was doing because, she admitted, "Often what I did *was* dangerous". But Tekka felt that her mother was overprotective, and this overprotectiveness was an attempt to "squash her energy".

Sarah disagreed about being overprotective and, in fact, felt she had been neglectful. After more of this exchange, I asked how this conversation was for the two of them. Sarah answered that it was useful because one of the things that was most painful in her life was that she hadn't been able to talk to her mother about what she was doing. Her mother was "completely naive". This, she thought, was part of why she used to get so angry when she felt Tekka was lying to her. All she wanted now, she said, was for Tekka to live her life safely. "Positively! Not safely!" Tekka exclaimed, correcting her.

### *Team reflections*
### *(Bill Lax, Brian Lewis, Lynn Hoffman)*

Opening the team's conversation, Lynn, who was meeting the family for the first time, talked about mothers and daughters. She likened what Tekka was doing to going out on thin ice. She felt that Tekka wanted to have her own life, but she also wanted to know that her mother is there in case she needs to be rescued. The problem, Lynn said, was that "if Mom gets too upset, communication breaks down". Lynn also wondered about "karmic issues" and the idea of danger. Was Sarah's mother unable to rescue Sarah? Perhaps there was a whole conversation from the past, a conversation with other generations. How do mothers allow daughters to share the experience of getting close to danger without everybody getting so upset that no new experiences are allowed?

Brian wondered why this family appeared so jovial, and he wondered what danger actually meant to them. Bill wondered if Tekka was trying to establish herself as an adult in relation to her family, and if past conversations had had similar themes about how much concern Sarah had and/or showed. Speaking again, Lynn reflected on the "mini-boomers"—the coming of age of children whose parents had been flower children themselves—and how much to repeat and yet not repeat the experiences of past generations.

### Family response

When the family returned, Sarah acknowledged that, in fact, she didn't know what Tekka meant by danger. Tekka responded by talking about creativity, suggesting that her struggle between being an artist and being practical was also her mother's struggle but that her mother had taken the safe road and had become a music therapist instead of a musician: "For myself, I need to be creating my own stuff! I'm making different choices."

With this conversation the session was ending, but I could not resist adding my own response to the reflections. In reference to Lynn's idea about karmic issues, I asked Tekka about how a conversation might go in the future when she and *her* adolescent daughter negotiated ideas about safety and creativity. "I'm not going to have a daughter", Tekka declared, "I'm going to have a son . . . because the universe has a sense of humour."

## THE FOURTH SESSION

Our next appointment was scheduled for two weeks later, but a medical emergency in my family forced me to postpone the meeting by a week. On the telephone with Sarah I shared some of the details of my son's illness, and she and I commiserated about the pain of seeing one's child sick or hurting. When I called Tekka with the message, she volunteered that she was thinking of spending a month in a treatment centre before starting her summer job on the Cape.

When the family arrived three weeks later for the fourth and last meeting, Tekka was less animated than usual and looked tired. I asked them how they wanted to use this last session. David answered that he wanted to talk about the future, but that Tekka didn't want to talk at all. "She's in a slump. School's over. Moving boxes."

Tekka responded by saying she was "not great, but okay". She had definitely decided on the treatment program, which had been recommended by her twelve-step sponsor. A conversation about this decision revealed that David was pleased about the plan as long as Tekka didn't see it as another hospital, but as "a resort with paid humans".

Sarah also thought it was a good idea, but was worried about something else: when she and David visited Tekka in her dorm room on the day of our cancelled meeting, they found on her door "a doll hanging herself". Sarah demonstrated with her hands around her neck. Although she was unable to comment on it at the time, Sarah talked briefly with Tekka about it the next day on the phone. Tekka told her it was her "recovery doll" and said: "This is what she [the doll] did to herself after she got out of the hospital. But I don't feel this way really."

The doll incident had upset Sarah profoundly, and I asked about the difficulty of talking about it. Sarah responded by talking about how "strangely hard" it was to talk with Tekka in light of the fact that in her work (dealing with troubled adolescents) she talked about "such things" regularly.

Exasperated, Tekka talked about how surprised she always was that her mother responded so intensely to her gestures rather than her words. "I think I make it pretty clear where I'm at. And when I'm not doing well, I say I'm not doing well. We went through this when I was living at home and I had my mohawk. Mom freaked out because I shaved my head. 'You must be very disturbed!'"

At this point, David interrupted. "I know your mother very well, and right now she is saying to herself: 'Does this mean Tekka is suicidal all the time?'"

T:  That's what I mean. I don't think people listen to me!

S:  So *are* you suicidal all the time?

T:   Do you think I'm suicidal all the time?

S:   I don't think you are.

T:   So okay! I don't think I am either. (*Family laughs*)

[Sarah went on here haltingly, trying to speak more about her confusion.]

J:   (*Feeling the need to help*) So the doll scared you.

S:   Yeah!

J:   And it was very hard for you to express that fear, hard to mention it to Tekka in a way that wasn't offensive to her?

S:   Yeah, I don't want to offend her. And David says "Of course she'll be offended. Of course she's not suicidal. Don't make a big deal. Why do you always react?" But the point is, if she does feel really bad and says it, maybe there's something that she could tell us . . . what she would like us to do to help.

As she was saying this, Sarah noticed that Tekka and David were looking at each other and beginning to smile. "That gets that look", she explained, as she turned to them and joined in their laughter. Deciding to give voice to my confusion, I asked if someone could please explain what "that look" meant. "It means", David said, "There she goes again". "What does, 'There she goes again' mean?" I asked Sarah. "Do you know?" "It means they think I'm over-psychologizing", she answered. I wondered here if this was some piece of private joke, another piece of the "unsaid"?

As talk about Sarah's overreacting went on, David explained that Tekka just wants Sarah to listen like a friend but not do anything. "Yeah", joined in Tekka, "or otherwise every time I say something, there's the threat that I'm going to be taken to a psych ward."

Sarah explained her hesitation to "just listen", saying that if Tekka really needed help and she (Sarah) didn't recognize it or do anything about it, it would be terrible. "In my work, when a kid has suicidal thoughts or does suicidal art work or writes suicidal songs, we set up a suicide watch. That is my framework and I know that's part of me. That's what I do. I spend a lot of time with children who are at risk. It scares me because I want you (*turning to Tekka*) . . . I wish you didn't feel that bad." "So do I", Tekka answered, and she and Sarah laughed identically.

## Team reflections
### (Bill Lax, Brian Lewis, Lynn Hoffman)

Brian began by commenting on how different the family seemed to him this time, how much less jovial. "Almost from a happy family to a sad family. But", he said, "as the session went on, the change made sense to me."

Lynn agreed that the change was striking and went on to say that even though they were talking about death she felt reassured in a peculiar kind of way because talking about it was possible. Recalling the previous conversation about danger and safety, Lynn thought that maybe it was now possible for Tekka to talk and for mother to listen and that that seemed to be an important part of the process. If they stopped being able to talk, that would be the real danger. Lynn went on: "Thinking as a mother—and I certainly have that particular piece of the territory seared in my head and my heart—that is the one reassurance I have."

Bill's comment had to do with the difference between "what you see is what you get", and "what else is there?" He asked whether Tekka's presentation to her family in the "what you see is what you get" mode was sufficient, or whether there was need for further inquiry? "And what happens when sometimes the 'what you see is what you get' mode stops further inquiry, such as with the doll? How can there be talk without an alarmed reaction to the talk? How can there be conversation around danger and safety without having to move to a 'suicide watch'?" Bill added, "Often what Tekka presents is 'I show you who I am'. And I can see from mother's point of view that sometimes that can be quite strange [laughter from behind the mirror]. There aren't many people who walk around the way Tekka does. Does that require further inquiry? Like, 'You have feathers in your hair. Does that mean you are thinking of becoming a bird?' [louder laughter]. 'No, there are just feathers in my hair.' That's 'what is, is'. Maybe there needs to be more of a balance of inquiry around that stuff." Bill went on to wonder if the plan for the treatment program was sufficient to allay concern about the danger: "Is this a plan that will allow them to move forward in such a way that then more conversation can take place?"

Lynn added here a reminder that mother was not alone. "There's not just mother, but there is also David. And even though mother could never just say 'it's immaterial to me how you feel' because she has to take action if she thinks certain things, David doesn't. That seems to me to be another strong piece in all of this." Lynn paused and added, "But I'm basically *not* relieved." Turning to Brian, she asked, "What is a recovery doll?"

Brian answered that he didn't know but had made the assumption that "somehow the doll symbolized part of the recovery process". Brian went on to wonder about David's multiple roles in the conversation: as one who enables Sarah to speak, as one who inhibits her speech, as one with different ideas of his own. He wondered whether at times David might join Sarah in her worries about Tekka.

## *Family's reflections*

David responded first, saying that although he personally had been feeling much better about the situation with each passing week, he was most interested in knowing what Lynn meant when she said she was not relieved. He also went on to respond to Brian's comment about the different roles he plays in the family and concluded that maybe he could be helpful because he was "not involved as a mother, but certainly involved as someone who cares very strongly for Tekka's well-being . . . and for Sarah's well-being".

Sarah responded next by asking if there was any chance of finding out from Lynn what she meant "instead of just speculating and wondering?" I assured her that the team could return before the end of the session to speak to their questions and asked if there were other thoughts about what the team had said. Laughing, Sarah confessed that she'd also wondered what a "recovery doll" was and, turning to her daughter, asked, "Would you mind telling us?" Tekka replied, "It's a doll when I was doing a lot of [recovery] work, my child doll . . . that I don't particularly like very much. But I had it for three years."

As Sarah and Tekka seemed unable to go beyond this single exchange, I decided to try to actively take up the metaphor as a resource in expanding this piece of the conversation. I asked Tekka, "You decided a few weeks ago to hang it on your door?"

T: I felt at the time that my recovery had been squashed in the hospital. Not taken away from me, but . . . kind of violated.

S: Because they made you take drugs or the whole thing?

T: That, and because they wouldn't let me go to group. No access to talking to people. People weren't listening to me the way I'm accustomed to having people listen to me.

J: That doll was a kind of statement about that experience?

T: Yeah.

J: (*Attempting to make space for a "not-yet-said" idea*) Where is she now?

T: Still there.

J: Will you be leaving that room soon?

T: Yeah. She'll have to come down.

D: She *could* stay there. (*Mother and daughter laugh as one*)

J: (*to Tekka*) If you could imagine a future past the summer or past this experience, where would you *like* her to be?

T: The doll?

J: Yeah.

T: Well, I would like *myself* to be back in control, in total recovery. So the doll can be in storage!

J: Do you have thoughts about what the team was saying?

T: Yeah. I thought it was interesting, their comments about our changing. I think that there are just so many different points [of view]. When we only come here for an hour once a week, you only get just so much. We have the ability to be humorous and we also have the ability to have a lot of shit going on and we deal with it. I know one of the accusations I got in the hospital was that I kept changing my mind. Every day a different idea.

S: That was from me?

T: Yeah, that was from you.

J: (*to Sarah*) Your thoughts about the team's comments?

S: Interesting . . . they were certainly looking at it from different ways, different frameworks. (*Pause*) I was just thinking as Tekka was talking about the hospital, I wish there was a way of communicating with her where she didn't feel I was accusatory, because that wasn't my perception. (*Pause*) What I'm learning in this period, is how I'm perceived. And I think often my state of worryness is, in turn, turned into feeling like accusation and criticism.

J: Uh huh.

S: I wish it could be different.

J: You're seeing her reaction, her response in a new way?

S: Yeah. I think I never really understood it. I felt bad or frustrated or whatever, but we couldn't relate somehow. But I never thought of what it was like for her. Or understood. I mean . . . what I'm learning is that what comes out of me is not what I think. Nor does it have the reaction I wish. I wish it could be different.

J: She hears you differently?

S: Yeah, like I was saying, I really have to listen to her in a more open way.

D: So that's positive.

After the silence that followed this last statement, I reminded the family that this was essentially the last meeting before the summer began, and I wondered how this time together could be made most useful. I was again attempting to open more space; I asked if there were some things they wished they could have said, or questions asked. How could we use this time best?

David answered first, saying that he didn't know if it was necessary to say this, but, turning to Tekka, said, "I am willing to help, give support" (*here Tekka put her hand out to David, rubbing her fingers together*) "including some money".

T: Thank you. (*Pause*) Not just for the money.

D: (*Gently*) I know.

T: I'm pretty burned out on the whole thing.

J: The whole thing?

T: The whole thing. I'm just tired of talking about it, dealing with it, being here—not here specifically, but where I am. (*Yawn*) Very tired . . . hoping after treatment I'll feel better.

S: I guess (*laughs*) I feel . . . hope . . . that if Tekka needs our support, she can ask for it. She can talk about it. Use us as an asset. She is grown up. At the age of stepping out on her own. But if there are things she may need from us, she'll be able to ask and not get caught up in power struggles. I know that she's hated all this stuff, but she has actually been very cooperative. Last time we weren't able to say this when we had all that trouble getting here; we didn't say (*looking directly at Tekka*) how good it was that you *were* able to get here. We don't get to say those things.

At this point I suggested that the team return to answer the questions the family raised.

## Team again

L:  I guess what I really want to say before I defend my position is that this family has changed again. It has all these sides to it. And it's a very tender family. And I feel also that there is one hero and two heroines here, truly. That Tekka has worked hard and lovingly, in whatever way she does it, and her mother and stepfather have been genuinely concerned. So I just wanted to say that. (*Pause*) But as far as this thing about not being relieved, I wanted to say to Sarah that I know how you must feel. That nobody says to women, and I guess to men, too, that every child you have is a hostage to the universe and you're vulnerable for the rest of your and their lives. So that's all I meant. Because actually I am very heartened by this meeting and the family. Tremendously impressed with how this family has pulled together.

Br: I was also primarily struck by how much love there was . . . and struck by the sadness, but maybe it makes sense. Maybe it has to do with the fact that things are changing. Tekka is definitely taking responsibility for herself and has made this decision and there's now not a whole lot that can be done. . . . Just a need to let whatever is going to happen, happen. And that *is* kind of sad. A new beginning and a letting go. The sadness for the past that is gone, and not quite sure about the future.

Bi: I'm viewing life from more of a philosophical position, like "children as hostages". Life is an ongoing unfolding of safety and danger. Sadness is a letting go of the idea that the rehabilitation program is going to be "it". It's another experience. It's not the perfect experience but a series of experiences—for the whole family. Tekka's experience, and Tekka's recounting of the experience. And I was thinking of something that took place here that I hadn't seen before that felt, to me, great—that was David's expressing of appreciation, "I'm here to support you emotionally, financially"—and Tekka's saying "Thank you". And Sarah saying to Tekka, "I wanted you to know how much I appreciated your being here". It sounds like they're moving to a different phase of interaction with one another . . . and the conversation is getting richer, more facets.

## *Family reflections*

As usual, I asked the family for their reactions to the team's comments.

J:  Any final comments, reactions—to their appreciation of your appreciation?

D:  I thought that this process here has been useful, actually. I've liked this crazy one-way mirror a lot because it creates a kind of artificial situation that lets you say some things that you probably couldn't say otherwise, and yet it is not so artificial that it seems bizarre. It doesn't close you up. To have all of these insightful and very different types of people give their thoughts and feelings about what they have just experienced is interesting—I'm gonna start worrying whether or not Tekka is going to become a bird (*all laugh*).

S:  Well, I really appreciated this process. It's given us a way to touch base with Tekka through this period, and it's allowed us to have conversations that wouldn't have happened. I'm more aware of some of the areas where I make it difficult for Tekka. I think I never heard it before. I don't think she didn't say it before. I just hadn't heard it before.

T:  I've enjoyed this—I think. I liked the mirror too. The switching back and forth, like they said, an experience among many to carry with me. I think the process will happen further down, but that's okay.

D: (*to me*) You've also been very good in terms of letting conversations develop, feeding them without intruding. Because if you had been intrusive, the conversations wouldn't have taken place.

By this time I was thinking it was my turn to respond, but I was surprised to find myself really choked up and barely able to contain my tears. I blurted out, "Happy family, sad family, I think you're a beautiful family; so much good stuff in there. I wish you the best" (through all you have yet to endure, I was thinking; without doubt, my tears were about my child as well as theirs).

To regain my composure, I tried to change the subject and insert some humour. When I'd called Tekka to reschedule the appointment, I couldn't make out what the message on her answering machine was: "You can't come to the phone because you're working on what?" I asked. "My basket case", Tekka answered. As I was slowly getting the joke, Sarah suggested, "You should hear what Tekka has on the machine now: 'I'm working on my anger, fuck you.'" With laughter and hugs we ended the meeting.

Although I don't know what meaning Sarah or David or Tekka made of the phone message, I suddenly felt hopeful. Maybe in some way, Tekka was needing to please less. Maybe she was beginning to feel she had some control over "who she wanted to talk to and how". And maybe this would make a difference in what got said and what got heard.


### Follow-up

Two months later when I called Sarah to ask how everyone was, she reported that Tekka had felt good about the treatment program, was off the lithium, and was living in her bus on the Cape. Sarah also reported that Tekka had cut off her hair but that it was cropped short, not shaved. "She looks much better now, and the sparkle is back in her eyes." Despite this positive picture, however, Sarah expressed continued anxiety. "I'm trying not to worry, but Tekka still seems so fragile to me. It's fifty-fifty whether she's fine or has another episode. But there's nothing I can do about it. I just have to trust she can take care of herself."

As the conversation ended, Sarah asked about my son's health, and the two of us reflected on Lynn's comment. No, no one does tell us ahead of time about hostages and the universe.

## Afterthoughts

As I write this account, I keep asking myself why we have chosen this experience to focus on. Clearly, we are not presenting it as proof that something "works". Instead, we are putting it down on paper as a way of looking back at the experience and asking ourselves what happened—that is, what we thought was happening at the time and what we now, in the context of writing about it, think was happening. We see this piece as an example of our notions about participating in a less hierarchical relationship with the people we see, one in which we reveal aspects of ourselves that connect us with them, that normalize their feelings, that speak from the heart as well as the head.

Obviously, we could not determine the "truth" about Tekka's potential to commit suicide. On the one hand, we felt torn between responding to the threat by encouraging the family to undertake a suicide watch and, on the other, refusing to buy into their fears lest we help make them come true. What allowed us to feel rescued from this dilemma was the reflecting stance, the stance that permitted us to hold a position of ambiguity and use the metaphors it produced.

It was this stance that allowed Randye to reflect on things getting better and better and yet worse at the same time, Brian to reflect on the family as both happy and sad simultaneously, Bill to reflect on the "what you see is what you get" mode being both enough and not enough, and Lynn to echo David and Sarah's differing positions, expressing simultaneously both their hopes and their fears.

What is the relationship between this therapeutic conversation and family change? It would be reassuring to believe that the conversation made space for:

- Sarah to ask questions directly first of the team and then of her daughter instead of just "speculating and wondering", as had apparently been her way.

- Tekka to articulate the family's strengths (and not just their failings).

- The family to give voice to their support and appreciation of each other.

- Tekka to change her answering machine's message (the message that contextualized all subsequent conversations) to "I'm no longer crazy, just angry".

- Mother to move away from the idea of a suicide watch to the idea that she cannot protect her grown daughter in this way. "I am no longer going to tell you what to do, but invite you to ask from us what you want, need."

It would be reassuring also to believe that in this family the need for strange actions or dramatic symbols was somehow lessened as the idea developed that dangerous thoughts could be expressed in words. But who can say?

## LYNN'S STORY

I had not been present for the first two interviews, so I was listening doubly hard behind the screen in order to catch up. I too was taken by Tekka's playful style of dress and her flair for exuberance; it was easy to miss her serious side until, boom, it tripped you up. When that happened I fell right down the rabbit hole to memories of frightening times with my own teenage daughter. I remembered how I seemed to be watching her struggle through a soundproof glass wall. So much for trying to be objective; during that last meeting, I might as well have been Tekka's mother myself. Luckily, David, by not being as drawn in as I was, acted like a firebreak. And when I went in to reflect, it was Bill who acted like a firebreak. Even with their help, I found this a particularly hard situation to be part of and at the time felt that I was not being very polished. When David drew attention to my contradictory statements, saying first that I was relieved and then that I was not, I wondered what I meant myself.

The answer, of course, was that I found myself in two places at once. One was a place of relief that the family could talk about the possibility of Tekka being in danger. My theory is that as long as people can keep talking about something they fear, nobody will give up and nobody will die. This is an idea I got from the late Harry Goolishian of the Galveston Institute, and it is an idea I try to take as literally as he did. The other place I was coming from was that I was

feeling exactly the way Sarah did: here was her own daughter, perhaps drowning, and shouldn't she go and rescue her? When I said I
was not relieved, I was simply validating Sarah's point of view. I
forgot I had just said the opposite, but when David asked if I could
clarify what I meant, I welcomed the chance. In the old days that
would have been against the rules because the therapist was supposed to be always in control and always skilful. But my style now is
to put anything that seems like a mistake or a feeling of being stuck
on the table for discussion. It certainly moves matters along.

As for Judy, I was very appreciative of what she was doing, even
more so after she transcribed all four sessions and I could read them.
I was already clear about the reflecting process. I think of it as a
Delphic commentary that is long on associations and stories and
short on interpretations and problem solving. What the interviewer
did, however, was less clear. It seemed that the interviewer did
nothing, at least compared to the sleuth-like questioning and complicated interventions of the approaches I had been trained in. But
there is always more than meets the eye. Let me try to lay out a few
characteristics of the way I think we work as interviewers now. I'll
confine myself to the fourth interview.

1. *Beginning the sessions.* We try to focus right away on this activity of talking together and what it means to people and how they
would like it to go. Our hope is to set things up so that people can
"take back the interview" from the professionals. Judy's question
"How would you like to use this session?" is a good example. Tom
Andersen's (1990) "What is the history of the idea to come here?"
was the prototype for this way of starting. Before, we used to ask
about the problem, and immediately it was a different ball game.

2. *Not controlling sessions.* As Judy said, we try to stay back, deliberately not asking provocative questions and not making interesting
interventions. This is harder than you think if you have been "prop-
erly" trained in family therapy. Judy tended to speak sparingly and
to use a soft voice, and she followed no pre-set schedule. This was to
allow maximum freedom for family members to come up with their
own ideas. Sometimes Judy made a space for someone, but that was
about it.

3. *Having less exact goals.* It seems to me that in this approach the
therapist does not set out to make something happen or find some-

thing out. Judy tried instead to keep the conversation going, nudging it so as to keep the pathways open between people but otherwise intervening little. For the most part she elicited ideas from people about whatever was uppermost in their minds, often using Milan-style agree/disagree questions. However, we don't do that much circular questioning, since it can so easily straitjacket the interaction. In the past we were always hunting for a particular animal—a hypothesis about the function of the symptom that we could connote positively—but the new way of working moves away from looking for patterns at all.

4. *Not taking a managerial position.* A common doctrine in cases of violence and threat of suicide is that the therapist should be an activist. No doubt that is often the best policy, as well as common sense, but there are a significant number of situations where the threat or use of force creates a worse outcome than if nothing at all is done. And not every therapist is comfortable with being an activist. So, as I often say, there ought to be a "different voice". Gandhi, for instance, provided a different voice in the fight against the British in India. This different voice, this softer voice, does not necessarily lack impact. As in Aesop's tale of the contest between the sun and the wind, the softer voice can be very strong.

5. *Asking special questions.* Judy asked a special kind of question from time to time; it is hard to describe, although it seems to fall into Peggy Penn's (1985) category of a "future question". A good example in the last interview is when the story of the recovery doll came up and Judy asked: "If you could imagine a future past the summer or past this experience, where would you like her to be?" And Tekka answers: "I would like myself to be back in control, in total recovery. So the doll can be in storage!" This is what I call looking for the windows, not the walls. People can often find the door on their own.

6. *Not pushing a particular outcome.* We had no aims in this last interview apart from the general ones that Tekka not hurt herself, not drop out of school, and not go back to a hospital ward. What did happen was that by the end of the meeting Sarah and David were expressing appreciation to Tekka, she was reciprocating, and there was an air of relief that maybe she was out of immediate danger. I think we expect that if we address the communication so that all parties can end up feeling that they are basically good persons, things will start to work better. That partly accounts for our relent-

lessly affirmative framework, one that many people object to, but that I think of as fundamental.

What I like about this approach is that it allows us to invite people to influence what happens in a much more creative way than we used to think was possible. Another thing: since there is a continual process of follow-up built into the work, there is great opportunity to change course, try different tacks, or go back and start again. What you lose, of course, is therapeutic predictability and elegance. I find this approach hard to teach and that is one reason I like formats like the reflecting team. Asking people to comment and to listen to each other's comments interferes with the usual process of problem solving, which we are trying to get away from. However, as this way of thinking gets built into the collective unconscious of those in the family therapy field, I think the use of a reflecting team in a formal sense will drop away.

Since we are writing a "story in retrospect", I would like to end with some remarks about a few theoretical ideas that have been in all our minds, ideas that have influenced and been influenced by our practice. As of now, I consider some of these influences to be:

1. *Ideas about the social construction of knowledge* (Gergen, 1991). The viewpoint that we create or invent what we think we know—in the field of human events, at least—challenges the legitimacy of "normal social science" as it applies to psychotherapy and family therapy. When we are dealing with the area of emotional distress, the concept of treatment becomes particularly questionable and the pressure to make a diagnosis even more so.

2. *Ideas about the harm done by normative models for psychotherapy* (Anderson & Goolishian, 1988). For me, most of the beliefs that surround the concept of psychology deserve to be challenged. I personally believe that all models of therapy that posit causes for pathology, whether of a structural nature (poor boundaries, lack of individuation) or of a process nature (growth impairments, developmental lags) should be thrown out. In fact, it might not be such a bad idea to decide that psychology is a flawed field and replace it with a new emphasis on human communication.

3. *Ideas about downplaying "texts"* (which belong to a culture of literacy) *and upgrading "conversations"* (which belong to a culture of

orality: Olson, submitted; Ong, 1982). Texts and formal vocabularies are what uphold the authority of the expert. Without such supports the art of therapy becomes local and perishable, like Christmas cookies or hamentashen. At the same time, I am in favour of ways in which the consumers of therapy can themselves become "authors", as when Peggy Penn (1991) helps people to compose letters to family members, or when a colleague of mine, social worker Catherine Taylor, assists client groups to compose and design their own newsletters.

4. *The idea that there are no patterns intrinsic to human affairs.* If one believes this, it makes no sense to look for patterns in the therapy process, in the family, or in the individual personality—except when doing so seems useful, and then only with a disclaimer or rationale attached.

5. *An idea about a "different voice", first advanced by Carol Gilligan.* After reading Gilligan's study (1982), which suggests that women value keeping relationships intact whereas men value right/wrong principles, I felt that we should make room for a style in family therapy that puts connection before truth and empathy before being right.

6. *Finally, ideas about discourse from French social historian Michel Foucault* (in Rabinow, 1984). Foucault calls attention to "the microfascism of everyday life". He holds that it is through the discourses that are built up around our institutions (e.g. penal institutions, legal institutions, medical institutions) that the modern state controls its subjects. Insofar as family therapists are more and more part of what Kearney, Byrne, and McCarthy (1989) call the "colonialism of mental health", I believe that we now have an obligation to critique and even alter our own roles.

A word about the format of this chapter. This is not the first time a family has been invited to contribute to an article (e.g. Roberts, "Alexandria", & "Julius", 1988). Neither is it the first time that article writers have broken ranks with the custom of starting pieces about therapy with a theoretical discussion (White, 1991). What feels different is having family members be part of a cumulative reflecting process in the writing *about* the sessions as well as during the sessions themselves. Another point is that this article was not written to fit any current scientific framework, unless one can say that the postmodern critique of Western thought is such a framework. We join this critique in questioning whether the study of human behaviour and communication can ever be a science at all. For this reason, we wanted to suggest an arrangement that places the "voice of the person" first, and the "voice of the text" second. If the text continues to lead the way, the automatic authority of the professional will never be challenged.

Finally, we decided to keep each voice individual and separate—there is no royal "we" producing this paper but a group of people with particular and local opinions. This is why we kept to a format something like Chaucer's *Canterbury Tales*, where each story conforms to the mode and manner of its teller. We hoped that this plethora of perspectives would invite the reader to contribute his or her own critical version.

* * *

Let us now consider the stories we haven't heard yet—namely, the contributions offered by Sarah, David, and Tekka.

## SARAH'S REFLECTIONS

*I appreciated the sessions at Brattleboro very much. They helped me get beyond my feelings of shock, panic, and helplessness which were the result of Tekka's episode and hospitalization, which came as a great surprise to me. I also took on my own private blame for everything in her life that might have contributed to her difficulties.*

*The sessions at Brattleboro gave us a format for conversations that we were unable to have by ourselves. The non-judgemental, supportive attitude of the team gave space for a larger perspective than I had at the time. I was able to take a look at my over-identification with Tekka. It would have been easier to have someone tell me what to do at the time—but, instead, I had to reach deeper inside myself.*

*The talk about mothers and daughters and being a hostage to the universe stayed with me throughout this year, which continued to have difficult moments. Tekka had another hospitalization, which was more benign but definitely took its toll. This time Tekka took charge of her own discharge and aftercare plans without us. I work at not following my impulses to take on her problems as my own, remembering that she is a very capable and strong woman and accepting that she has a condition that she will have to find her own way to deal with. I have also been working with my mother in therapy this year, and the quality of our relationship is improving. I am becoming more sensitive to the times when I do to Tekka exactly what I have been angry at my mother for doing to me.*

*My gratitude to David for being there during all this keeps deepening, as does my respect for Tekka as a person who is separate from me. The Brattleboro experience taught me the importance of daring to talk about my concerns without getting "freaked out". I will need many years of practice.*

## STEPFATHER'S REFLECTIONS: COMMENTS FROM DAVID

*The following is my view of the Brattleboro Family Center as I experienced it with Sarah and Tekka in the Spring of 1991. I am writing the first section of this without reading what the team in Brattleboro has written. I would rather get on paper my own views of the experience first, before making comments about the others' perceptions. For the same reason, I have not read Sarah or Tekka's comments beforehand.*

*Sarah and I contacted the Brattleboro Family Institute to look for some form of therapy that would be useful to Tekka in dealing with what had been diagnosed as manic-depressive or bi-polar behaviour. Looking back, I do not know if we found what we were looking for, something primarily for Tekka. What we did find was something Sarah and I needed: a way to relate to Tekka about her condition. Tekka also gained; she got closer to her family and thus I think found more support than she had expected. Our ways of relating to her on our own were frustrating, too filled with our fears and guilt, sometimes even exploding in anger. None of us could help it, even though I think we all saw what was taking place.*

*The sessions at Brattleboro presented a kind of a safety net. Judy Davis provided an extremely neutral forum for discussion. Comments later by the "hidden therapists" behind the mirror allowed for subsequent clarification of our statements. Often what we say may not be what we mean, especially as interpreted by another. Having the chance to hear the interpretations of the "hidden therapists" gave us all an opportunity to see how we had been misunderstood, and the ending part of each session allowed for restating in clearer words what we meant to say the first time.*

*Implications of our thoughts and feelings also came to light. The sessions were specifically helpful to me by allowing a forum where we could discuss Tekka's plans for the future. In sum, although I am writing this as a critique of an experience and certainly not as an advertisement, I think very highly of the Brattleboro Institute and would certainly recommend it to any of my friends needing ways of communicating in a crisis.*

*There is still a part of me, however, that wishes the sessions had been more specific in helping Tekka directly with her psychological difficulties. Nonetheless, it was refreshing to find help oneself, especially when one is looking for help for someone else! And in finding help in communicating, we all gained a stronger, or at least more positive, sense of our family together.*

## David's comments
## on Brattleboro's comments

*I see that the "hidden therapists" ought to be called "the reflecting team". I really have no particular comments to add after reading the narrative by Judy Davis and the comments by Lynn Hoffman. I find I view the actual situations that took place similarly. I probably do not agree with some of the theoretical statements regarding therapy but appreciate the effort to not get stuck in preconceptions of what therapy ought to be. I say "probably do not agree" because upon reflection I might come around to the same views. I will give one example: Lynn Hoffman states: "I personally believe that all models of therapy that posit causes for pathology . . . should be thrown out." At first reading, this statement implies to me that looking for possible causes is itself a mistake. I have a hard time with this notion of throwing out the search for causes. If therapy is to some extent a curative process, this in itself means that there is something that needs curing. Whatever it is that needs curing came about somehow; trying to find out what that "somehow" is seems worthwhile to me. And yet I know the problem that Lynn is addressing by her statement. Too often theories are imposed on what we see and hear, and what we get back is only what we used as a filter to begin with. With Tekka, various therapists presented to us with equal conviction conflicting theories regarding her episode. Stress caused it; biological defects caused it; having an addictive personality caused it; lack of a chemical in the brain caused it; the perils of a spiritual quest caused it. All or none may actually be true. Imposing these theories on Tekka's behaviour changes how one looks at her, stifles dialogue, prevents one from dealing with the situation as it is.*

*And yet I still believe that one ought to at least be interested in what a possible cause could be. If there is a cause that can be identified, then perhaps others need not be subjected to that cause; this would be preventive mental health. Or perhaps the cause can be counteracted, and thus cured. Or perhaps nothing can be done, in which case greater emphasis needs to be put on acceptance. I realize that the therapist is in a rough position. On the one hand, the therapist must be open to what is taking place. On the other hand, past experience and the search for understanding lead to theories, even if the theory is that there should be none.*

*Thank you for permitting me this small indulgence of commenting on one of the theoretical points. Thinking about this stuff makes me glad I am not in your shoes.*

*Sincerely,*
*David*

## TEKKA'S REFLECTIONS

*Dear Judy,*

*Here are my thoughts and reflections on both our work together and the material written about it. I had not given that time any thought until you asked me to write this, but I have sat down many times in the past week to put my ideas and feelings into any cohesive or articulate statement. I don't think I have fully succeeded, but since time is running out I will share what I have at this moment.*

*Before I begin I would like to thank you and the rest of the Brattleboro Institute team for showing so much interest in our case and for investing so much energy into "it"—whatever "it" is worth.*

*I find myself torn between a feeling of excitement to be part of a project that focuses on going beyond existing structures of communication and therapeutic approach—and revulsion at delving into personal territory in a pointless venture into nothingness. I resent the focus on myself as suicidal or even having problems—or at least I resent it in the context it was in last spring, where I am clearly the "patient" and the pivot point of our "family gathering".*

*Nonetheless, I love things that have to do with me (whatever you choose to call it) and I thoroughly enjoyed the process of our work and getting to hear the team's impressions of me as a person. The concept of transient realities and perceived realities has always interested me; and to voice and hear the realities of me as a person was a worthwhile opportunity. Especially in relationship to my mother and David, since we all clearly have different perceptions of our dynamics. It felt like a safe environment to do this because I felt that my voice was respected by the team, and I remember at times feeling as though my views were being defended and protected.*

*I believe the concept of freedom versus safety that surfaced is a profound one—that was seen clearly in our case and that I see clearly in society as well. I have thought about my mother's comment that "in my work, when a kid has suicidal thoughts or does suicidal art work or writes suicidal songs, we set up a suicide watch". In my life it is played out with emotional concern on her behalf—that there must be something wrong and she wants to help, and feels powerless. Yet her approach leaves me resentfully in a "victim" role that I don't adhere to—because I see myself more as a survivor . . . I guess that's why.*

*I see this same scenario on a larger scale. Where do we draw the line between putting a stop to exploitative pornography and taking away the endowed rights of expression? The line quickly moves to the right, putting censorship restrictions on art.*

*This week I have been listening to the new Tracy Chapman tape, Matters of the Heart. The chorus of the first song is "Bang Bang Bang. He shoots you dead." It is played all the time on the radio and people at my job are reciting the chorus constantly. I told my friend of the fear/vision I had of little kids hearing the song and running around with toy guns singing, "Bang Bang Bang, I'll shoot you dead." My friend responded that Tracy Chapman was probably concerned with singing about reality, period.*

*Freedom or safety? Jimmy Cliff sings: "I'd rather be a free man in my grave than living as a beggar or a slave." I think it is an issue of oppression—personal and societal, and that once "a kid" gets to the point where he/she is able to consciously think, draw, sculpt, sing, or in any other way express suicide, that they are actually in a more healthy place.*

*To respond to the idea of a suicide rather than the act of expression gives the suicide even more power. For example, I felt very violated to have the topic of my "recovery doll" even be a topic. To me it was a very sensitive personal thing to begin with (the doll, that is) and to hang it on the door was my way of consciously expressing how I was feeling in relation to others. To have the "others" then react to it only perpetuated the feeling: the feeling of violation, oppression, infringement. So where does one go with that? It can become a vicious circle quickly.*

*But what if the response was gratitude or hopefulness? What if when the black slaves sang of freedom rather than oppression the white people said, "Wow you are human beings with a voice to be heard and respected instead of worrying about riots and revolution?" What if when ugly things are put before our eyes we can say, "Yes they are ugly; yes they are real, let's get on with it and do something with it"?*

*I can be a rebel to the point of hurting myself, and I can be responsible to the same point. But if I were the ideal—a Responsible Rebel—or especially so, it would be dangerous. My mother once taught me a song Janis Joplin sings which says, "Freedom's just another word for nothing left to lose, nothing ain't worth nothing unless it's free" . . . something like that. Anyway, Freedom/oppression/ and then safety. I don't know if there is room for safety when you are dealing with such big issues. Look at Ghandi, Kennedy, Martin Luther King, Jr., Karen Silkwood. Safety certainly wasn't their first choice and yet they were not put on a suicide watch.*

*If every artist that ever dealt with the issue of suicide and death were put on watch, we would be missing out on a lot of our culture. And what if Freud was questioned about his cocaine addiction, etc.?*

*I am definitely rambling a bit—but my point is that it is a fundamental question and one that affects me personally for many reasons. The fact that my mother is a therapist makes her not only a mother—but an institution and an approach as well—and so there are many levels to question and disagree with her on—of course they are also a part of me.*

*In closing, I will say that I'm opposed to the exaggeration that I "attempted to walk into or through the side of a subway car" since it was not the car but the wall of the station. This was the point of conflict between my family and me, because it was the incident that would determine if my episode was "a threat to myself". Obviously if I had tried to run through the subway car it would have been dangerous!*

*I realize this letter is long—but I don't expect you to use it all. It's the best I can do at this point. However, I would be very willing and interested to continue this discourse if there is an interest on your side for any reason.*

*If you have any questions feel free to contact me. Thank you again.*

*Sincerely*
*Tekka*

## EDITOR'S QUESTIONS

Q: *Most of us learned that it is important to have a theoretical framework to guide our clinical activities. You describe the therapy process as "a canoe trip on a river. It starts when we 'put in' and ends when we 'put out.'"* In a *previous paper* [see chapter three] *you* [Lynn] *refer to Judy's idea of the therapist as an "accidental ethnographer". Would you expand on these ideas and compare your approach with more traditional family therapy models? Your work is a major step away from the therapist as an active, directive, more intrusive presence in the therapy process. Would you comment on how your work evolved in this direction?*

A: *Lynn*: My earliest influences came from reading Haley's ideas about "directive therapy" and watching Virginia Satir's magisterial family interviews. Haley defined strategic therapy as a therapy designed by the therapist. I followed this model until I became aware, just after his death, of the immense discomfort Gregory Bateson felt with the growing family therapy industry with its emphasis on manipulation and control. His book *Angels Fear* (Bateson & Bateson, 1987) had just been posthumously put together by Mary Catherine Bateson, and the dangers of conscious purpose was a major thesis of the book. I began to feel more and more impressed by this point of view.

Then came my awareness of the unusual work of Harlene Anderson and Harry Goolishian (1988) in Texas, Tom Andersen (1987) in Norway, and Ben Furman and Tappi Ahola (1992) in Finland, which altered the therapist-driven model, giving the ordinary citizen much more say in what went on. It was I who added the ingredient of the "different voice", taking this idea from the germinal work of Carol Gilligan. This became the basis for my own protest against a managerial style associated mostly with the men with whom I had trained but adopted by many women too.

*Judy*: My first post-doctoral training was an externship at the Brattleboro Family Institute with Bill Lax and Lynn Hoffman. I had just completed a dissertation in the field of family systems that had quite accidentally, by the time it was over, led me to what was then being called the "new ethnography". In contrast to traditional ethnography, this was a reflexive approach that understood the field-worker as an actor in the very drama he or she was attempting to describe. In my case, the drama centred on the way in which four families planned and experienced the bar mitzvah of a first child (Davis, 1988b).

The ethical, intellectual, moral, and methodological issues with which I had been wrestling in my attempt to "write up" my experience with these families were, it turned out, many of the same issues about which postmodern ethnographers were then writing (e.g. Clifford & Marcus, 1986; Geertz, 1988; Meyerhoff & Ruby, 1982; Ruby, 1982). Their ideas gave me a language for understanding the "ethnographic" portraits I had unintentionally produced. (My goal had been to write more traditional case studies, but the nature of my immersion in the process had made that impossible.)

It was only a short time later that these issues (of voice, position, authority, text, etc.) began appearing prominently in the family therapy literature. They were, it seemed, the very same issues with which social theorists on the constructionist, narrative end of the field had themselves been struggling (e.g., Andersen, 1987; Anderson & Goolishian, 1988; Miller & Lax, 1988) [see also "Beyond Power and Control", in chapter one]. My attraction, therefore, to the reflecting process I encountered in Brattleboro was immediate and deep. It was, for me, both a natural extension of my research and a personally more comfortable fit (vis-à-vis client–therapist positioning) than the Milan approach in which I had originally trained.

It was in my early conversations with Lynn that I came to recognize that my idea of open-ended, collaborative research resonated with her distrust of therapies that are too tightly planned. Both my research design and the reflecting interview were non-directive. My intention as researcher was to follow the family in their journey over time and to talk with them periodically about their experience of that journey and (secondarily) their experience of talking about that experience; it was not to put them through an exercise or experiment that I had set up. Similarly, a reflecting conversation also follows, rather than directs; it elicits the family's ideas about what brought them to therapy, and also asks about their ideas about the process. With such research and with such therapy, the duration of the conversation and the direction in which it moves is placed actively in the hands of the families rather than being a function of a particular methodological or theoretical model.

I had no preconceived notion, as researcher or as therapist, about how the family was supposed to do what they were doing. Although I had some culturally preconceived ideas about the "proper" way to do a bar mitzvah, I had none about how families use the experience to work on issues of emotional process (Friedman, 1980, 1985). I had no normative ideal against which to measure the family culture I had been permitted to enter. My only plan was to remain as unobtrusive and as non-threatening as possible so that they'd let me stay. Likewise, as the interviewer in Tekka's family, I had no preconceived plan about how the family had to do the work they'd come in to do. My only plan was to keep the conversation going so that ideas other than the ones they had come in with might emerge. In both cases what I was hoping for was what Arthur Penn (1991) calls a "felicitous accident", a convergence of people, events, ideas such that something new and exciting gets created.

The idea of accident was not only in the research and the therapy but in the write-ups as well. In both instances I attempted to tell the story in such a way as to include as much detail as feasible, and as much of the other people's voices as possible. I also wished to expose myself as much as I exposed them, all in the service of allowing readers to construct their own meanings.

Q:  *As therapists you put yourselves directly into the story as equal partners with family members. You provide space for the family to offer their ideas and then have a reflecting team comment on these ideas in a recursive process of multiple conversations. In this particular situation family members are talkative and articulate and, as you say, "especially informed consumers". How do you modify your approach with families whose members are not so talkative or articulate as this one, families who might not so easily make use of the space the therapist provides?*

A:  *Lynn*: I don't feel that families have to be articulate to profit by this approach. What is important is the invitation to comment on the *process of therapy* rather than on the *problem*. We are talking about a shift that changes the nature of the professional relationship towards a more equitable one, if only symbolically, not a technique that works better with some people than others. Of course, there may be a good reason not to ask people to comment publicly. If people would be endangered by open talking, you would probably not see the family together anyway, so the question wouldn't come up.

*Judy*: I would add to what Lynn mentioned, that families don't have to be particularly articulate to respond to the invitation to switch positions. For instance, we ask the family how they would like to use the time rather than authoritatively choosing what to talk about. We also invite them to listen to us or to each other from new positions, thus increasing the chance of new ways of seeing.

This is precisely the situation that Bill Lax recounts in a chapter on postmodern practice (1992). In that piece he describes a family for whom the process of therapy was intimidating and who found it difficult to talk about their situation. I was the therapist in the room and Bill was behind the mirror. We asked the child to watch from behind the mirror with Bill while the parents talked in the room with me. Then we switched and the parents watched as their son spoke with Bill. From that position, they were able to, as the mother put it, "see their baby grow up in front of their eyes". It was a dramatic example of the difference a new position can make.

Q: *You comment that your work is "not attached to outcome" and yet you appear to have certain goals in mind with this family, namely to prevent Tekka from attempting suicide and from a return visit to the psychiatric hospital. Doesn't this count as a preferred outcome? Also, Tekka says in the fourth session that "I would like myself to be back in control, in total recovery. So the doll can be in storage." Isn't this a goal of the therapy, as well? How do your goals in therapy differ from goals set by more traditional family therapists? Doesn't the therapist have a responsibility to get family members to specify their goals for therapy so that you can know whether you're moving in their preferred direction?*

A: *Lynn and Judy*: You ask about our bias against having a preferred outcome. In a setting that demanded clearly defined goals we would always give priority to those demands, but we would share with the family our dilemma about setting up such goals. Then we would work with the families or persons on what goals we might choose to set up, including goals that might keep changing.

However, the phrase "not attached to outcome" is probably unfortunate because it has so many meanings. One meaning is that we are not attached to any *particular* outcome, only to one that would remove or diminish the reason people came to talk to us. Here we paid attention to what the family wanted, which was to "improve communication" and to help get Tekka off medication and find a plan, at least short-term, that would be acceptable to her and reassuring to the parents. In that sense we do try to listen to what family members want. Of course, sometimes there is a concern that people can't come right out with or that there is disagreement about. In this case self-harm was such a concern, and within the constraints that defined that issue we naturally paid attention to it.

But there is another meaning to "not attached", and this is the one Bateson was talking about in *Angels Fear*. If as a therapist you try to control the therapy towards some normative outcome, you may get into trouble. First, this kind of goal often hides a therapeutic or social bias; second, getting too attached to it can seriously get in the way— the more you push, the less likely it is that it will happen. That is a principle of Zen, but it is a principle of therapy as well.

Q: *You met with this family only four times over a six-week period. Is it standard practice for you to see families for only a few sessions over a relatively short span of time? Who decides about the frequency of meetings and about the duration of therapy?*

A: *Lynn and Judy*: The time intervals and length of therapy are decided by the group or depend on the circumstances of the situation. There is a flexible negotiation from session to session dictated by the logic of events and people's wishes. But by drawing on the participation of the group as we do, we find we meet less frequently and more episodically, depending on the situation. With this family, the school year was ending and Tekka was leaving the area, so that limited our contact.

Q: *When you, Lynn, talk about the importance of people "taking back the interview from the professionals", you're talking about a radical philosophic shift in perspective. In light of the prominence, power, and pervasiveness of the medical-expert model, how can these new methods of inquiry grow and flourish?*

A: *Lynn*: There is a growing pile of complaints about the profession of psychotherapy, and my twig is but a small addition to the pyre.

Perhaps this criticism is growing *in proportion to* the increasing importance of the medical model in justifying insurance reimbursement and simplifying managed care. The point is exactly that: to affront the trend towards professionalizing every problem.

Actually, I see the support group movement, even when I don't agree with all of its rationales, as a much more useful and inexpensive way of managing many common miseries than traditional psychotherapy. Where psychotherapy does seem advisable, I would want to see it become much more comfortable and collaborative. I would like professionals to share far more broadly with families the techniques we have mostly kept to ourselves. I would also like to see the process of therapy demystified by the use of ordinary language, even in conferences between professionals. Finally, I would like to see banished for once and all the idea of therapists as doctors, healers, or priests. This would not mean abandoning our hard-won skills: it would mean that instead of subjecting people to them, we would explain and teach people how to use them.

## NOTES

1. Special thanks to William D. Lax, Ph.D., Director of Training, Brattleboro Family Institute, for his generosity in offering us this research site.

2. Team membership fluctuated from session to session, depending on individual schedules. William Lax, Ph.D., was present for all four sessions. Randye E. Cohen, Ph.D., in private practice in Norwich, Vt., was present only for the first session, and Brian Lewis, Ph.D., in private practice in Montpelier, Vt., joined the group for the last two sessions, as did Lynn.

3. Further thanks are due to Mary Olson (submitted), who shared her ideas about applying Walter Ong's (1982) theories of literacy and orality to therapy during an evening's conversation with Judy Davis and Lynn Hoffman before this paper was finished.

# CONCLUSION

In summarizing, let me say that the journey from my first to my last essay has crossed a continental divide that is not peculiar to the field of family therapy alone. Most fields today are coping with the pell-mell criss-crossing of the new influences I have described: French deconstructionism, German critical theory, Foucault-type discourse analysis, poststructuralism, narrative theory, hermeneutics, social constructionism, and feminist critical theory. All these strands come together to make up the dense tapestry called postmodern thought.

Despite its diversity, this movement marks a major shift in human studies from a belief in objective, bias-neutral research to a kind of self-conscious and sophisticated subjectivity. This is not a new direction. Charles Cooley, quoted earlier in this century by the American social philosopher George Herbert Mead (1964), stated that "the imaginations which people have of one another are the solid facts of society".

The postmodernists add that these imaginations are not confined to peoples' minds but are part of a Penelope's web that is continually woven and rewoven between them. The line between individual and social becomes tenuous here, as what is called the hermeneutic circle comes into play: an idea is constructed together with others; then is internalized in the private mind; then rejoins the common mind; and so forth. Behind such a shifting surface, it is hard to find a joist into which to plant a nail.

This challenge to what could be called native realism has created a split in the postmodern arena. There is a contradiction between the position of postmodern feminists who use neo-Marxist critical theory to support their ideals and that of social constructionists who do not believe in any "truth discourse" at all. Within the field of psychotherapy, especially in work with violence, this is the basis for a quarrel between activists and relativists. There are those, however, who feel that the concept of binary opposites itself should be jettisoned along with other attributes of patriarchal thought.

The anti-oppression camp has two faces, too. One face looks outward, seeing the personal as political. Moral values and social issues replace the psychological framework, and the therapist becomes an advocate of the victimized person. Another face turns inward, seeing the political as personal. The hurt is within, characterized by phrases like the inner child, low-self esteem, survivor. Here the therapist becomes a healer, helping people tell and retell the stories of their victimhood in order to move past them. Again, these views often seem simply incompatible, and each side irritates the other.

Since I am uncomfortable with the inordinate power we have given to therapists, whether as advocates or healers, I tend to share a distrust of moral absolutes. Foucault's notion of what he called "the micro-fascism of everyday life" offers a framework for an activism of a different kind. Instead of the leap to the barricades, he sets us up for a kind of low-key institution watch. It is not the people in power that we need to rebel against, he says, but our modern institutions and the discourses that flow from them. These discourses affect our daily thoughts and actions at the most local level; being invisible, they are all the more insidious.

I would like to apply this watch to the institution that family therapy has become. I would like all of us who engage in this activity to maintain a deeply critical attitude towards what constitutes professional identity. I would like us to question methods of working that cause us to "practise down" to the people we see. And for clinical speech, which despite its scientifically neutral veneer is imbued with unkind meanings, I would like us to substitute ordinary speech.

The late Harry Goolishian, who has helped to give us this benign legacy, told me a story once about an exchange between himself and the legendary Ronnie Laing. Laing said to him, "What language do you use with the people you work with?" Harry said: "I use the vernacular." Laing replied: "Horseapples, why don't you use their own language?" This is not as easy as it sounds, but it represents an ideal that in my work and writing I will continue to pursue.

# POSTSCRIPT

*Margaret Robinson*

It may or may not be a coincidence that I am writing this post-script to Lynn's collected papers in the same garden where she, her soon-to-be husband Noel Hennessy, Robin Skynner with his partner Josh Partridge, Ros Draper, my husband, and myself were sitting in the sun some two years ago. After attending her seminar at the Tavistock Clinic, I had followed Lynn's writings and teaching on family therapy over the years with eager delight, as much because of her literary lucidity as for her therapeutic insights. She always seemed to be either just that little bit ahead of where I was, but not so far as to be unreachable, or, to be putting into words thoughts that I was struggling with myself.

Now Lynn's papers have been collected into this one volume and her philosophical literary and therapeutic excursions linked together by a commentary that describes her journey since writing the *Foundations of Family Therapy* twenty years ago. For many of her readers who are also busy practitioners and teachers, this collection of her papers will have been a relief as well as a joy, because the effort of tracking down papers in the multifarious family therapy, systems, psychological, and psychiatric journals, as well as being time-consuming, rarely seems congruent with the reflective waysides of one's own journey at the time. I had read almost all of these papers before, and always Lynn had something illuminating to say to me. Rereading them has helped me to retrace my steps to and set forth afresh—as I now like to think of it—on the journey towards wisdom.

In 1985 she set out the case against power and control, defining second-order cybernetics, and, by refusing to accept epistemology as psychobabble, but as how we know our knowing, she went on to elucidate what she at that time described as the constructivist view. She also "stepped down" from the compulsory production of change in favour of introducing the idea of the conversational domain. Two years later and soon after reading that paper, I began writing my own book, *Family Transformation Through Divorce and Remarriage* (1991), in which I wanted to write a succinct chapter on families as systems and describe the models of intervention which I found most useful. Then, as since, I drew heavily on Lynn's clarifying of complex ideas as, influenced by the work of Goolishian and Anderson, she described how the problem creates the system. I am still reflecting on this in my current work on the interacting belief systems of lawyers and the legal system, and counsellors, therapists, and the families caught in the conflict of divorce in which they intervene, not always usefully.

Lynn's 1988 paper, "A Constructivist Position for Family Therapy", set out even more clearly the new epistemology and stressed that in our attempts to understand the world we should look for fit between our perceptions of items in the environment and those of significant others. According to Lynn the target of therapy was to find some kind of meaning for the significant system that was created around a given problem. It was at this time that she became interested in Tom Andersen's ideas about the reflecting team which led to the concept of position: where one stands in relation to the significant system created around a particular problem. Also at this time, feeling very stuck in my own thinking, I took myself off to a summer course organized by Carlos Sluzki in Williamstown, where I met Lynn again, was reintroduced to Gianfranco Cecchin, and also met Tom Andersen and Michael White. This led to my rewriting the theory chapters of my book, as well as giving me the courage to abandon the somewhat rigid and explicit avoidance in my therapy of the importance of my own values that psychoanalytic theory and treatment had taught me. In fact I began freely to admit my step-mother status where it seemed that it might be helpful to my client stepfamilies, and even sometimes the way that my husband and I had resolved a similar problem to those of my client. particularly those who had not had a good-enough co-parental model. At this time Lynn herself made a significant shift, abandon ng some of her earlier ideas in literary criticism that she had been taught at college, towards what is now known as postmodernism.

The delightful and incisive interview by Richard Simon for the *Family Therapy Networker*—the issue that had a Batman-type cover, with the slogan, "The Constructivists Are Coming"—gave Lynn the opportunity to clarify her current position even more clearly, and she refused to be deflected from her explanation of constructivism, or to get back on the mountaintop of being the expert to the families down below. Therapy, as she explained, is not an adversarial process, but a special kind of conversation, and once again—the mistress of modern metaphors—she contrasted the first-order therapist as an environmental engineer trying to change the course of a river, with the second-order therapist as a white-water canoeist, navigating upon a river. She reminded her readers that we are always operating from our own value system or that of the agency and that she often shares this with her clients.

In 1990 there followed a further seminal theoretical paper, "Constructing Realities: An Art of Lenses", which set out the dimensions of her own move to social construction theory, with the addition of two other lenses: that of a second-order view and that of a sensitivity to gender. She has described, as lucidly as ever, social construction theory as part of an ideological shift in family therapy and has explained how, after reading Carol Gilligan's research *In a Different Voice*, she became stunningly aware of gender bias in psychological research. Never afraid to declare herself mistaken, she explains why she has given up what she called her Rosetta Stone fallacy whereby only the therapist as a Master Interpreter can be in charge of the field.

I am sad that Lynn did not find her own excursions into therapy all that helpful, as long ago I was considerably helped by personal psychoanalysis, there being no family therapy at that time. About two years ago, more by chance than by judgement, I became involved in seeing couples both individually and together with a psychoanalyst friend and colleague. This has allowed me to become reacquainted and to some extent updated with psychoanalytic theory, and also to co-work with a male colleague. I have begun to persuade him of the value of the two of us reflecting in front of the couple during our quartet sessions (as Ros Draper and I used to do) and hope to move to asking them to comment back to us.

Lynn's reflexive stance paper—new to me—describes a trip to Buenos Aires, where, influenced by Furman and Ahola, she began to deconstruct the pathologizing of almost all the symptoms of people in trouble who sought help. I was relieved to read the honest openness with which Lynn describes what I had recently begun to do myself—often saying to clients who fearfully described their symptoms as if they were nearing madness, that the older I get, the less I know what normal is. I particularly liked Dora Schnitman's idea of her focus as balls of light over people's heads, and I have a game I play with children where I start telling them a story by holding onto a circular glass paperweight with stars inside and then hand it to them, asking them to continue. Maybe I could extend this game to some of the family work I do.

Lynn's introductory paper in McNamee and Gergen's book *Therapy as Social Construction* not only points out the revolution in social sciences, but describes what she calls the five sacred cows in modern psychology. In doing so, she weaves a seamless thread between between so-called objective social research, the self (a delightful reference to Bruce Chatwin's *Songlines* here), developmental psychology, the whole question of levels, and the introduction of the idea of partnership, the final death blow to the therapist as expert. Synchronicity is apparently working again here. because in order to write this postscript I had temporarily set aside reading Eisler's *The Chalice and the Blade,* to which Lynn refers in this paper. She concludes by taking a fresh look at Pearce and Cronen's levels of communication and moves on to explore the usefulness of playing with stories in her own work.

The penultimate paper, *Kitchen Talk,* describes her experience on her Australian tour in 1992, in which she clarifies her current way of conducting workshops: talking openly with the therapist in front of the family, and inviting them to comment on their conversation later.

"Tekka with Feathers" is a composite piece contributed by Lynn and by Judy Davis—the therapist to a young artist, Tekka, who had just come out of a mental hospital to which she had been admitted following an apparent attempt at suicide—and also by Tekka's mother and stepfather. Here Lynn and Judy have extended the idea of the reflecting team in order to invite the family to write their comments on the therapy, and they conclude with a description of their visit to Tekka's qualifying exhibition of her sculptures. It reminded me of my visit to a client's exhibition of her textile tapestries and to her pianist husband's concert, something I had previously kept to myself. So let me give thanks to Lynn for conveying complex ideas with lucid simplicity, for giving us the encouragement to change our therapeutic ways, and for her honesty in sharing herself with her clients.

*Winchester, England, 1993*

# REFERENCES

Allman, L. (1982). The aesthetic preference. *Family Process* 21: 43–56.

Andersen, T. (1987). The reflecting team. *Family Process*, 26: 415–428.

Andersen, T. (Ed.) (1990). *The Reflecting Team*. New York: W.W. Norton.

Anderson, H., & Goolishian H. (1988). Human systems as linguistic systems. *Family Process*, 27: 371–393.

Anderson, H., Goolishian, H., & Winderman, L. (1986). Problem-determined systems: towards transformation in family therapy. *Journal of Strategic and Systemic Therapies, 5*: 1–13.

Anderson, H., Goolishian, H., Pulliam, G., & Winderman, L. (1986). The Galveston Family Institute: some personal and historical perspectives. In: D. Efron (Ed.), *Developments in Strategic and Systemic Therapies*. New York: Brunner/Mazel.

Anderson, S. R., & Hopkins, P. (1991). *The Feminine Face of God*. New York: Bantam Books.

Andersson, M., Gravelius, K., & Salamon, E. (1987). AGS–Uppdragsmodellen. Presentation given at the First Northern Family Therapy Congress, Stockholm, Sweden, August.

Bateson, G. (1972) *Steps to an Ecology of Mind*. New York: Ballantine.

Bateson, G. (1979). *Mind and Nature*. New York: E. P. Dutton.

Bateson, G. & Bateson, M.C. (1987). *Angels Fear: Toward an Epistemology of the Sacred.* New York: Macmillan.

Bateson M. C. (1972). *Our Own Metaphor.* New York: Alfred A. Knopf.

Bateson, M. C. (1990). *Composing a Life.* New York: Penguin.

Bateson, M. C. (1992). *Composers and Improvisers.* Plenary address. Family Therapy Network Symposium (March).

Beer, S. (1980). Preface. In: H. Maturana & F. Varela, *Autopoiesis and Cognition.* Dordrecht, Holland: D. Reidel.

Belenky, M., Clinchy, B., Goldberger, N., & Tarule, J. (1986). *Women's Ways of Knowing.* New York: Basic Books.

Berger, P., & Luckmann, T. (1966). *The Social Construction of Reality.* Garden City, NY: Doubleday.

Berman, A. (1988). *From the New Criticism to Deconstruction.* Chicago, IL: University of Illinois Press.

Bogdan, J. (1984). Family organization as an ecology of ideas. *Family Process, 23:* 375–388.

Boscolo, L., Cecchin, G., Hoffman, L., & Penn, P. (1987). *Milan Systemic Family Therapy.* New York: Basic Books.

Braten, S. (1987). Paradigms of autonomy: Dialogical or monological? In: G. Teubner (Ed.), *Autopoiesis in Law and Society.* New York: De Gruyter.

Braten, S. (1984). The third position. In: F. Geyer & J. van der Zouwen (Eds.), *Sociocybernetics Paradoxes.* London: Sage Publications.

Campbell, D., & Draper, R. (1985). Creating a concept for change. In: D. Campbell & R. Draper (Eds.), *Applications of Systemic Family Therapy: The Milan Method.* New York: Grune & Stratton.

Carter, B., & McGoldrick, M. (1988). *The Changing Family Life Cycle: A Framework for Family Therapy* (2nd ed.). New York: Gardner Press.

Chatwin, B. (1987). *The Songlines.* London: Jonathan Cape.

Clifford, J., & Marcus, G. E. (Eds.) (1986). *Writing Culture: The Poetics and Politics of Ethnography.* Berkeley, CA: University of California Press.

Cooper, B. (1982). *Michel Foucault: A Study of His Thought.* New York: Mellen.

Cronen, V. E., Johnson, K. M., & Lannamann, J. W. (1982). Paradoxes, double-binds, and reflexive loops. *Family Process, 21:* 91–112.

Davis, J. (1988a). Learning about women through (of all things) a study of bar mitzvah. Presented at the Association for Jewish Studies, Boston, Dec. 18.

Davis, J. (1988b). Mazel tov: The bar mitzvah as a multigenerational ritual of change and continuity. In: E. I. Black, J. Roberts, & R.

Whiting (Eds.), *Rituals in Families and Family Therapy* (pp. 177–208). New York: W. W. Norton.

Dell, P. F. (1989). Violence and the systemic view: the problem of power. *Family Process, 28*: 1–14.

Dell, P. F. (1985). Understanding Bateson and Maturana: toward a biological foundation for the social sciences. *Journal of Marital and Family Therapy, 11*: 1–20.

Dell, P. F. (1982). Beyond homeostasis. *Family Process, 21*: 21–42.

Dell, P. F. (1980). Researching the family theories of schizophrenia. *Family Process, 10*: 321–326.

Dell, P. F., & Goolishian, H. (1979). Order through fluctuation: an evolutionary paradigm for human systems. Presentation given at the Annual Scientific Meeting of the A.K.A. Rice Institute, Houston, Texas.

Derrida, J. (1978). *Writing and Difference.* Chicago, IL: University of Chicago Press.

Eisler, R. (1987). *The Chalice and the Blade.* New York: Basic Books.

Erickson, G. (1988). Against the grain: decentering family therapy. *American Journal of Marital and Family Therapy, 14*: 225–236.

Eyer, D. (1993). *Mother–Infant Bonding: A Scientific Fiction.* New Haven, CT: Yale University Press.

Fisch, R., Weakland, J., & Segal, L. (1982). *The Tactics of Change.* San Francisco, CA: Jossey-Bass.

Forrester, J. W. (1961). *Industrial dynamics.* Cambridge MA: M.I.T. Press.

Foucault, M. (1977). *Discipline and Punishment.* London: Allen Lane.

Foucault, M. (1975). *The Archaeology of Knowledge.* London: Tavistock.

Fraser, N., & Nicholson, L. (1990). Social criticism without philosophy. In: L. Nicholson (Ed.), *Postmodernism and Feminist Theory.* London: Routledge.

Freidson, E. (1972). *Profession of Medicine.* New York: Dodd Mead.

Friedman, E.H. (1985). *Generation to Generation: Family Process in Church and Synagogue.* New York: Guilford Press.

Friedman, E.H. (1980). Systems and ceremonies: a family view of rites of passage. In: E.A. Carter & M. McGoldrick (Eds.), *The Family Life Cycle* (pp. 429–460). New York: Gardner Press.

Friedman, S. (Ed.) (1993). *The New Language of Change: Constructive Collaboration in Psychotherapy.* New York: Guilford Press.

Fruggeri, L., Dotti, D., Ferrara, R., & Matteini, M. (1985). The systemic approach in a mental health service. In: D. Campbell & R. Draper

(Eds.), *Applications of Systemic Family Therapy: The Milan Method.* New York: Grune & Stratton.

Furman, B., & Ahola, T. (1992). *Solution Talk: Hosting Therapeutic Conversations.* New York: W. W. Norton.

Gadamer, H. (1975). *Truth and Method,* trans. by G. Barden & J. Cumming. New York: Continuum.

Geertz, C. (1988). *Works and Lives: The Anthropologist as Author.* Stanford: Stanford University Press.

Geertz, C. (1983). *Local Knowledge.* New York: Basic Books.

Geertz, C. (1973). *The Interpretation of Cultures.* New York: Basic Books.

Gergen, K. (1991). *The Saturated Self.* New York: Basic Books.

Gergen, K. (1985). The social constructionist movement in modern psychology. *American Psychologist, 40:* 266–275.

Gergen, K. (1982). *Toward Transformation in Social Knowledge.* New York: Springer-Verlag.

Gergen, K., & Gergen, M. (1986). Narrative form and the construction of psychological science. In: T. Sarbin (Ed.), *Narrative Psychology.* New York: Praeger.

Gergen, M. (1988). *Feminist Thought and the Structure of Knowledge.* New York: New York University Press.

Gilligan, C. (1982). *In a Different Voice.* Cambridge, MA: Harvard University Press.

Gleick, J. (1987). *Chaos.* New York: Penguin Books/Viking Press.

Gluck, S., & Patai, D. (1991). *Women's Words: The Feminist Practice of Oral History.* London: Routledge.

Goldner, V. (1988). Generation and gender: normative and covert hierarchies. *Family Process 27:* 17–31.

Goolishian, H., & Winderman, L. (1988). Constructivism, autopoiesis and problem-determined systems. *The Irish Journal of Psychology, 9:* 130–1437.

Gould, S. J. (1980). *The Panda's Thumb.* New York: W. W. Norton.

Haley, J. (1976). *Problem-Solving Therapy: New Strategies for Effective Family Therapy.* San Francisco CA: Jossey-Bass.

Haley, J. (1969). *The Power Tactics of Jesus Christ.* New York: Grossman, Publishers.

Haley, J. (1963). *Strategies of Psychotherapy.* New York: Grune & Stratton.

Hare-Mustin, R. T. (1988). The meaning of difference. *American Psychologist 43:* 455–464.

Harré, R. (1986). *The Social Construction of Emotions.* New York: Basil Blackwell.

Harré, R. (1984). *Personal Being*. Cambridge, MA: Harvard University Press.

Heims, S. (1977). Bateson and the mathematicians. *Journal of the History of the Behavioral Sciences, 10*: 141–159.

Held, D. (1980). *Introduction to Critical Theory*. Berkeley, CA: University of California Press.

Hewstone, M. (1983). *Attribution Theory: Social and Functional Extensions*. Oxford: Blackwell.

Hoffman, L. (1981). *Foundations of Family Therapy*. New York: Basic Books.

Howe, G. (1984). Changing the family mind. Paper presented at The Fourth Annual Symposium on Family Therapy at the University of Tennessee, Knoxville (November).

Howe, R., & von Foerster, H. (1974). Cybernetics at Illinois. *Forum, 6*: 15–17.

Imber-Black, E. (1985). Families and multiple helpers: a systemic perspective. In: D. Campbell & R. Draper (Eds.), *Applications of Systemic Family Therapy: The Milan Method*. New York: Grune & Stratton.

Jackson, D. D. (1957). The question of family homeostasis. *Psychiatric Quarterly Supplement, 31*: 79–90.

Kaplan, A. (Ed.) (1988). *Postmodernism and Its Discontents*. New York: Verso.

Kearney, P., Byrne, N., & McCarthy, I. (1989). Just metaphors: marginal illuminations in a colonial retreat. *Family Therapy Case Studies, 4*: 17–31.

Keeney, B. (1983). *The Aesthetics of Change*. New York: Guilford Press.

Keeney, B., & Ross, J. (1985). *Mind in Therapy*. New York: Basic Books.

Keeney, B., & Sprenkle, D. (1982). Ecosystemic epistemology. *Family Process, 21*: 1–22.

Kelly, G. (1983). *A Theory of Personality*. New York: W. W. Norton.

Lane, G., & Russell, T. (1987). Neutrality vs. social control: a systemic approach to violent couples. *The Family Therapy Networker, 11* (3): 52–56.

Lane, G., & Russell, T. (1984). Circular replication: a systemic intervention. Paper presented at The Fourth Annual Symposium on Family Therapy at the University of Tennessee, Knoxville, Tennessee (November).

Lax, W. D. (1992). Postmodern thinking in a clinical practice. In S. McNamee & K. Gergen (Eds.), *Therapy as Social Construction* (pp. 69–85). London: Sage.

Lax, W. D. (1989). Systemic family therapy with young children and their families: use of the reflecting team. *Journal of Psychotherapy and the Family, 5*: 55–74.

Lax, W., & Lussardi, D. (1989). "Systemic" family therapy with young children in the family: use of the reflecting team. In: J. J. Zilback (Ed.), *Children in Family Therapy*, New York: Haworth.

Leitch, V. (1983). *Deconstructive Criticism.* New York: Columbia University Press.

Linde, C., & Goguen, J. (1978). The structure of planning discourse. *Journal of Social and Biological Structures.* (Quoted in F. J. Varela, *Principles of Biological Autonomy.* New York: Elsevier/North Holland, 1979.)

Luepnitz, D. (1988). *The Family Interpreted.* New York: Basic Books.

Masson, J. (1990). *Against Therapy.* New York: Fontana Paperbacks.

Maturana, H. R., & Varela, F. J. (1980). *Autopoiesis and Cognition.* Dordrecht, Holland: D. Reidel.

McCarthy, I. C., & Byrne. N. O'R. (1988). Mis-taken love: conversations on the problem of incest in an Irish context. *Family Process, 27*: 181–198.

McKinnon, L., & Miller, D. (1987). The new epistemology and the Milan approach: feminist and socio-political considerations. *Journal of Marital and Family Therapy, 13*: 139–155.

Mead, G. H. (1964). *George Herbert Mead on Social Psychology: Selected Papers*, edited by A. Strauss. Chicago, IL: University of Chicago Press.

Messer, L., Sass, L. A., & Woolfolk, R. L. (Eds.). (1988). *Hermeneutics and Psychological Theory.* New Brunswick, NJ: Rutgers University Press.

Meyerhoff, B., & Ruby, J. (1982). Introduction. In: J. Ruby (Ed.), *A Crack in the Mirror: Reflexive Perspectives in Anthropology* (pp. 1–35). Philadelphia: University of Pennsylvania Press.

Miller. D. (1988). Women in pain: substance abuse—self starvation. In: M. Merkin (Ed.), *The Social and Political Context of Family Therapy.* New York: Gardner Press.

Miller, D., & Lax, W. (1988). A reflecting team model for working with couples: interrupting deadly struggles. *Journal of Strategic and Systemic Therapies, 7* (3): 17–23.

Miller, J. (1978). *Living Systems.* New York: McGraw-Hill.

Miller, J. (1976). *Toward a New Psychology of Women.* Boston: Beacon Press.

Mishler, E. (1986). *Research Interviewing: Context and Narrative.* Cambridge, MA: Harvard University Press.

Moore, T. (1992). *The Care of the Soul.* New York: Harper Collins.

Nicholson, L. (Ed.). (1990). *Postmodernism and Feministic Theory.* New York: Routledge.

Olson, M. (submitted). "Conversation" and "text": a media perspective for therapy. *Family Process.*

Ong, W. (1982). *Orality and Literacy.* New York: W. W. Norton.

Pask, G. (1976). *Conversation Theory.* New York: Elsevier Press.

Pearce, W. B., & Cronen, V. E. (1980). *Communication, Action and Meaning: The Creation of Social Realities.* New York: Praeger.

Penn, A. (1991). A conversation on cybernetics and film. Public discussion between Fredrick Steier and Arthur Penn at the annual conference of the American Society for Cybernetics. Amherst, MA (July).

Penn, P. (1991). Letters to ourselves. *The Family Therapy Networker, 15*: 43–45.

Penn, P. (1985). Feed-forward: future questions, future maps. *Family Process, 24*: 299–311.

Penn, P., & Sheinberg, M. (1988). Family therapy and all that jazz. Paper presented at the Institute on Violence and the Family, AAMFT Annual Conference, New Orleans (October).

Penn, P., & Sheinberg, M. (1986). A systemic model for consultation. In: L. Wynne, S. McDaniel, & T. Weber (Eds.), *The Family Therapist as Systems Consultant.* New York: Guilford Press.

Poster, M. (1989). *Critical Theory and Poststructuralism.* Ithaca, NY: Cornell University Press.

Prigogine, I. & Stengers, I. (1984). *Order out of Chaos.* New York: Bantam Books .

Rabinow, P. (Ed.). (1984). *The Foucault Reader.* New York: Pantheon Press.

Rappaport. R. (1979). *Ecology, Meaning and Religion.* Richmond, CA: North Atlantic Books.

Roberts, J., "Alexandra", & "Julius" (1988). Use of ritual in "redocumenting" psychiatric history. In: E. I. Black, J. Roberts, & R. Whiting (Eds.), *Rituals in Families and Family Therapy* (pp. 307–330). New York: W. W. Norton.

Robinson, M. (1991). *Family Transformation Through Divorce and Remarriage.* London: Routledge.

Rosener, J. (1990). Ways women lead. In: *Harvard Business Review.* Cambridge, MA.

Ruby, J. (Ed.). (1982). *A Crack in the Mirror: Reflexive Perspectives in Anthropology.* Philadelphia, PA: University of Pennsylvania Press.

Ruesch, J., & Bateson, G. (1951). Communication. In: *The Social Matrix of Psychiatry*. New York: W.W. Norton.

Russell, B. & Whitehead, A. N. (1910–13). *Principia Mathematica*, 2nd ed. (3 vols.). Cambridge: Cambridge University Press.

Sarbin, T. (1986). *Narrative Psychology*. New York: Praeger Press.

Satir, V. (1964). *Conjoint Family Therapy*. Palo Alto, CA: Science & Behavior Press.

Saussure, F. de (1959). *Course in General Linguistics*, edited by C. Bally & A. Sechehave, trans. by W. Baskin. New York: Philosophical Library.

Selvini-Palazzoli, M., Boscolo, L., Cecchin, G., & Prata, G. (1980). Hypothesizing–circularity–neutrality: Three guidelines for the conductor of the session. *Family Process, 19*, 3–12.

Selvini-Palazzoli. M., Boscolo, L., Cecchin, G., & Prata, G. (1978). *Paradox and Counterparadox*. New York: Jason Aronson.

Shotter, J. & Gergen, K. (Eds.). (1989). *Texts of Identity*. London: Sage.

Sluzki, C. E. (1983). Process, structure and world views: toward an integrated view of systemic models in family therapy. *Family Process, 22*: 469–476.

Sluzki, C. E., & Ransom, D. C. (Eds.). (1976). *Double Bind: The Foundation of the Communicational Approach to the Family*. New York: Grune & Stratton.

Spence, D. (1982). *Narrative Truth and Historical Truth*. New York: W. W. Norton.

Surrey, J. (1984). The "self-in-relation": a theory of women's development. In: *Work in Progress, No. 13*. Wellesley, MA: Stone Center Working Papers Series.

Tannen, D. (1990). *You Just Don't Understand*. New York: Ballantine Books.

Taylor, M. (1986). *Deconstruction in Context*. Chicago, IL: University of Chicago Press.

Telfner, U., & Ceruti, M. (Eds.). (1987). *Heinz von Foerster, Sistemi che Osservano*. Rome: Casa Editrice Astrolabia, Ubaldini Editore.

Thom, R. (1975). *Structural Stability and Morphogenesis*. Reading, MA: Benjamin.

Tomm, K. (1987a). Interventive interviewing: Part I. *Family Process, 26*: 3–15.

Tomm, K. (1987b). Interventive interviewing: Part II. Reflexive questioning as a means to enable self-healing. *Family Process, 26*: 167–184.

Tyler, S. (1978). *The Said and the Unsaid*. New York: Academic Press.

Ugazio, V. (1985). Hypothesis-making: the Milan approach revisited. In: D. Campbell & R. Draper (Eds.), *Applications of Systemic Family Therapy: The Milan Method*. New York: Grune & Stratton.

Varela, F.J. (1979). *Principles of Biological Autonomy*. New York: North Holland.

Varela, F. J. (1976). Not one, not two: position paper for the Mind–Body Conference. *Co-Evolution Quarterly*: 62–67.

von Foerster, H. (1983). Plenary address. Presentation at the Sixth Biennial MRI Conference: Maps of the Mind: Maps of the World, San Francisco.

von Foerster, H. (1981). *Observing Systems*. Seaside, CA: Intersystems Publications.

von Glasersfeld, E. (1987a). *The Construction of Knowledge: Contributions to Conceptual Semantics*. Seaside, CA: Intersystems Publications.

von Glasersfeld, E. (1987b). The concepts of adaptation and viability in a radical constructivist theory of knowledge. In: *The Construction of Knowledge*. Seaside, CA: Intersystems Publications.

von Glasersfeld, G. (1984). An introduction to radical constructivism. In: P. Watzlawick (Ed.), *The Invented Reality*. New York: W. W. Norton.

von Glasersfeld, E. (1979). The control of perception and the construction of reality. *Dialectica, 33*: 37–50.

Walters, M., Carter, E., Papp, P., & Silverstein, O. (1988). *The Invisible Web*. New York: Guilford Press.

Watzlawick, P. (Ed.) (1984). *The Invented Reality*. New York: W. W. Norton.

Watzlawick, P., Weakland, J., & Fisch, R. (1974). *Change: Principles of Problem Formation and Problem Resolution*. New York: W. W. Norton.

White, M. (1991). Deconstruction and theory. *Dulwich Centre Newsletter*, No. 3.

White, M., & Epston, D. (1990). *Narrative Means to Therapeutic Ends*. New York: W. W. Norton.

Wiener, N. (1961). *Cybernetics*. Cambridge, MA: M.I.T. Press.

# INDEX

abuse: *see* violence
"accidental ethnographers" (Davis), 100
    therapist as, 197
Ackerman Institute of Family Therapy, 6, 24, 46, 95, 70, 146
Adelphi School of Social Work, 146
Adorno, T., 105
affirmative framework, 154, 155
Ahola, T., 197, 209
Allman, L., 13
allopoietic systems, 37
Andersen, T., 23, 48, 57, 58, 63–68, 77, 78, 82, 115, 131, 194, 198, 207
Anderson, H., 3, 19, 40, 59, 74, 81, 89, 93, 101, 106, 115, 116, 127, 131, 189, 197, 198, 207
Anderson, S. R., 1
Andersson, M., 49
anthropologists, 117, 149
association causality, 143
associative formats, 113, 130–132
attributions:
    causal, 26
    negative, 27
autonomous system, 18
autopoiesis, 12, 13, 16, 71, 89
    concept of (Varela), 17
    definition of, 16
autopoietic (autonomous) systems, 37, 38

Bahktin, M., 52
Bateson, G., 2, 3, 6, 8, 10–22, 28–31, 35, 36, 39, 43–48, 79, 92, 94, 95, 98, 112, 121, 136, 143, 146, 168, 197, 201
Beer, S., 21
behaviour, problem-maintaining, 28
Belenky, M., 136, 147
beliefs:
    as social inventions, 88
    focus on, 57
Berger, P., 25, 88
Berman, A., 103, 107

Bogdan, J., 20
Boscolo, L., 22, 23, 30, 40, 44, 45, 47, 48, 50, 57, 79
Braten, S., 42, 43
Brattleboro Family Institute, 58, 67, 115, 167–196
Byrne, N., 49, 122, 150, 190

Campbell, D., 49
Carter, B., 93
case history, as a text, 163
catastrophe theory (Thom), 90
causality, linear, 35
Cecchin, G., 22, 23, 40, 44, 45, 47, 48, 50, 57, 78, 79, 207
Ceruti, M., 49
chaos theory (Gleick), 90, 120
Chatwin, B., 119, 209
"chicken soup" therapy, 125
Chomsky, N., 98
circular causality, 45, 84, 94
circular organization, model of, 27
circular questioning, 22, 45, 46
circular replication, 24, 49
circularities, cybernetic, 21
circularity, 71, 89
client, belief system of, 25
Clifford, J., 88, 107, 117, 132, 142, 149, 198
Clinchy, B., 136
clinical hate speech, banning, 152
cognitive social psychology, and family therapy, 26
collaborative approach, 154, 163
collaborative language systems, 131
colonial mentality, perpetuation of, 122
colonial official, metaphor of, 122
colonial stance, objection to, 137
colonial therapist, 112, 149–151
colonialism of mental health, 122–124
communication:
    and control, science of, 87
    hierarchies of, 122
    level of, 130

220